HISTORIES
and
MYSTERIES

From Abracadabra to Zeus

WORD HISTORIES *and* MYSTERIES

From Abracadabra to Zeus

From the Editors of the
AMERICAN HERITAGE®
DICTIONARIES

HOUGHTON MIFFLIN COMPANY
BOSTON   NEW YORK

Visit our website: www.houghtonmifflinbooks.com

ISBN-13: 978-0-618-45450-1
ISBN-10: 0-618-45450-0

Library of Congress Cataloging-in-Publication Data

Word histories and mysteries : from abracadabra to Zeus / from the editors of the American Heritage dictionaries.
    p. cm.
Includes index.
ISBN 0-618-45450-0
1. English language--Etymology--Dictionaries. I. American Heritage dictionary. II. Houghton Mifflin Company.
PE1580.W665 2004
422'.03--dc22

2004014798

Manufactured in the United States of America

QUM 10 9 8 7 6 5 4 3 2

Table of Contents

v

Editorial and Production Staff

Vice President, Publisher of Dictionaries
Margery S. Berube

Vice President, Executive Editor
Joseph P. Pickett

Vice President, Managing Editor
Christopher Leonesio

Project Editor
Patrick Taylor

Contributing Editors
Michael Adams
Benjamin W. Fortson IV

Copyeditor
Ann-Marie Imbornoni

Administrative Coordinator
Kevin McCarthy

Database Production Supervisor
Christopher Granniss

Art and Production Supervisor
Margaret Anne Miles

Manufacturing Supervisor
James W. Mitchell

Editorial Production Associate
Brianne M. Lutfy

Text Design
Catherine Hawkes, Cat & Mouse

Introduction

The Origins of English

The roots of English run deep into the past and reach all around the world. Today English is the first language of over 350 million people all over the globe, and the great diversity of English speakers is matched by the great diversity of English words. This diversity has arisen through a variety of historical processes, and in order to illustrate these processes vividly, this book traces all the twists and turns taken by over four hundred words on their journey into modern English. When we examine the origins of English words, even the words we use everyday, we find that English has drawn its vocabulary from a great variety of sources, and readers can discover in these pages a representative sample of these wide-ranging borrowings. However, English also has a considerable number of words that have been in continuous use for thousands of years, inheritances from the prehistoric ancestor of English spoken many thousands of years ago, Proto-Indo-European.

The Prehistoric Ancestors of English

All around us as we speak, we can observe the kinds of linguistic change that have transformed Proto-Indo-European into English. In this century, most of the inhabitants of the United States speak English, but many regional differences in American speech can be heard easily. Some of these regional differences reflect the different areas of Britain and Ireland from which settlers arrived, but after all these years, it would be difficult to find a dialect back in the old country that sounds exactly the same as an American dialect. Linguistic change is continually at work transforming people's speech. Occasionally we hear an elderly person use an old-fashioned word or expression, and we have to ask them what it means. I, for example, cherish a vivid memory of hearing my grandfather jokingly use the word *moxie* and asking him what it meant. Or we find that older people have a slightly different accent. Parental complaints about the incomprehensibility of young people's slang are a cliché. Over time, the differences that we can hear in our daily lives accumulate and eventually transform a language utterly. I spoke to my grandfather, and he spoke to his grandfather, and he spoke to his grandfather, and that's halfway to Shakespeare. The results of thousands of years of such change have led to Modern English as we know it today.

The story of English begins far from the shores of the United States, and even far from England. English belongs to the Indo-European family, one of the largest language families, which includes the languages of most of Europe and much of Asia, ranging from Ireland and Iceland to Iran and India. Linguists have demonstrated that such languages as Irish Gaelic, Welsh, English, German, French, Polish, Russian, Albanian, Armenian, Persian, Hindi, and a hundred more are descended from a single language spoken at least six thousand years ago, most probably in the region of the Black Sea. Linguists call this language Proto-Indo-European. We have no written records of this language, and we never will have any, since it must have been spoken long before the invention of writing. Nevertheless, many of the most common words in English are inherited from this prehistoric ancestor.

Proto-Indo-European was notable in that many of its words could be broken down into roots, the minimal meaningful units from which larger words are built. Many roots had the basic shape of *consonant-vowel-consonant*. For example, the Proto-Indo-European root meaning "woman" was *g^wen-*. (This root is discussed at the note on the word *queen*.) As another example, the basic form of the root meaning "bright" or "bright sky" was *dyeu-, which can be seen in the name *Zeus*, originally the god of the bright sky. From this root, speakers of Proto-Indo-European could also make other words by rearranging the sounds of the root and adding suffixes. The derived noun *deiwos meant "god" (that is, a "sky-dweller") in Proto-Indo-European. (The *w* in this word is the consonantal form of the *u*– notice that the lips are rounded when making both the consonant *w* and the vowel *u*.) In English, this noun *deiwos shows up in the first part of the word *Tuesday*. Most of the words of Indo-European were formed in ways similar to *deiwos, by being derived from roots with suffixes.

The asterisk (*) in front of the roots and words mentioned above indicates that these words are not attested–that is, there is no written document or sound recording in which these words exist as such. Instead, such words are reconstructed, or recovered by linguists through the comparison of words in related languages. Linguists are sure that reconstructed words as *deiwos once existed because of evidence from attested languages, such as Sanskrit *devas*, Avestan *daēuuō*, Latin *deus*, and Irish *día*, all meaning "god." These languages are widely separated in time and space, as well as by cultural differences, so it is unlikely that the similarity between these words for "god" represents borrowing between the languages. Instead, they must have inherited the word from a common source. On the evidence of the different words for "god" above, linguists reconstruct the word *deiwos. All of the other reconstructed forms marked with an asterisk in this book are supported by similar evidence.

The Old English Period

The distant ancestor of English, Proto-Indo-European, broke up into several branches, which are illustrated in the diagram on pages 346–347. The branch in which English developed is called the Germanic branch. The first Germanic tribes speaking early dialects of Old English began to move into Great Britain in the middle of the fifth century of our era. The medieval scholar Bede gives the exact date as A.D. 446, and from around this time we can begin to trace the history of English separately from its Indo-European and Germanic cousins.

Many of the most common words in English today are inherited from Old English and are the direct descendants of ancient Proto-Indo-European terms as well. Such basic words as *fire* and *water,* or *heart* and *tooth,* have been used continuously over six thousand years in the course of the development of English from Proto-Indo-European. Many Modern English terms relating to religious beliefs, such as *bless, Easter, god,* and *Yule,* have their roots in the ancient paganism of the Germanic peoples.

A great deal of Old English vocabulary has not survived into Modern English, however. Much of the vocabulary of Modern English is borrowed from other languages, many of which also happen to be Indo-European languages. Greek, Latin, and the Romance languages have been the most important sources of new words grafted onto the stock of Old English. After many centuries of borrowing, English now contains words that have originated in, or at least passed through, most of the major branches of Indo-European. In this way, English has been lucky enough to reacquire many of the Proto-Indo-European roots that it had previously lost during the course of its development. For an example, see *fire.*

The earliest major source of these "non-English" English words is Old Norse, and specifically the dialect of the Danes who began to make permanent settlements in the northern half of England in the middle of the ninth century of our era. The Old Norse word for settlement was *bȳr,* and this is continued in the Modern English word *bylaw.* Another Old Norse contribution to legal vocabulary is *outlaw.* The Danes who settled in England fought intermittently with the English, even gaining control of theEnglish throne for a few years, and during the long interaction between Old English and Old Norse, almost one thousand words of Norse origin entered the English language. These are found in all areas of culture and include such common items of vocabulary as *fellow* and *window.* In fact, the fellowship between the two languages even led to the replacement of some of the most basic, everyday Old English words by their Old Norse equivalents. The verb *take* (see *numb* in this book) and the pronoun *they* offer interesting cases of such borrowing.

The Middle English Period

The conquest of England by the Normans in 1066 is traditionally used to separate the Old English Period from the Middle English period, even though features characteristic of Middle English began to appear in Old English texts before this date. There were already several dialects of Old English, and in Middle English dialectal developments increased. Standard Modern English today contains a mixture of elements from these Middle English dialects. *Bury, kale,* and *raid* provide examples of such mixture.

The Middle English period was also marked by increasing borrowing from French, and such borrowing has continued since this period into modern times. The earliest French words borrowed into English often aren't immediately apparent as French. They may not sound French anymore, unlike more recent borrowings such as *nonchalant* or *chagrin.* In words borrowed from French at an early date, English sometimes preserves sounds that have since disappeared from the word in French in the intervening centuries. The *ch* sound of *chase* (see *catch*) is an example of an English word preserving such sounds, since *ch* in French *chasser* is now pronounced like English *sh.* However, French words that have been in English for only a few centuries, such as *envelope,* sometimes hesitate between Anglicizing pronunciations on the one hand and pronunciations that attempt to approximate the French sounds on the other.

The Normans who conquered England spoke a dialect of French different from that used in Paris, and a dialect of French called Anglo-Norman or Anglo-French based on their speech, with an admixture of other elements, became the second language of England for a while. Especially characteristic of Anglo-Norman was the preservation of the Latin consonant *c* before the vowel *a.* In the French of Paris, however, *c* before *a* had developed into *ch.* Many of the earlier borrowings from French into English were from Anglo-Norman, but later it sometimes happened that the same word was borrowed again in a form closer to the standard Parisian form. This has led to a certain number of doublets (words derived from the same historical source by different routes of transmission) in English, such as *chattel* and *cattle* (see *cattle*). French has also made a notable contribution to English vocabulary describing the good things in life, with words such as *banquet, beef,* and *victual* that tellingly illustrate the relationship between the culture of the ascendant Anglo-Norman aristocracy and that of rest of the population, which spoke English.

Other Languages That Have Influenced English

Widespread direct borrowing from Latin has also characterized the history of English, from the Old English period onwards. In medieval times, Latin was the preeminent language of religion, scholarship, and government in western Europe. *Dirge, hearse, patter,* and *short shrift* find their origins in the Medieval Latin of the Church. In more recent centuries, thousands of scientific terms of Greek and Latin origin have poured into the dictionary. Some scientific and medical words of Latin origin with unexpected etymologies include *oscillate* and *testis.*

Since the medieval period onward, Arabic has also made a substantial contribution to the vocabulary of English. Words of Arabic origin include *alcohol, average, racket,* and *zero.* Many other languages began to add to the wealth of English words as British mercantile interests stretched around the world and the British Empire began to emerge. Borrowings from Dutch are especially numerous and include such words as *bumpkin, pickle, walrus,* and *yacht.* British ships brought *ketchup, tea,* and *typhoon* back from China. Recently the word *tea* has been imported again in the form of its doublet *chai.* Irish and Scottish Gaelic have given English such words as *galore, slogan,* and *spree.* As another example of the varied sources of English words, we may recall a borrowing from Romany (the language of the Gypsies), *pal.* And we must not forget the many loanwords from Yiddish found in American English, such as *glitch.*

However, borrowing is not the only process that has brought new words into the dictionary. Many linguistic processes like clipping (shortening or abbreviation) have made new words out of old, such as *cute* from *acute* or *za* from *pizza.* Avoidance of taboo words has led to the appearance of newer, less offensive-sounding words, such as *donkey.* The glossary at the end of this book will help readers explore more of these processes in depth.

All of the processes outlined above have been working together over thousands of years to give us the English words that we use today. If you open the dictionary, you will find that we know the history of most of these words quite well. But still a certain number remain mysteries. Often it is the most recent words that remain the most obscure, such as *gremlin*. Legions of scholars pore over old newspapers, dime store novels, and photographs of nineteenth-century cityscapes and billboards, searching for the attestation that will clear up the remaining mysteries. For an example of the importance of this work, see *hooker.*

English speakers are uniquely privileged by the variety of their linguistic heritage, from Indo-European and from other language families. And since English is now the first truly global language in the history of humanity, as well as the language of the majority of webpages, English can expect to grow even richer with new words.

A Note on Sources

Many different editors have worked over the years to produce the word history notes collected in this volume. Major sources of evidence that they have used in compiling this book are the great historical dictionaries of English and other languages, and readers who seek to know more about the history of English are encouraged to consult these works for further enlightenment. Most important among these sources is the *Oxford English Dictionary*, 2nd Edition (Oxford University Press, 1989). Also essential are the *Middle English Dictionary*, edited by Hans Kurath, Sherman E. Kuhn, et al. (University of Michigan Press, Ann Arbor, 1952-2001), the *Dictionary of American Regional English*, edited by edited by Frederic G. Cassidy and Joan Houston Hall (4 volumes, A-Sk; Belknap Press of the Harvard University Press, 1985-2002), and the *Random House Dictionary of American Slang*, edited by J. E. Lighter (2 volumes, A-O; Random House, 1994). When we have given dates at which words or meanings entered the English language, we have often given the dates recorded in these large historical dictionaries. To the editors—past and present—of all these great works we are heavily indebted.

For the study of the history of the pronunciation of English, we have consulted *Accents of English* by J. C. Wells (3 volumes, Cambridge University Press, 1982) and *The Pronunciation of English in the Atlantic States* edited by Hans Kurath and Raven I. McDavid, Jr. (University of Michigan Press, Ann Arbor, 1961).

Another important resource in tracing the history of words is the work of linguists who reconstruct unrecorded languages, such as Germanic and Indo-European. *The American Heritage Dictionary of Indo-European Roots*, 2nd edition, edited by Calvert Watkins (Houghton Mifflin, 2000) has been especially helpful to us in this respect. The *Lexicon of Reconstructed Pronunciation in Early Middle Chinese, Late Middle Chinese, and Early Mandarin* by Edwin Pulleyblank (University of British Columbia Press, Vancouver, 1991) was consulted for the etymologies of words of Chinese origin.

We are also greatly indebted to the many authors who have devoted their time to researching individual English words and publishing their findings in scholarly works. In particular, we would like to thank Allen Koenigsberg, whose research has contributed greatly to our understanding of the word *hello*. We are also grateful to Ward Cunningham for sharing the story of the genesis of the word *wiki*.

abracadabra

```
A B R A C A D A B R A
A B R A C A D A B R
A B R A C A D A B
A B R A C A D A
A B R A C A D
A B R A C A
A B R A C
A B R A
A B R
A B
A
```

Magicians still use the word *abracadabra* in their performances, unaware that at one time the word was both more and less magical than it is today. *Abracadabra* couldn't pull a rabbit out of a hat, but it was used to ward off disease or trouble.

In order to work its magic, the word was worn as an amulet on which the letters ABRACADABRA were arranged in an inverted pyramid. One less letter appeared in each line of the pyramid until only *a* remained to form the vertex of the triangle. As the letters disappeared, so supposedly did the disease or trouble. The use of an amulet such as this is prescribed as a treatment for fever in a poem on medical subjects from the third century A.D., called *Liber Medicinalis,* by the Roman physician Quintus Serenus Sammonicus.

accolade

People usually have to stick their necks out to earn accolades, and this is as it should be. In tracing *accolade* back to its Latin origins, we find that it was formed from the prefix *ad-*, "to, on," and the noun *collum*, "neck," which may bring the word *collar* to mind. From these elements came the Vulgar Latin word **accollāre*, which was the source of French *accolade*, "an embrace." An embrace was originally given to a knight when dubbing him, a fact that accounts for *accolade* having the technical sense "ceremonial bestowal of knighthood," the sense in which the word is first recorded in English in 1623.

acorn

A thoughtful glance at the word *acorn* might lead one to think that it is made up of *oak* and *corn*, especially if we think of *corn* in its sense of "a kernel or seed of a plant," as in *peppercorn*. The fact that others thought the word was so constituted partly accounts for the present form *acorn*. Here we see the workings of the process of linguistic change known as folk etymology, an alteration of the form of a word or phrase so that it resembles a more familiar term mistakenly regarded as analogous. *Acorn* actually goes back to Old English *æcern*, "acorn," which in turn is derived from the Indo-European root **ōg-*, meaning "fruit, berry."

acre

Today an acre is known as 4,840 square yards, but to a speaker of Old English an *æcer,* the immediate ancestor of *acre,* meant "a field, land," as well as "a particular quantity of land," known in Anglo-Saxon times to be the amount of land a yoke of oxen could plow in one day. Although the size of the measure of land varied in different places and at different times (depending on the strength and stamina of one's oxen), it was set at the current measure by statute during the Middle Ages.

Old English *æcer* descended from the Proto-Indo-European word **agros.* The *c* in the Old English word was changed from the *g* by the action of GRIMM'S LAW (see glossary). In Latin, Proto-Indo-European **agros* developed into *ager,* "field, land," which we can see in such Modern English words as *agriculture.* The English word *pilgrim* is ultimately derived from Latin *peregrīnus,* "foreigner," itself a derivative of the Latin adjective *pereger,* "away from home, on a journey." This in turn was derived from *per,* "through," and *ager,* a traveler being one who has crossed many acres of land.

admiral

Long before most European countries had navies, North African Arabs ruled the waves. Although American and British admirals would not think that they had much in common with an emir, the words *admiral* and *emir* spring from the same source, the Arabic word *'amīr,* meaning "commander."

In twelfth-century Sicily, a naval commander was designated by words going back to the Arabic word

ʾamīr in the phrase ʾamīr-al- "commander of the." The *al* in *admiral* is actually the definite article of the noun that designated what was being commanded. The *d* in *admiral* appeared first in the Medieval Latin and Old French forms, from which *admiral* came into English during the sixteenth century. The *d* is perhaps suggested by forms of the Latin verb *admīrārī,* source of our verb *admire,* an admiral probably being someone who is looked up to.

Emir was borrowed into English through French in the seventeenth century as an Arabic title. The *e* here probably represents an Arabic dialectal feature in which an *a* acquires an *e*-like pronunciation, a feature still common in Arabic dialects today.

a-hunting

Prefixing *a-* to verb forms ending in *-ing,* as in *a-hunting* and *a-fishing,* was once fairly common in vernacular American English speech, particularly in the highland areas of the South and in the Southwest. Many folk and blues songs just wouldn't be the same without this construction, which is heard in the opening lines "Froggy went a-courting and he did ride, uh-huh!" as well as in "John Brown's body lies a-mouldering in the grave," a song sung during the Civil War by Union soldiers marching to the tune now used for the "Battle Hymn of the Republic." Such verb forms derive from an Old English construction in which a preposition, usually *on,* was placed in front of a verbal noun (a noun made from a verb by the addition *-ing*) in order to indicate that the action was extended or ongoing. Gradually such prepositions were shortened to *a-* by the common linguistic process that shortens or drops unaccented syllables. The

-*ing* forms came to be regarded as present participles rather than verbal nouns, and the use of *a-* was extended to genuine present participles as well as to verbal nouns. Eventually *a-* disappeared from many dialects, including Standard English in the United States and Great Britain, though it has been retained in some isolated dialect areas, particularly among older speakers. Today, speakers from the American South who use the *a-* prefix do not use it with all -*ing* words (or - *in'* words, as the ending is usually pronounced in these dialects), nor do they use it randomly. Rather, *a-* is only used with -*ing* words that function as part of a verb phrase, as in "She was a-runnin'." Speakers would not prefix *a-* to the -*ing* words in phrases such as "I can't stand this fussin' and fightin'," since these nouns function as direct objects, not participles. Also, the prefix *a-* is never added to verbs stressed on the second syllable or to verbs beginning with a vowel. No one would say "The hound was a-retrievin' the duck" or "I was a-eatin' my supper." Although speakers of Standard American English unfamiliar with the regional dialects of the United States may not perceive these complexities, the nonstandard dialects of English have grammatical rules that are just as intricate and subtle as those of the standard variety.

alcohol

The *al-* in *alcohol* may alert some readers to the fact that this is a word of Arabic descent, as is the case with *algebra* and *alkali, al-* being the Arabic definite article corresponding to *the* in English. The origin of -*cohol* is less obvious, however. Its Arabic ancestor was *kuḥl*, a fine powder most often made from antimony and used by women to darken their eyelids; in fact, *kuḥl* has given us the word *kohl* for such a preparation. Arabic chemists came to use *al-kuḥl* to mean "any fine powder produced in a number of ways, including the process of heating a substance to a gaseous state and then recooling it." The English word *alcohol,* derived through Medieval Latin from Arabic, is first recorded in 1543 in this sense. Arabic chemists also used *al-kuḥl* to refer to other substances such as essences that were obtained by distillation, a sense first found for English *alcohol* in 1672. One of these distilled essences, known as "alcohol of wine," is the constituent of fermented liquors that causes intoxication. In time, this became the sole meaning of *alcohol,* which then came to refer to the liquor that contains this essence as well as to a class of chemical compounds such as methanol.

alibi

With the word *alibi,* the technical Latin legal terminology of the courts enters everyday English. When the Latin adverb *alibi,* "elsewhere," first appeared as an English noun in the eighteenth century, it meant "the plea of having been elsewhere at the time when any alleged act took place." Perhaps because frail human beings cannot have too many words that mean "excuse" or "apology," we have appropriated this term simply to mean "an excuse," prompted by the frequent use of *alibi* in crime novels, films, and television shows.

aloof

The origin of *aloof* is uncertain. It may be made up of the prefix *a-,* meaning "in the direction of," as in *aback,* and *luff,* "the windward side of a ship." *Luff* is recorded in English from the fourteenth century, but no one is sure of how it entered the language. *Aloof* appears first in the sixteenth century and probably translates Dutch *te loef,* which, in nautical terms, means the same thing. As a result of Anglo-Dutch trade, English borrowed many Dutch nautical terms. Thus both *luff* and *aloof* may have been borrowed from Dutch at different times.

A ship sailing *aloof* would sail with its bow into the wind, keeping the ship from being blown by the wind toward the shore, or *alee.* This term was adapted much earlier than *aloof,* from Old Norse *á hlé.*

The fact that the ship kept its distance from something, such as a shore, when it sailed aloof led to the development of the senses "away at some distance" and "from a distance," which were later extended to mean "without community of feeling; distant, indifferent."

Two other nautical terms that have seeped into everyday life and lost their salty tang are **average** (see below) and *ahead,* one of the earliest senses of which was "in front of a moving company of ships."

See also **yacht.**

Amazon

In classical legend the Amazons were a tribe of warrior women. Their name is supposedly derived from Greek *a-mazos,* "without a breast," because according to the legend they cut off their right breasts so as to be better able to shoot with a bow and arrow. This folk etymology, like most folk etymologies, is incorrect, but the Amazons of legend are not so completely different from the historical Amazons, who were also warriors. The historical Amazons were probably Scythians, an Iranian people renowned for their cavalry. The first Greeks to come into contact with the Iranians were the Ionians, who lived on the coast of Asia Minor and were constantly threatened by the Persians, a powerful Iranian people. *Amazōn* is probably the Ionian Greek form of the Iranian word *ha-mazan,* "fighting together." The regular Greek form would be *hamazōn,* but

Roman copy of a marble statue of an Amazon, the original of which was attributed to the Greek sculptor Kresilas (fl. 450 BC)

because the Ionians dropped their *h*'s like Cockneys, *hamazōn* became *amazōn,* the form taken into the other Greek dialects.

ambition

The Latin word *ambitiō* meant "desire for advancement"; however, an earlier sense of the word was "a soliciting of votes, canvassing." *Ambitiō* comes from *ambīre,* a combination of *ambi-,* "about," and *īre,* "to go." *Ambīre* could mean "to canvass, solicit for political support," as well as "to canvass for an office, prize, etc." Corresponding senses of *ambitiō* were "a standing for public office" and "rivalry for honors." Related to these senses of *ambitiō* were "currying favor" and "desire for advancement." The word, borrowed directly from Latin and also from Old French, appears in Middle English as *ambicioun,* and at first it had only negative connotations. By Shakespeare's time, however, *ambition* had developed the positive sense that it has today.

an

The forms of the indefinite article *an* are good examples of what can happen to a word when it becomes habitually pronounced without stress. *An* is in fact a weakened form of *one;* both *an* and *one* come from Old English *ān,* "one." In early Middle English, besides representing the cardinal numeral "one," *ān* came to function as an indefinite article, and in this role the word was ordinarily pronounced with very little or no stress. Sound changes that affected unstressed syllables elsewhere in the language affected the word also. First, the vowel was shortened and eventually reduced to a schwa (ə). Second, the *n* was lost before consonants. This loss of *n* affected some other words as well and created such pairs as *my* and *mine, thy* and *thine.* Originally these were doublets just like *a* and *an,* with *mine* and *thine* occurring only before vowels, as in Ben Jonson's famous line "Drink to me only with thine eyes." By the time of Modern English, though, *my* and *thy* had replaced *mine* and *thine* when used before nouns (that is, when not used predicatively, as in "This book is mine"), just as some varieties of Modern English use *a* even before vowels ("a apple").

Metaphorical extension is a common phenomenon in language change: two dissimilar things resemble each other enough in some way so that the name of one ends up being applied to the other. The Greeks, for instance, saw a resemblance between, on one hand, the spar or yard that jutted from the bow of a ship to hold a sail and, on the other, an insect feeler, or what we now call an antenna. They used *keraia* for both things; no one knows which meaning came first and which followed as a meta-phor. Medieval scholar Theodorus Gaza, who translated Aristotle's *History of Animals,* confronted the problem of translating the Greek *keraia,* meaning "an insect horn or feeler," into Latin. He knew that *keraia* also meant "yardarm, a projecting 'horn' or end of a sail yard," and therefore thought that the Latin word *antenna,* meaning "sail yard, yardarm," was an appropriate translation. While English scholars knew the Latin word from Latin scientific texts well into the Renaissance, *antenna* didn't become a natural English word until the seventeenth century. *Antenna* seems to invite metaphorical application—by the twentieth century, *antenna* was extended to refer to a radio aerial wire, perhaps because of its resemblance to an insect feeler. It was then only natural to use *antenna* to refer to a television aerial as well.

apron

At the beginning of the fourteenth century, folks spread *naprons* on their tables, drilled holes with *naugers,* avoided *nadders,* and turned to *noumperes* to settle their disputes. By the end of the century, *apron, auger, adder,* and *umpire* (or at least early forms of them) had emerged as new words due to a trick of the ear. When preceded by the indefinite article *a*, the article attracted the initial *n* in all of these words, so that *a* became *an* and the noun that followed was left *n*-less. The change occurred regardless of etymology. *Apron*, originally *napron*, came from Old French *naperon*, "tablecloth," a word with connections to *napkin* and *napery*. Likewise, *umpire*, originally *noumpere*, was derived from Old French *nonper*, which is made up of *non*, "not," and *per*, "equal," as is someone requested to act as arbiter of a dispute between two parties. *Auger*, was originally *nauger*, from Old English *nafogār*, a compound word made from *nafa*, "wheel hub" (related to *navel*), and *gār*, "spear." An auger is a tool for piercing and boring holes, like the hole in a wheel through which the axle passes. *Adder*, too, descends from Old English *næder*, "serpent." In the case of *nuncle*, a late-sixteenth-century regional variant of *uncle*, the article divided in the opposite way and *uncle* became *nuncle*.

arena

Fans watching contact sports such as boxing, hockey, or football being played in modern arenas may be struck by the connection between the word *arena* and the notion of gladiatorial combat. This word is from Latin *harēna* (also spelled *arēna*), "sand." *Harēna* then came to mean the part of a Roman amphitheater that was covered with sand to absorb the blood spilled by the combatants. *Arena* is first recorded in English during the seventeenth century, denoting this area of a Roman amphitheater.

artichoke

Those who have been warned to watch out for the small, sharp-tipped leaves toward the innermost part of an artichoke may wonder whether the name of this vegetable has anything to do with choking. Originally it did not. Our word goes back to an Arabic word for the same plant, *al-ḫaršuf.* Along with many other Arabic words, it passed into Spanish during the Middle Ages, when Muslims ruled much of Spain. The Old Spanish word *alcarchofa* was variously modified as it passed through Italian, a northern dialect form being *articiocco,* the source of the English word. It was further modified in English, where a potpourri of spellings and explanations are found since its appearance early in the sixteenth century. For example, people who did not know the long history of the word explained it by the notion that the flower had a "choke," that is, something that chokes, in its "heart."

asparagus

The history of the word *asparagus* is a good illustration of one of the peculiarities of English etymology. After the rebirth of classical learning during the Renaissance, Greek and Latin achieved a lofty status among the educated. As a result, etymologists and spelling reformers of the sixteenth and seventeenth centuries tried to give English a classical look by Latinizing or Hellenizing the spelling of words that had Latin or Greek ancestry (and even some that didn't). For example, Medieval Latin had a word *sparagus,* from Classical Latin *asparagus,* that was borrowed into Middle English and rendered as *sparage* or, more commonly, *sperage.* Botanists were familiar with the proper Latin version *asparagus,* and their use of that term together with the efforts of the etymologists caused the Latin form to become more widespread, eventually supplanting *sperage.* Thus, it is difficult to say whether the Modern English word *asparagus* is a direct continuation of Middle English *sperage* or a borrowing directly from Latin, a difficulty one encounters with hundreds of other words whose spellings and even pronunciations were Latinized during this time. The Latin form *asparagus* lives on in another guise as well; in the 1600s it was shortened in popular speech to *'sparagus,* which became *sparagrass* and *sparrowgrass* by folk etymology.

asset

In England after the Norman Conquest in 1066, French, the language of the conquerors, became the language of law. *Asset* comes from the old legal term *assets,* which was not a plural noun *(asset* plus *-s).* *Assets* was originally *asetz* or *asez,* an Old French word meaning simply "enough," as the modern French form *assez* still does. *Assets* was used as legal shorthand for "enough wealth to settle the claims made against a deceased person's estate." Because *assets* looked like a plural form and had a collective meaning, the word was mistakenly analyzed by a process known as *back-formation,* which gives us the verb *burgle* from the noun *burglar.* Speakers took *asset* as the base word with the plural suffix *-s,* thus inventing a noun where there wasn't one before. The singular form *asset* appeared in the nineteenth century to denote a single item in the assets column of a balance sheet, and from that usage the extended meanings of "valuable item" and "beneficial quality" developed.

atlas

18th-century French engraving of Atlas holding up the heavens

The word *atlas,* used to refer to a collection of maps, comes from the name of the Greek mythological figure Atlas, the Titan condemned to support the heavens on his shoulders. In 1585 the great sixteenth-century Flemish geographer Gerhardus Mercator, who devised the Mercator projection commonly used to represent the entirety of the earth's surface on a map, published *Atlas, or Cosmographical Meditations upon the Creation of the Universe.* Mercator's work consisted of two parts: a treatise on cosmology and a collection of maps. It was a new idea to publish a group of maps together for reference, and Mercator's work was very influential. On the title page of his collection there was a depiction of Atlas holding the globe. The title *Atlas* and images of the god were retained in subsequent publications of map collections, and the word became generic for any similar work.

attic

Nowadays, most attics just fill up with junk, belying the elegant origins of the word *attic. Attic* goes back through French and Latin to the Greek word *Attikos,* "relating to Attica or its chief city Athens."

The French word *attique* refers to, among other things, "a decorative architectural structure placed above another decorative structure of much greater height." This structure usually made use of the Attic order, an architectural order having square columns of any of the basic five orders, such as Doric or Corinthian, with pilasters rather than pillars. The English, who also built these structures, borrowed the French term for them. In English, the part of the building enclosed by this decorative structure was, from the seventeenth century, called the *Attic story,* a phrase in which *attic* is actually an attributive noun. Story later disappeared from the phrase and left us with just plain *attic,* stripped of its elegant associations, for the top story of a house.

average

An average day may not be wonderful, but we might at least emerge from it unscathed. The English *average,* however, originated from the Old French *availe,* which meant "damage to shipping." The Old French in turn is a borrowing of the Arabic word *ʾawāriyah,* "damaged goods," a derivative of *ʾawār,* "blemish." *Average* entered English around 1500, via Italian, as a maritime term referring in general to any expense, such as a loss from damage, over and above the cost of shipping freight. These expenses were usually distributed proportionally among the interested parties in the venture—for instance, the ship owners and the cargo owners. The idea of a mathematical average, or the arithmetic mean, developed from the notion of distributing a sum among a number of persons, and the senses of the adjective *average,* "typical" and "usual," are derived from this sense of a "mean" figure.

The history of *avocado* takes us back to the Aztecs and their language, Nahuatl, which contained the word *ahuacatl,* meaning both "fruit of the avocado tree" and "testicle." The word *ahuacatl* was compounded with others, as in *ahuacamolli,* meaning "avocado soup or sauce," from which the Spanish-Mexican word *guacamole* derives. In trying to pronounce *ahuacatl,* the Spanish who found the fruit and its Nahuatl name in Mexico came up with *aguacate,* but other Spanish speakers substituted the form *avocado* for the Nahuatl word because *ahuacatl* sounded like the early Spanish word *avocado* (now *abogado*), meaning "lawyer." In borrowing the Spanish *avocado,* first recorded in English in 1697 in the compound *avogato pear* (with a spelling that probably reflects Spanish pronunciation), we have lost some traces of the more interesting Nahuatl word.

baby-sit

The verb *baby-sit* is of interest to parents, children, and linguists. It is interesting to the last group because it illustrates one of two types of the linguistic process called *back-formation.* The first type is based on misunderstanding, as in the case of our word *pea.* In Middle English the ancestor of *pea* was *peṣe* or *peaṣe,* forms that functioned as both singular and plural. In other words, the *ṣ* was part of the word, not a plural ending. But around the beginning of the seventeenth century people began to interpret the sound represented by *ṣ* as a plural ending, and a new singular, spelled *pea* in Modern English, was developed. In the second type of back-formation, as seen in the case of *baby-ṣit,* first recorded in 1947, and *babyṣitter,* first recorded in 1937, no misunderstanding is involved. The agent noun *babyṣitter* with its *-er* suffix could have been derived from the verb *baby-ṣit,* as *diver* was from *dive,* but the evidence shows that the pattern was reversed, and the agent noun preceded the verb from which it would normally have been derived.

badger

Our name for the Eurasian species of this mammal, which is noted for defending its burrow like a knight of old, may come from the badger's knightly emblem. The creature's white head with a broad black stripe on each side of the snout may have brought to mind a badge, hence *badger.* Good evidence supporting this theory is that an earlier name for the animal was *bauson,* which comes from the Old French word *baucenc,* usually referring to a white patch on a horse and also meaning "badger." *Badger* was later used of the species native to North America.

ballot

The earliest meaning of *ballot* in English is "a small ball used to register a vote." The source of the English word was Italian *ballotta,* the diminutive form of *balla* "ball." In order to prevent others from learning who had cast which votes, those voting would drop balls into a box or other container. When yea and nay votes were recorded with different colored balls, a black ball was often used to register a negative vote. This practice gave rise to the verb *blackball,* recorded in English from the eighteenth century, meaning "to exclude someone from membership by a negative vote." The Italian word *balla* is ultimately of Germanic origin, and is thus kin to the English word *ball.* A word ancestral to English *ball,* "spherical object," is not attested in Old English, however. Old English does attest a closely related word, *beallucas,* meaning "testicles," source of the rather vulgar modern British slang *bollocks.* Some scholars suggest that Old English did have a word *beall, which would have developed into Modern English *ball,* but the Old English word has simply not shown up in any surviving texts. Although linguists usually do not like to postulate unattested forms for real languages such as Old English, nevertheless they sometimes must. Our knowledge of ancient and medieval languages usually depends upon written records, and since we possess only a fraction of the many manuscripts that must have been written in the past, we can expect that a few words have fallen through the cracks.

banquet

The linguistic stock of the word *banquet* has been fluctuating for a long time. The Old French word *banquet,* the likely source of our word, was derived from Old French *banc,* "bench," ultimately of Germanic origin. The sense development in Old French seems to have been from "little bench" to "meal taken on the family workbench" to "feast." The English word *banquet* is first recorded in a work possibly composed before 1475 with reference to a feast held by the god Apollo, and it appears to have been used from the fifteenth to the eighteenth century to refer to the feasts of the powerful and the wealthy. Perhaps this association led a nineteenth-century newspaper editor to label the word "grandiloquent" because it was being appropriated by those lower down on the social scale.

barnacle

The word *barnacle* is known from as far back as the early thirteenth century. At that time it did not refer to the crustacean, as it does nowadays, but rather to a species of waterfowl today known as the barnacle goose; more than three hundred years went by before *barnacle* was used to refer to the crustacean. One might well wonder what the connection between these two creatures is. The answer lies in natural history. Until fairly recent times, it was widely believed that certain animals were engendered spontaneously from particular substances. Maggots, for instance, were believed to be generated from rotting meat. The barnacle goose breeds in the Arctic, a fact not known for a long time; since no one ever witnessed the bird breeding, it was thought to be spontaneously generated from trees along the shore, or from rotting wood. Wood that has been in the ocean for any length of time is often dotted with barnacles, and it was natural for

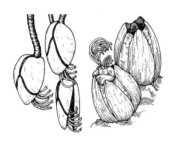

two types of barnacles: goose (left) *and acorn*

people to believe that the crustaceans were also engendered directly from the wood, like the geese, and to make a connection between the two. In fact, as different as the two creatures might appear to us, they share a similar trait: barnacles have long feathery appendages that are reminiscent of a bird's plumage. This led one writer in 1678 to comment on the "multitudes of little Shells; having within them little Birds perfectly shap'd, supposed to be Barnacles [that is, barnacle geese]." In popular conception the two creatures were thus closely linked. Over time the crustacean became the central referent of the word, and the bird was called the *barnacle goose* for clarity.

bayonet

It is not unusual for a word to come from a place name. *Cheddar,* from the name of a village in southwest England; *hamburger,* after Hamburg, Germany; and *mayonnaise,* possibly from Mahón, the capital of

Minorca, are often found together on our tables. The word *bayonet,* a very undomestic sort of word, also derives from a place name, that of Bayonne, a town in southwest France where the weapon was first made. The French word *baïonnette* could also mean "a dagger or a knife," and the English word *bayonet* is first found in 1672 with this meaning. The word is first recorded in its present sense in 1704.

bead

The connection between a bead and the Old English word *bed* or *gebed,* "prayer," from which it derives, is in the Christian practice, begun in the Middle Ages, of keeping count of prayers by means of beads threaded on a string. *Telling one's beads*—or saying one's prayers—with the aid of a rosary was such a common way of praying that the Middle English descendant of the Old English word gradually became the word for the counter as well as the prayer that was counted. By modern times *bead* no longer meant "prayer" at all but had been extended to signify other small round objects, such as drops of water.

bed

When we lie down in our beds at night, on a comfortable mattress or futon, we are far removed in terms of comfort from the users of an earlier form of the word *bed.* Our word goes back to the Indo-European root **bhedh-,* meaning "to dig." In prehistoric Common Germanic, the reconstructed ancestor of languages such as English, German, and Swedish, the word derived from the Indo-European root meant "a garden plot, flower bed" and "a sleeping place." The connection between digging and a place for sleeping lies in the notion that beds, or resting places, were at one time dug out of the ground. In English, we still say that a river digs its *bed* out of the surrounding terrain.

beef

That beef comes from cows is known to most, but the close relationship between the words *beef* and *cow* is hardly household knowledge. *Cow* comes via Middle English from Old English *cū*, which is descended from the Indo-European root **gwou-*, also meaning "cow." This root has descendants in most of the branches of the Indo-European language family. Among those descendants is the Latin word *bōs*, "cow," whose stem form, *bov-*, eventually became the Old French word *buef*, also meaning "cow." The French nobles who ruled England after the Norman Conquest of course used French words to refer to the meats they were served, so the animal called *cū* by the Anglo-Saxon peasants was called *buef* by the French nobles when it was brought to them cooked at dinner. Thus arose the distinction between the words for animals and their meat that is also found in the English word-pairs *swine/pork, sheep/mutton,* and *deer/venison.* What is interesting about *cow/beef* is that we are in fact dealing with one and the same word, etymologically speaking.

belfry

The words *bell* and *belfry* seem obviously related, but in fact the *bel-* portion of *belfry* had nothing to do with bells until comparatively recently. *Belfry* goes back to a compound formed in prehistoric Common Germanic. It is generally agreed that the second part of this compound is the element *frij-, meaning "peace, safety." The first element is either *bergan, "to protect," which would yield a compound meaning "a defensive place of shelter," or *berg-, "a high place," which would yield a compound meaning "a high place of safety, tower." Whatever the meaning of the original Germanic source, its Old French descendant *berfrei,* which first meant "siege tower," came to mean "watchtower." Presumably because bells were used in these towers, the word was applied to bell towers as well. The Old North French alteration *belfroi,* which reminded English speakers of their native word *belle* (our *bell*), entered Middle English with the sense "bell tower," first recorded in 1272.

berserk

When we say that we are going berserk, we may not realize how extreme a state this might be. Our adjective comes from the noun *berserker,* or *berserk,* which is from the Old Norse word *berserkr,* "a wild warrior or champion." Such warriors wore hides of bears, which explains the probable origin of *berserkr* as a compound of *bera,* "bear," and *serkr,* "shirt, coat." These *berserkers* became frenzied in battle, howling like animals, foaming at the mouth, and biting the edges of their iron shields. *Berserker* is first recorded in English in the early nineteenth century, long after these wild warriors ceased to exist.

Betelgeuse

The history of the curious star name *Betelgeuse* is a good example of how scholarly errors can creep into language. The story starts with the pre-Islamic Arabic astronomers, who called the star *yad al-jawzā'*, "hand of the *jawzā'*." The *jawzā'* was their name for the constellation Gemini. After Greek astronomy became known to the Arabs, the word came to be applied to the constellation Orion as well. Some centuries later, when scribes writing in Medieval Latin tried to render the word, they misread the *y* as a *b* (the two corresponding Arabic letters are very similar when used as the first letter in a word), leading to the Medieval Latin form *Bedalgeuze.* In the Renaissance, another set of scholars trying to figure out the name interpreted the first syllable *bed-* as being derived from a putative Arabic word **bāṭ,* meaning "armpit." This word did not exist; it would correctly have been *ibṭ.* Nonetheless, the error stuck, and the resultant etymologically "improved" spelling *Betelgeuse* was borrowed into French as *Bételgeuse,* whence English *Betelgeuse.*

bigot

Bigots may have more in common with God than one might think. Legend has it that Rollo, the first duke of Normandy, refused to kiss the foot of the French king Charles III, uttering the phrase *bi got,* his borrowing of the assumed Old English equivalent of our expression *by God.* Although this story is almost surely apocryphal, it is true that *bigot* was used by the French as a term of abuse for the Normans, but not in a religious sense. Later, however, the word, or very possibly a homonym, was used abusively in French for the Beguines, members of a Roman Catholic lay sisterhood. From the fifteenth century on Old French *bigot* meant "an excessively devoted or hypocritical person." *Bigot* is first recorded in English in 1598 with the sense "a superstitious hypocrite."

bless

The verb *bless* comes from Old English *blædsian* (also spelled *blēdsian* or *blētsian*), "to bless, wish happiness, consecrate." Although the Old English verb has no cognates in any other Germanic language, it can be shown to derive from the Germanic noun **blōdan*, "blood." *Blædsian* therefore literally means "to consecrate with blood, sprinkle with blood." The Angles, Saxons, and Jutes, the early Germanic migrants to Britain, used *blædsian* for their pagan sacrifices. After they converted to Christianity, *blædsian* acquired new meanings as a result of its use in translations of the Latin Bible, but it kept its pagan Germanic senses as well.

blurb

In a lifetime of reading the fluff on book jackets we may never have stopped to think about the origin of *blurb,* the term for this kind of prose. *Blurb,* in fact, does not come to us from another language, nor does it go back to an Indo-European root. The American humorist, illustrator, and author Gelett Burgess coined *blurb* in the early 1900's. He did so on an amusing book jacket that he designed for his book *Are You a Bromide?* (first published in 1906). The cover pictured a young woman whom Burgess christened Miss Belinda Blurb. Burgess himself had these words to say about *blurb* in 1914: "On the 'jacket' of the 'latest' fiction, we find the blurb; abounding in agile adjectives and adverbs, attesting that this book is the 'sensation of the year.'" Although we are indebted to Burgess for *blurb,* his other inventions somehow failed to catch on. They included *oofle,* "a person whose name you cannot remember," and *tintiddle,* "a witty retort, thought of too late."

For an example of another recently invented word that shows signs of staying power, see **wiki.**

book

From an etymological perspective, *book* and *beech* are branches of the same tree. The Germanic root of both words is **bōk-,* ultimately from an Indo-European root meaning "beech tree." The Old English form of *book* is *bōc,* from Germanic **bōk-ō,* "written document, book." The Old English form of *beech* is *bēce,* from Germanic **bōk-jōn,* "beech tree." The early Germanic peoples used strips of beech wood to write on, which makes the semantic connection between *beech* and *book* clear. A similar development occurred in Latin. The Latin word for book is *liber,* whence *library. Liber,* however, originally meant "bark"—that is, the smooth inner bark of a tree, which the early Romans likewise used to write on.

boomerang

The words we have borrowed from native languages of Australia, such as *billabong, budgerigar, dingo, kangaroo, koala, kookaburra, waddy,* and *wallaby,* generally have the exotic sound of down under, and *boomerang* is no exception. In a book about the languages of New South Wales published in 1790 is found the native term *boo-mer-rit,* glossed "the scimitar," because of the curved shape of the boomerang. In 1825 in a passage containing the first recorded instance of the English form *boomerang,* we are told it is "a short crested weapon which the natives of Port Jackson [now part of Sydney] project with accurate aim into a rotary motion." In 1827 another commentator says that this term "may be retained for want of a more descriptive name."

boutique

You would not go to an apothecary for the same products that you would look for in a boutique or a bodega, yet all three words—*apothecary, boutique,* and *bodega*—are derived from the Greek word *apothēkē,* "storehouse." These words came into English by way of Latin, which borrowed the Greek word as *apothēca.* The addition of the Latin suffix *-ārius* formed a new word, *apothēcārius,* meaning "clerk, warehousekeeper." In postclassical times the Latin word came to refer primarily to one storing and selling medicines and drugs, and with such meanings the word *apothecary* was borrowed into English. *Boutique* and *bodega* are both derived from Latin *apothēca* and came to English from French and Spanish, respectively. *Boutique* originally meant a small shop of any kind but now refers to a small, fashionable retail store. *Bodega* in Spanish means "wine cellar"; only in American Spanish has it been extended to mean "grocery store" as well.

boycott

Charles C. Boycott seems to have become a household word because of his strong sense of duty to his employer. An Englishman and former British soldier, Boycott was the estate agent of the Earl of Erne in County Mayo, Ireland. The earl was one of the absentee landowners who as a group held most of the land in Ireland. Boycott was chosen in the fall of 1880 to be the test case for a new policy advocated by Charles Parnell, an Irish politician who wanted land reform. Any landlord who would not charge lower rents or any tenant who took over the farm of an evicted tenant would be given the complete cold shoulder by Parnell's supporters. Boycott refused to charge lower rents and ejected his tenants. At this point members of Parnell's Irish Land League stepped in, and Boycott and his family found themselves isolated— without servants, farmhands, service in stores, or mail delivery. Boycott's name was quickly adopted as the term for this treatment, not just in English but in other languages such as French, Dutch, German, and Russian.

bridal

Champagne, not ale, flows at many modern bridal celebrations. *Bridal,* however, is a compound of two Old English words that meant "bride" and "ale." In the days when heartier drink was imbibed, the compound meant "wedding feast," but by late medieval times it was used to refer to the ceremony itself. The word *bridal* as an adjective probably arose from the widespread interpretation of -al as the common adjectival suffix.

broker

Giving gifts to one's broker might be justifiable from an etymological point of view because the word *broker* may be connected through its Anglo-Norman source, *brocour* or *abrocour,* with Spanish *alboroque,* meaning "ceremony or ceremonial gift after the conclusion of a business deal." If this connection does exist, "business deal" is the notion shared by the Spanish and Anglo-Norman words because *brocour* referred to the middleman in transactions. The English word *broker* is first found in Middle English in 1355, several centuries before we find instances of its familiar compounds *pawnbroker,* first recorded in 1687, and *stockbroker,* first recorded in 1706.

buccaneer

The Errol Flynn-like figure of the buccaneer pillaging the Spanish Main may seem less dashing if we realize that the term *buccaneer* corresponds to the word *barbecuer.* The first recorded use of the French word *boucanier,* which was borrowed into English, referred to a person on the islands of Hispaniola and Tortuga who hunted wild oxen and boars and smoked the meat in a barbecue frame known in French as a *boucan.* This French word came from a Tupi word meaning "a rack used for roasting or for storing things," or "a racklike platform supporting a house." The original barbecuers seem to have subsequently adopted a more remunerative way of life, piracy, which accounts for the new meaning given to the word. *Buccaneer* is recorded first in 1661 in its earlier sense in English; the sense we are familiar with is recorded in 1690.

buffalo

The buffalo is so closely associated with the Wild West that one might assume that its name comes from a Native American word, as is the case with the words *moose* and *skunk*. In fact, *buffalo* can probably be traced back by way of one or more of the Romance languages through Late and Classical Latin and ultimately to the Greek word *boubalos,* meaning "an antelope or a buffalo." The buffalo referred to by the Greek and Latin words was of course not the American one but an Old World mammal, such as the water buffalo of southern Asia. Applied to the North American mammal, *buffalo* is a misnomer, *bison* being the preferred term. As far as everyday usage is concerned, however, *buffalo,* first recorded for the American mammal in 1635, is older than *bison,* first recorded in 1774.

bumpkin

The term *bumpkin* may at one time have been directed at an entire people rather than that segment of the population living in a rural area. The first recorded appearance of the word in 1570 is glossed by the Latin word *Batavus,* "Dutchman," making plausible the suggestion that *bumpkin* may come from either the Middle Dutch word *bommekijn,* "little barrel," or the Flemish word *boomken,* "shrub." The connection would be between a squat object and the short, rotund figure of the Dutchman in the popular imagination. Any bumpkin would surely prefer this etymology to the suggestion that *bumpkin* is a derivative of *bum,* "the rear end."

bury

Why does *bury* rhyme with *berry* and not with *jury?* The answer goes back to early English times. The late Old English form of the verb *bury* was *byrgan,* pronounced approximately (bür'yən). The symbol (ü) represents a sound like the vowel found, for example, in French *tu,* made by saying the vowel in the English word *tea* while rounding the lips to say the *oo* in *too.* During Middle English times this (ü) sound changed, but with different results in different regions of England: to (oͦo) as in *put* in the Midlands, to (ĭ) as in *pit* in southern England, or to (ĕ) as in *pet* in southeast England. London is located in the East Midlands, but because of its central location and its status as the capital, its East Midlands dialect was influenced by southern (Saxon) and southeastern (Kentish) dialects. The normal East Midlands development of (ü) was (oͦo). Because scribes from the East Midlands pronounced the word with this vowel, they tended to spell the word with a *u,* and this spelling became standard when spellings were fixed after the introduction of printing. The word's pronunciation, however, is southeastern. *Bury* is the only word in Modern English with a Midlands spelling and a southeastern pronunciation. Similarly, the word *busy,* from Old English *bysig, bisig,* and its verb *bysgian, bisgian,* "to employ," is spelled with the East Midlands dialect *u,* but pronounced with the southern (Saxon) development of (ü), (ĭ).

bus

If we did not know the correct etymology, the existence of a word *bus,* meaning "large motor vehicle for carrying many passengers," and the verb *bus,* "to clear dishes from a table," might lead us to speculate that the word *bus* originally had something to do with the notion of transport before buses were invented. In fact, the word *bus* has a curious history. It is short for *omnibus*, a form of the Latin word *omnis*, "all," with the plural ending *-ibus*, meaning "to or for," attached. *Omnibus* was used in the French phrase *voiture omnibus*, "vehicle for all." This phrase appeared in French around 1830 and was both borrowed and shortened to *bus* by the English before the end of the decade. *Omnibus* was also used to designate a waiter's assistant at a restaurant, though whether this usage derived from the use of *omnibus* to mean "vehicle," or whether it was an independent use of the word, is not clear. *Busboy* is derived from the clipping of *omnibus* in this sense of "waiter's assistant." But the verb *bus*, meaning "to work as a busboy," and by extension, "to clear dishes from a table," comes from *busboy*, and not directly from the word *omnibus*.

butterfly

It is difficult to resist the temptation to find an etymology for the charming word *butterfly*. But what exactly is the connection between butterflies and butter? The modern English word descends from Middle English *butterflye*, from Old English *butorflēoge*, which does indeed look like a compound of *butor*, *butere*, "butter," and *flēoge*, "fly." Some believe that the butterfly is named for the butterlike appearance of its excrement. This theory rests on the fact that an early Dutch name for the butterfly was *boterschijte*, which seems like a compound of the Dutch words corresponding to English *butter* and *shit*, respectively. However, it is hard to imagine that anyone ever noticed the color or consistency of butterfly droppings. Others have suggested that the name derives from the insect's reputation for stealing butter, since there is an old belief that the butterfly was really a larcenous witch in disguise.

bylaw

A casual glance at the word *bylaw* might make one think that the element *by-* means "secondary, subsidiary," especially since *bylaw* can mean "a secondary law." It is possible that *by-*, as in *byway,* has influenced *bylaw* in the sense "secondary law"; however, *bylaw* existed long before the sense in question. The word is first recorded in 1283 with the meaning "a body of customs or regulations, as of a village, manor, religious organization, or sect." *By-* comes from Old Norse (as may the whole word *bylaw*) and is related to the element *-by* in the names of many places where Scandinavians settled when they invaded England during the early Middle Ages, such as Whitby. We get the sense of this *-by* if we compare the related Old Icelandic word variously spelled *bær, bœr, bȳr,* meaning "a town or village" in Norway, Sweden, and Denmark and "a farm or landed estate" in Iceland. We thus see why *bylaw* would mean "a body of customs of a village or manor" and why we use the word to mean "a law or rule governing the internal affairs of an organization."

candidate

Candidates for political office nowadays must convince voters of their spotless records, and it was no different in the past. The word *candidate* derives from Latin *candidātus,* "a person standing for office," which is in turn derived from *candidus,* "white," with the suffix *-ātus.* A Roman *candidātus* wore a bleached white toga as, perhaps, a symbol of his political purity when he went to the forum to seek election to the magistracy. This association between the color white and the quality of purity is common across cultures. For instance, the Latin word *candor* (from the same root as *candidātus*) meant both "brilliant whiteness" and "naturalness, honesty," and in Modern English *candor* is still used in the second sense. The white-clad Roman *candidātus,* however, was accompanied to the forum by *sectātōrēs,* "followers," who helped him get votes by bribery and bargaining.

Candidate was borrowed into English in the late seventeenth century, after appearing in French a little earlier. This illustrates the principle that new institutions often motivate the use of new words. As Anglo-American politics became increasingly democratic, English needed a term for someone whose ascent to office was a matter of public choice. English lacked such a word, and so one was borrowed, ultimately from the political vocabulary of Rome.

canter

Most of those who have majored in English literature, and many more besides, know that Chaucer's *Canterbury Tales* were told by a group of pilgrims on their way to Canterbury to visit the shrine of England's famous martyr Thomas à Becket. Many pilgrims other than Chaucer's visited Canterbury on horse, and phrases such as *Canterbury gallop, Canterbury pace,* and *Canterbury trot* described the easy gait at which they rode to their destination. The first recorded instance of one of these phrases, *Canterbury pace,* is found in a work published before 1636. However, in a work written in 1631 we find a shortened form, the noun *Canterbury,* meaning "a canter," and later, in 1673, the verb *Canterbury,* meaning "to canter." This verb, or perhaps the noun, was further shortened, giving us the verb *canter,* first recorded in 1706, and the noun *canter,* first recorded in 1755.

cappuccino

The history of the word *cappuccino* exemplifies how words can develop new senses because of resemblances that the original coiners of the terms might not have dreamed possible. The Capuchin order of friars, established after 1525, played an important role in bringing Catholicism back to Reformation Europe. Its

Italian name came from the long pointed cowl, or *cappuccino*, derived from *cappuccio*, "hood," that was worn as part of the order's habit. The French version of *cappuccino* was *capuchin* (now *capucin*), from which came English *Capuchin*. The name of this pious order was later used as the name (first recorded in English in 1785) for a type of monkey with a tuft of black cowl-like hair. In Italian *cappuccino* went on to develop another sense, "espresso coffee mixed or topped with steamed milk or cream," so called because the color of the coffee resembled the color of the habit of a Capuchin friar. The first use of *cappuccino* in English to refer to coffee is recorded in 1948.

caprice

When we think of the word *caprice*, hedgehogs and goats don't immediately come to mind. Yet both animals play a part in the history of *caprice*. The word comes to us from the Italian word *capriccio*, originally *caporiccio*, which first meant "fright, a state of being startled, shivering." The Italian word combined two words, *capo*, "head," and *riccio*, "hedgehog," because in a state of fright one's hair stands on end like the spines of a hedgehog. After the word changed in form from *caporiccio* to *capriccio*, the *capr-* part of the word was associated

African pygmy hedgehog

with the similar sounding word *capra*, "goat," after the characteristic capering of goats. Other goatlike behavior then became part of the meaning of the word *capriccio*, including impulsiveness and sudden changes of mind. *Caprice* then came into English through French from Italian with the sense it has today, "an impulsive change of mind." *Capriccio* and *caprice* also came into use as musical terms for pieces in improvisatory style written in free form. The word *caper* itself is also related to *caprice*. English *caper* is an alteration of French *capriole*, a borrowing of Italian *capriole*, "somersault," from the word *capriolo*, "roebuck, wild goat."

caricature

The history of the word *caricature* takes us back through the centuries to a time when the Romans occupied Gaul (roughly modern France and Belgium), offering the blessings of civilization to the Gauls but also borrowing from them as well. One such borrowing, the Gaulish word **karros*, meaning "a wagon or cart," became Latin *carrus*, "a Gallic type of wagon." This Latin word has continued to roll through the English language, giving us *car, career, cargo, carry*, and *charge*, among others. *Caricature*, came to us via French from Italian, in which *caricatura*, the source of the French word, was derived from Italian *caricare*, "to load, burden, or exaggerate." *Caricare* in turn came from Late Latin *carricāre*, "to load," derived from *carrus*. *Carricāre* is also the source of English *charge*.

carouse

The origin of the word *carouse* can be found in a German interjection that meant "time to leave the bar." German *garaus*, which is derived from the phrase *gar* ("all") *aus* ("out"), meaning "all out," then came to mean "drink up, bottoms up," and "a last drink before closing time." The English borrowed this noun, with the meaning "the practice of sitting around drinking until closing time," sometimes spelling the word *garaus* but usually spelling it closer to the way it is spelled today. Soon after the word is first recorded as a noun in 1559, we find the verb *carouse,* in 1567.

catch

When hunters chase their quarry, they do not necessarily catch the animal. However, *catch* and *chase* are ultimately two forms of the same word, derived from two different dialects of Old French. Both dialectal forms come from Vulgar Latin *captiāre,* an alternation of attested Latin *captāre,* "catch." English *catch* descends from the Anglo-Norman form *cachier,* which meant only "to chase" and not "to catch." The Middle English word *cacchen,* the ancestor of *catch,* is first recorded in the early thirteenth century. In Middle English *cacchen* seems to have become associated with the native English word *lacchen* (the descendant of which, *latch,* occurs in our phrase *latch on to*), since it shared certain meanings including the sense "to capture." The word *chase,* on the other hand, comes from a form closer to the Parisian, or Francien, verb *chacier.* This word, like the Anglo-Norman form *cachier,* meant only "to chase." "To chase" is still the meaning of its descendant in modern French, *chasser.* After the adoption of *chacier* as *chase* in English in the fourteenth century, *catch* became used exclusively to mean "to capture."

caterpillar

L arvae of moths and butterflies are popularly seen as resembling other larger animals. Consider the Italian dialect word *gatta*, "cat, caterpillar"; the German dialect term *tüfelskatz*, "caterpillar" (literally "devil's cat"); the French word *chenille*, "caterpillar" (from a Vulgar Latin diminutive, **canīcula*, of *canis*, "dog"); and last but not least, our own word *caterpillar*, which appears probably to have come from an unattested Old North French word **catepelose*, meaning literally "hairy cat." Our word *caterpillar* is first recorded in English in 1440 in the form *catyrpel*. *Catyr*, the first part of *catyrpel*, may indicate the existence of an English word **cater*, meaning "tomcat," otherwise attested only in *caterwaul*. *Cater* is probably related to Middle High German *kater* and Dutch *kater*. The latter part of *catyrpel* seems to have become associated with the word *piller*, "plunderer." By giving the variant spelling -*ar*, Samuel Johnson's *Dictionary* (1755) set the spelling *caterpillar* with which we are familiar today.

cattle

A rancher driving his *cattle* to market could technically say that they were his *chattels* or his *capital*, but he would be unlikely to realize that all three words go back to the same Latin adjective *capitalis*, "of the head, principal." *Cattle* and *chattel* go back through medieval French to the Medieval Latin word *capitale*, "property," which comes from the Latin word *capitalis*. *Cattle* is derived from Anglo-Norman *catel*, which in medieval times meant "movable property" in general. The word became restricted to animals because livestock was then one of the most important forms of wealth. The further narrowing of *cattle* to refer only to bovines occurred in the nineteenth century. The current English word *Chattel* descends from the form used in central France, *chatel*. The alternation between the *c* and *ch* sounds in this case is the same as that illustrated in *catch* and *chase* above, reflecting dialectal differences in northern (Norman) and central France. *Chatel* was adopted in medieval England as a legal term for "movable property," supplanting *cattle*. *Capital* was also borrowed from French in medieval times. It represents not the regular French development of Latin *capitāle,* but instead a direct borrowing of the Latin adjective *capitālis* into French. The original use of *capital* in English was as an adjective, first meaning "relating to the head" and later meaning "principal" or "chief." *Capital* came to denote wealth when it was used to mean someone's principal substance or property. The further developments of word are quite recent: *capitalist,* "one who possesses wealth," dates from the eighteenth century, while *capitalism,* denoting the economic system in which the means of production and distribution are privately or corporately owned, first appears in the nineteenth century.

caviar

Although caviar might seem to be something quintessentially Russian, the word *caviar* is not, the native Russian term being *ikra. Caviar* first came into English in the sixteenth century, probably by way of French and Italian, which borrowed it from Turkish *havyar.* The source of the Turkish word is apparently an Iranian dialectal form related to the Persian word for "egg," *khāyah,* and this in turn goes back to the same Indo-European root that gives us the English words *egg* and *oval*. This rather exotic etymology is appropriate to a substance that is not to everyone's taste, giving rise to Shakespeare's famous phrase, " 'twas caviary to the general," the general public, that is.

chagrin

The ultimate etymology of the word *chagrin,* which comes directly to us from French, is considered uncertain by many etymologists. At one time *chagrin* was thought to be the same word as *shagreen,* "a leather or skin with a rough surface," derived from French *chagrin.* The reasoning was that in French the word for this rough material, which was used to smooth and polish things, was extended to the notion of troubles that fret and annoy a person. It was later decided, however, that the sense "rough leather" and the sense "sorrow" each belonged to a different French word *chagrin.* Other etymologists have offered an alternative explanation, suggesting that the French word *chagrin,* "sorrow," is a loan translation of the German word *Katzenjammer,* "a hangover from drinking." A loan translation is a type of borrowing from another language in which the elements of a foreign word, as in *Katzen,* "cats," and *Jammer,* "distress, seediness," are translated literally by corresponding elements in another language, in this case, *chat,* "cat," and *grigner,* "to grimace." The actual etymology is less colorful, with the word probably going back to a Germanic word, **gramī,* meaning "sorrow, trouble." *Chagrin* is first recorded in English in 1656 in the now obsolete sense "anxiety, melancholy."

When we order a *chai* at a café in the United States, we expect a hot milky tea with plenty of sugar, and usually cardamom, cloves, and other spices. If we order *tea,* we expect just tea leaves infused in hot water—unless we are in the South, where plain old *tea* usually means iced tea. In fact, *chai* and *tea* are in origin the same word, borrowed twice from two different dialects of Chinese and transformed by the journey over the sea or the Silk Road from China to the many countries where tea is enjoyed.

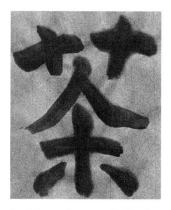

the Chinese character for "tea"

Words for tea around the world fall into two groups. One group includes Russian *chaĭ,* Persian *chây,* and Hindi *chai.* The Hindi word, which means simply "tea," is the source of the new English word, often used in the United States specifically to mean the spiced tea properly called *masala chai* in Hindi. The other group of words for tea includes Spanish *té,* Italian *tè,* French *thé,* and German *Tee,* and of course English *tea,* all beginning with the sound *t.* Within each group, it is often unclear who borrowed from whom. However, the ultimate source of all these words is Chinese, and the two different groups of pronunciations represent variations found among the dialects of Chinese in the different areas from which tea was imported. In the Mandarin dialect of the north of China, the word for tea is pronounced as *cha,* with a rising tone, and similarly in the Cantonese dialect of southernmost China, it is pronounced *cha* with a low falling tone. Mandarin and other dialects like it were the source of the first group of words like *chai.* However, in the dialect of Xiamen (or Amoy) in the southeast-ern province of Fujian, the word is pronounced *tê,* with a tone rising from the midrange of the voice. Xiamen was a major port through which tea was exported, and its dialect is the source of the second group of pronun-ciations with *t* such as English *tea.* All of these Chinese dialectal variations go back to an original **drai* or **drε̄;* in Middle Chinese, the spoken Chinese of the seventh century.

It has been proposed that most pronunciations in the first group, like Hindi *chai,* reflect pronunciation along the route by which tea was first brought to the lands speaking these languages—namely, the Silk Road across Asia.

A great deal of British trade also passed through Cantonese-speaking areas, but English *tea* begins with the *t* of the Amoy dialect rather than a *ch* typical of Cantonese. There is, however, a slang word for tea, *cha* or *char* (as it is more usually spelled in dialects which "drop their *r*'s") found all around the English-speaking world. Thus English has three different words all descended from the same Chinese word for what is perhaps the world's most popular beverage.

See also **tea.**

chameleon

The words referring to the animal chameleon and the plant chamomile are related etymologically by a reference to the place one would expect to find them, that is, on the ground. The first part of both words goes back to the Greek form *khamai,* meaning "on the ground." What is found on the ground in each case is quite different, of course. The *khamaileōn* is "a lion [*leōn*] on the ground," a term translating the Akkadian phrase *nēš qaqqari.* The *khamaimēlon* is "an apple [*mēlon*] on the ground," so named because the blossoms of at least one variety of this creeping herb have an applelike scent. Both words are first found in Middle English, *chameleon* in a work composed before 1382 and *chamomile* in a work written in 1373.

chaperon

The chaperon at a high-school dance seems to have little relationship to what was first signified by the English word *chaperon,* "a hood for a hawk," and not even that much to what the word later meant, "a woman who protects a young single woman." The sense "hood for a hawk," recorded in a Middle English text composed before 1400, reflects the original meaning of the Old French word *chaperon,* "hood, headgear." In order to understand why our *chaperon* came to have the sense "protector," we need to know that in French the verb *chaperonner,* meaning "to cover with a hood," was derived from *chaperon* and that this verb subsequently developed the figurative sense "to protect." Under the influence of the verb sense the French noun *chaperon* came to mean "escort," a meaning that was borrowed into English, being found first in a work published in 1720. In its earlier use English *chaperon* referred to a person, commonly an older woman, who accompanied a young unmarried woman in public to protect her. The English verb *chaperon,* "to be a chaperon," is first recorded in Jane Austen's *Sense and Sensibility,* begun in 1796 as a sketch called "Elinor and Marianne" and published as a novel in 1811.

charming

The first full English translation of the Bible, dating from around 1388, describes the witch of Endor, asked to raise the spirit of the prophet Samuel, as "a womman havynge a charmynge goost" (1 Samuel 28:7). Speakers of modern English are familiar with friendly ghosts, but charming ones? "Charmynge goost" really means "a familiar spirit that can work magic." The English words *charm* and *charming* originally only had meanings related to magic.

Charming is first recorded in its present sense of "highly pleasing" in the seventeenth century as a figurative extension of the previous magical sense "putting a spell on somebody."

English borrowed the word *charm* from French *charme,* which also originally meant "magic, magical charm." The French word is the direct descendant of Latin *carmen,* "song, sung spell." (For another example of the regular change of Latin *c* to French *ch* before *a,* see **catch**). The Latin word developed from an earlier form **kanmen,* which contains the Indo-European root **kan-,* "sing." The *r* in *carmen* is the result of dissimilation—the original nasal consonant **n* became a non-nasal consonant before the following nasal *m.*

English speakers are familiar with the root **kan-* in many other borrowings, such as Italian *cantata,* originally "something sung." In yet another derivative of the root **kan-, enchant,* we can observe exactly the same change in meaning from "cast a spell over" to "delight" as in *charm. Enchant* ultimately comes from Latin *incantāre,* "to sing magical spells over." English *incantation* is a direct borrowing of the Latin noun *incantātiō,* made from this verb. In French, however, the verb *incantāre* developed into *enchanter,* which English then borrowed as *enchant.* Both English and French then show the shift in meaning from "to put a spell on" to "to attract, please." Perhaps in the future the same thing will happen again, and English speakers won't even notice the *witch* in a *bewitching* smile.

chauvinism

A few lucky people over the ages have had their names become everyday words, such as Julius Caesar, whose name eventually came to be used in many languages as the title for a king or other ruler, such as German *Kaiser* or Russian *tsar.* Others, like Charles C. **Boycott** and Nicolas Chauvin, have not been quite so fortunate, and their names have given rise to somewhat less positive words. Chauvin was a French soldier who served under Napoleon and received seventeen wounds during the Napoleonic Wars. Because of his unerring and vehemently expressed devotion to his leader, he was made a humorous character in several nineteenth-century French comedies. Many legendary details were tacked on to his story—for instance, that he was born on the fateful date of July 4, 1776, along with the American Revolution. Just as *Pollyanna,* a modern literary and film character, became a term for someone blindly optimistic, so did the legendary character of Chauvin lend his name to an attitude of exaggerated patriotism called in French *chauvinisme.* The English word, first recorded in 1870, derived from the French and was generalized to mean "an exaggerated devotion to one's own group or place." Recently *chauvinism* has come to be applied quite often to a particular kind of prejudice. First it became part of the phrase *male chauvinism,* and then it shed the *male* and acquired the simple meaning "prejudiced belief in the superiority of men."

The family name *Chauvin,* is derived from the French word for "bald," *chauve,* from Latin *calvus.* The

Northern French equivalent of this name, *Calvin,* was borne by reformer Jean Calvin, the founder of Calvinism. Calvinism and chauvinism, however, remain quite different things, which goes to show that in the practice of etymology, a shared origin is no guarantee of shared meaning.

check

The words *check, chess,* and *shah* are all related. *Shah,* as one might think, is a borrowing into English of the Persian title for the monarch of that country. The Persian word *shāh* was also a term used in chess, a game played in Persia long before it was introduced to Europe. One said *shāh* as a warning when the opponent's king was under attack. The Persian word in this sense, after passing through Arabic, probably Old Spanish, and then Old French, came into Middle English as *chek* about seven hundred years ago. *Chess* itself comes from a plural form of the Old French word that gave us the word *check. Checkmate,* the next stage after *check,* goes back to the Arabic phrase *shāh māt,* meaning "the king is dead." Through a complex development having to do with senses that evolved from the notion of checking the king, *check* came to mean something used to ensure accuracy or authenticity. One such means was a counterfoil, a part of a check, for example, retained by the issuer as documentation of a transaction. *Check* first meant "counterfoil" and then came to mean anything, such as a bill or bank draft, with a counterfoil—or eventually even without one.

child

Cat, cats; dog, dogs. We all know how plurals in Eng-lish are usually made. *Sheep, sheep* is a familiar exception, as is *ox, oxen. Child, children* is one of the oddest of the exceptions because *child* has had its plural formed in three different ways over the course of its history. The earliest Old English form, *cild,* "child, infant," formed its plural by adding no suffix, like the Modern English *sheep* and *deer.* Other Old English nouns, however, formed plurals by adding the suffix *-ru,* and in later Old English times a new plural, *cildru,* was used for *cild.* This form developed into *childer.* Still other nouns in Old English formed the plural with the suffix *-an,* which survived in Mid-dle English as *-en. Oxen* is a modern plural with this suffix. In some dialects of Middle English *-en* was the usual plural suffix, and it was added to *childer* to make it conform to other nouns, producing forms spelled variously as *childeren, childern,* and *children.* This last has survived as the modern spelling of the plural of *child.*

china

*O*ur term *china* for porcelain or ceramic ware is a shortening of *chinaware* and probably *china dish-es.* Although the word *china* is identical in spelling to the name of the country, there are sixteenth- and seventeenth-century spellings like *chiney, cheny,* and *cheney* that reflect the borrowing into English of the Persian term for this porcelain, *chīnī.* The Persian word and the Sanskrit word *cīnāḥ,* "Chinese people," which gave us the English name for the country, go back to the Chinese word *Qín,* the name of the dynasty that ruled China from 221 to 206 B.C.

chivalry

The Age of Chivalry was also the age of the horse. Bedecked in elaborate armor and other trappings, horses were certainly well dressed, although they might have wished for lighter loads. That the horse should be featured so prominently during the Age of Chivalry is etymologically appropriate because *chivalry* goes back to the Latin word *caballus,* "horse, especially a riding horse or packhorse." Borrowed from French, as were so many other important words having to do with medieval culture, the English word *chivalry* is first recorded in works composed around the beginning of the fourteenth century and is found in several senses, including "a body of armored mounted warriors serving a lord" and "knighthood as a ceremonially conferred rank in the social system." Our modern sense, "the medieval system of knighthood," could not exist until the passage of several centuries had allowed the perspective for such a conceptualization, with this sense being recorded first in 1765.

chortle

'Ofrabjous day! Callooh! Callay!' He chortled in his joy." Perhaps Lewis Carroll would chortle a bit himself to find that people are still using the word *chortle,* which he coined in *Through the Looking-Glass,* published in 1872. In any case, Carroll had constructed his word well, combining the words *chuckle* and *snort*. This type of word is called a *blend* or a *portmanteau word*. In *Through the Looking-Glass* Humpty Dumpty uses *portmanteau* ("a large leather suitcase that opens into two hinged compartments") to describe the word *slithy*, saying, "It's like a portmanteau—there are two meanings packed up into one word" (the meanings being "lithe" and "slimy").

churl

The word *churl* comes almost unchanged in meaning and pronunciation, though not in spelling, from Old English *ceorl*, "freeman of the lowest class." An Anglo-Saxon *ceorl* had a social position above a slave but below a *thegn*, "thane." *Ceorl* comes from Germanic **karilaz*, whose basic meaning is "old man." In Finnish, which is not a Germanic language, the Germanic word was borrowed and survives almost unchanged as *karilas*, "old man." The Old Norse descendant of the Germanic word, *karl*, meant "old man, servant," and the Old High German equivalent, *karal*, meaning "man, lover, husband," became the name *Karl*. The Germanic word was adopted into French as the name *Charles*, from which we also have the name *Charles*. The Medieval Latin form *Carolus* was based on the Old High German *karal*. The fame of *Carolus Magnus*, "Charles the Great," or Charlemagne, added luster to the name *Carolus* and explains why the Slavic languages borrowed the name as their general word for "king," *korol'* in Russian.

ciao

Ciao first appears in English in 1929 in Hemingway's *A Farewell to Arms*, which is set in northeast Italy during World War I. It is likely that this is where Hemingway learned the word, for *ciau* in Venetian dialect means "servant, slave," and, as a casual greeting, "I am your servant." *Ciau* corresponds to standard Italian *schiavo;* both words come from Medieval Latin *sclavus,* "slave." A similar development took place with *servus,* the Classical Latin word for "slave," in southern Germany, Austria, Hungary, and Poland, where *servus* is used as a casual greeting like *ciao.* At the opposite end of the world, in Southeast Asia, one even sees words meaning "slave" or "your slave" that have developed into first person pronouns, again to indicate respect and humility.

cleric

Cleric, clerk, and *clark* all come from Latin *clēricus,* "a man in a religious order, a man in holy orders." *Cleric* appeared in Old English about 975 and lasted into the thirteenth century. *Clerc* appeared in late Old English, around 1129, and was identical in spelling and pronunciation with Old French *clerc,* "belonging to the (Christian) clergy." In the Middle Ages the clergy were the only literate class and were often employed as scribes, secretaries, or notaries. By about 1200 *clerc* had acquired the meaning "pupil, scholar," as we see in Chaucer's "clerk of Oxenford" in *The Canterbury Tales* (around 1386). Clerks were also of necessity employed in keeping accounts and recording business transactions; this is the source of the modern sense of *clerk.* By the early seventeenth century, the word *clerk* had become completely ambiguous; it could refer equally to a clergyman or to an accountant. For this reason *cleric* was introduced or reintroduced from Latin or Greek as both a noun and an adjective to refer specifically to a member of the clergy. The pronunciation (klärk) having the vowel of *father* and spelled both *clark* and *clerk,* arose in the south of England during the fifteenth century, and this pronunciation of the word is still widespread in the United Kingdom today. The modern American pronunciation (klûrk) with the vowel in *work* represents a different development of the Middle English sounds. The pronunciation (klärk) is used in the United States only in the proper name *Clark.* The sound change in southern England responsible for the pronunciation (klärk) also gave rise to *parson* (beside *person*), *varsity* (beside *university*), and even *varmint* (beside *vermin*).

cloud

The weather in medieval England must not have been very sunny because two modern English words meaning "sky" meant "cloud" in earlier times. *Welkin,* from Old English *wolcen,* meant "cloud" until the twelfth century, as the German word *Wolke* still does. *Sky* comes from the Old Norse word *sky,* meaning "cloud." The Old Norse word was borrowed into English with the meaning "cloud" in the thirteenth century and was not used to mean "sky" until about a century later. The word *cloud* itself, from Old English *clud,* is quite down to earth, for it meant "hill" or "rock" until about the fourteenth century. The ordinary word for "sky" in Old English was *heofan,* the ancestor of our word *heaven,* which retains that sense in Modern English only in the plural *heavens.* The use of *heaven* as the abode of God is recorded as early as the word itself.

clove

It may seem odd that *clove,* "a section of a garlic bulb," and the spice called *cloves* in English should share the same name, but the two words are not at all related. The *clove* that means "bulb section" comes from Old English *clufu,* a noun related to the verb *clēofan,* "to split," the ancestor of *cleave,* "to split or separate." The past participle of this verb is seen in English *cloven,* as in the split hooves of cattle and other ungulates. *Cleave,* meaning "to stick fast," the opposite of "to split or separate," actually derives from another Old English verb, *clifian.* The name of the spice called *cloves* has an entirely different origin. In Old French, the dried flower bud of the clove tree was called a *clou de girofle,* a "nail of cloves." *Clou* is the French word for "nail," and the dried bud resembles a small nail or tack. English shortened the full French name of the spice to *clove.* The spice was known in antiquity, and French *girofle* ultimately comes from Greek *caryophyllon.* In Middle English, the spice was also called *gilofre* (a metathesis of French *girofle*), and an altered form of this word has survived in *gillyflower,* a name for various clove-scented flowers like the carnation.

clue

Clue and *clew* were at one time simply two spellings of the same word meaning "ball," especially a ball of yarn or thread, an obsolescent sense of *clew* today. The meaning "guide to a solution" developed from the story of Theseus and the Minotaur. Theseus, a great Athenian hero, was to be sacrificed to the Minotaur, a monster that was half-man and half-bull and lived in the Labyrinth, King Minos's maze on Crete. Finding the Minotaur was no problem, but discovering the way out of the Labyrinth would have been impossible if Ariadne, Minos's daughter, had not provided Theseus with a clew—or ball—of string. Theseus unwound the ball as he entered and wound it up as he returned, thus following a sure path out of the maze. Allusions to this "clew of thread" or a "clew to a maze" have been common from Chaucer's day to modern times and have appeared in contexts that referred to various kinds of difficulties. As a result, the figurative import of the word *clew* was lost by the seventeenth century, and all associations with a ball of twine were cut. In very recent times, especially since the advent of detective fiction, the spelling *clue* has primarily signified the meaning "guide to a solution."

coach

Coach, used to mean "a tutor" or "a trainer," alludes to the speed of stagecoaches and railway coaches. In the days before automobiles and airplanes, the fastest method of travel was by coach—at first horse-drawn and later steam-powered. A *coach* in the parlance of a British university is an instructor who brings his students along at the fastest possible rate, a sense of the word that first appeared in the nineteenth century. The origin of *coach* for a vehicle is somewhat unexpected. Words similar to English *coach* appear in most of the major languages of Europe in the sixteenth century, and they are all ultimately borrowed from Hungarian *kocsi,* "from Kocs," in the phrase *Kocsi szeker,* "a wagon from Kocs." Kocs is a town in Hungary where light carriages featuring an innovative suspension system and favored by the nobility of Europe were manufactured, beginning in the fifteenth century.

cockroach

The word for *cockroach* in Spanish is *cucaracha,* which should certainly set anyone with an eye for etymology to thinking. Users of English did not simply borrow the Spanish word. Instead, they made it conform in appearance to other English words: *cock,* the word for rooster, and *roach,* the name of a fish. We do not know exactly why these words were chosen other than their resemblance to the two parts of the original Spanish word. We do know that the first recorded use of the word comes from a 1624 work by the colonist John Smith. The form Smith used, *cacarootch,* is closer to the Spanish. A form more like our own, *cockroche,* is first recorded in 1657.

cocoa

The confusion of *cocoa,* the beverage, with *coco,* the tree, can be traced to Samuel Johnson's great dictionary, published in 1755. Johnson maintained the distinction between the two words in his own writing, but by some editorial or printing error the definitions for *coco* and *cocoa* appeared together under the word *cocoa.* That was unfortunate, because *coco* and *cocoa* are two different words that refer to two different trees. The cacao tree of tropical America produces both cocoa and chocolate. The name *cacao* comes from *cacahuatl,* "cacao bean," in Nahuatl (the language of the Aztec), while *chocolate* comes from *xocolatl,* "article of food made from cacao," an unrelated word in the same language. The word *cocoa* is simply a variant spelling of *cacao,* influenced by *coco.* The coconut or coco palm originated in the East Indies. Its name is not a native name like *cacao* but comes

from Portuguese *coco,* "goblin," referring to the face-
like appearance of the three holes at the bottom of
the fruit.

cologne

The word *cologne,* denoting toilet water, is from
Cologne, the French (and English) name of the German city Köln, where cologne has been made since the
beginning of the eighteenth century. The first use of
cologne for toilet water is recorded in English in 1814,
with the word being used in the compound *cologne
water,* a translation of *eau de Cologne,* the French
name for this liquid. The ultimate source of the word
lies in the history of the city, which stretches back to
the Roman Empire: its Latin name was *Colōnia,* meaning "colony."

colonel

The improbable pronunciation of the word spelled
colonel represents the triumph of popular speech
over learned respellings. *Colonel* goes back to Old Italian *colonnello,* from *colonna,* "column (of soldiers)."
The officer named *colonnello* led the first company of
a regiment. In English, *colonel* did not come directly
from Italian but by way of French, during the sixteenth century. The French word was at one time
spelled *coronel* showing the effects of a process called
dissimilation, in which two similar or identical
sounds, such as the two *l* sounds in *colonnello,* become
less alike. Later in literary French *coronel* was
replaced by *colonnel* because the latter looked more
like the original Italian. Influenced by this French
usage as well as their perusal of Italian military

treatises, English writers began to use the more Italianate form *colonel,* spelled with an *l,* in the seventeenth century. However, a pronunciation based on the spelling *colonel* did not win out over the earlier pronunciation with an *r* based on French *coronel.*

comet

Comets have been feared throughout much of human history, and even in our own time their goings and comings receive great attention. Perhaps a comet might seem less awesome if we realized that our name for it is based on a figurative resemblance between it and humans. This figurative name is recorded first in the works of Aristotle, in which he uses *komē,* the Greek word for "hair of the head," to mean "luminous tail of a comet." Aristotle then uses the derived word *komētēs,* "wearing long hair," as a noun meaning "comet." The Greek word was adopted into Latin as *comētēs,* which was refashioned in Late Latin and given the form *comēta,* furnishing Old English with *comēta,* the earliest English ancestor of our word *comet.*

comfort

Comfort, as a noun and verb, is ultimately derived from the Latin prefix *con-,* an intensifier, and *fortis,* meaning "strong." The Latin verb *confortare* and its descendants in the medieval Romance languages meant "to strengthen." The verb and the noun were borrowed into English from French in the thirteenth century. The sense "to strengthen" for the verb and "strengthening" and "solace" for the noun both occurred at that early date, while the verb senses "to support" and "to console" developed quickly in the next century. The meaning "ease" for the noun is not recorded until the early nineteenth century, although the meaning "at ease" for *comfortable* developed earlier, during the eighteenth century, by which time the sense "to strengthen," except in emotional terms, had become obsolete.

coroner

Coroner comes from Anglo-Norman *corouner,* a word derived from *coroune,* "crown." *Corouner* was the term used for the royal judicial officer who was called in Latin *custos placitorum coronae,* or "guardian of the crown's pleas." The person holding the office of coroner, a position dating from the twelfth century, was charged with keeping local records of legal proceedings in which the crown had jurisdiction. He helped raise money for the crown by funneling the property of executed criminals into the king's treasury. The coroner also investigated any suspicious deaths among the Normans, who, as the ruling class, wanted to be sure that their deaths were not taken lightly. At one time in England all criminal proceedings were included in the coroner's responsibilities. Over the years these responsibilities decreased markedly, but coroners have continued to display morbid curiosity. In the United States, where there is no longer the crown, a coroner's main duty is the investigation of any sudden, violent, or unexpected death.

costume

A costume is a custom of dress, a fact that is partly explained by the origin of both *custom* and *costume* in the Latin word *consuētūdō,* "custom, habit, usage." English borrowed both words from French, but at different times. *Custom* appeared first; it was used about 1200 in the sense "habitual practice," which is still current. *Costume* was borrowed from French much later, in the eighteenth century, as a term from the technical vocabulary of the fine arts. It meant "the features characteristic of a particular historical period represented in painting or sculpture." This was the meaning of the Italian word *costume,* from which the French and then later the English word derived. Such characteristic features naturally included styles of dress, and the use of *costume* was ultimately restricted to clothing styles. *Habit,* which also means "apparel," as in "a nun's habit," followed the semantic course opposite from *custom.* It entered English from Old French *abit,* "apparel," in the thirteenth century, developing later, in the sixteenth century, the current, more frequent senses "tendency" and "custom."

cot

People might assume that there is nothing particularly exotic about the history of the word *cot.* However, *cot* is a good example of how some words borrowed from other cultures become so firmly naturalized over time that they lose their émigré flavor. The British first encountered the object denoted by *cot,* a light frame strung with tapes or rope, in India, where their trading stations had been established as early as 1612. The word *cot,* first recorded in English in 1634, comes from *khāṭ,* the Hindi name for the contrivance. During subsequent years, *cot* has been used to denote other types of beds, including, in British usage, "a crib."

coward

A coward is one who turns tail. The word comes from Old French *couart* or *coart*, "coward," and is related to Italian *codardo*, "coward." *Couart* is formed from *coe*, a northern French dialectal variant of *queue*, "tail" (from Latin *cōda*), to which the derogatory suffix *-ard* was added. This suffix appears in *bastard*, *laggard*, and *sluggard*, to name a few. A coward may also be one with his tail between his legs. In heraldry a *lion couard*, "cowardly lion," was depicted with his tail between his legs. So a coward may be one with his tail hidden between his legs or one who turns tail and runs like a rabbit, with his tail showing.

crayfish

The crayfish, also known as the crawfish, owes its name to a misunderstanding. The actual source of the word may be the Old High German word *krebiz*, "edible crustacean," or a word related to it. From this Germanic source came Old French *crevice*, which when taken into English became *crevise* (first recorded in a document written in 1311-1312). In Old French and Middle English these words designated the crayfish. People began to pronounce and spell the last part of this word as if it were *fish*, the first such spelling being recorded in 1555. Because of a variation in Anglo-Norman pronunciation, two forms of the word have come down to Modern English: *crayfish* and *crawfish*.

Crisscross is a phonetic spelling of *Christ('s)-cross,* "the cross of Christ." The word originally denoted a mark of two crossed lines resembling the Christian religious symbol. This mark had two main functions: it was placed at the head of alphabets used for the teaching of children, and it was a figure used in place of a signature by uneducated persons. Both senses of *crisscross* are first recorded in the sixteenth century, though the latter sense describing a signature may well have been used even earlier than that. In the nineteenth century the religious association was lost, and *crisscross* was applied to any pattern of crossed lines. The *criss-* in *crisscross* is the same as *Kriss* in *Kriss Kringle. Kringle* is a fanciful American alteration (some would call it a misunderstanding) of German *kindl,* the diminutive form of *kind,* "child." *Kriss Kringle* comes from German *Christkindl,* or "the Christ child," but since 1830, the date at which it is first recorded, *Kriss Kringle* has meant "Santa Claus" rather than the child in the manger. In Pennsylvania German tradition, it is the Christ child, rather than St. Nicholas (Santa Claus), who delivers presents to good children on Christmas Eve.

croissant

The words *croissant* and *crescent* illustrate double borrowing, each coming into English from a different form of the same French word. In Latin the word *crēscere,* "to grow," when applied to the moon meant "to wax," as in the phrase *lūna crēscēns,* "waxing moon." Old French *croissant,* the equivalent of Latin *crēscēns,* came to mean "the time during which the moon waxes," "the crescent-shaped figure of the moon in its first and last quarters," and "a crescent-shaped object." However, this word was first borrowed into Middle English in its Anglo-Norman form *cressaunt.* It is recorded in a document dated 1399–1400, in the meaning "a crescent-shaped ornament." *Crescent,* the Modern English descendant of Middle English *cressaunt,* owes its second *c* to Latin *crēscere. Croissant,* as it is used in English today, is not an English development but rather a borrowing of the modern French descendant of Old French *croissant.* It is first recorded in English in 1899. French *croissant* was used to translate German *Hörnchen,* the name given by the Viennese to this pastry, which was first baked in 1689 to commemorate the raising of the siege of Vienna by the Turks, whose symbol was the crescent moon.

cuckold

The allusion to the cuckoo on which the word *cuckold* is based may not be appreciated by those unfamiliar with the nesting habits of certain varieties of this bird. The female of some Old World cuckoos lays her eggs in the nests of other birds, leaving them to be cared for by the resident nesters. This parasitic tendency has given the female bird a figurative reputation for unfaithfulness as well. Hence in Old French we find the word *cucuault,* composed of *cocu,* "cuckoo, cuckold," and the pejorative suffix *-ald,* used to designate a husband whose wife has wandered afield like the female cuckoo. An earlier assumed form of the Old French word was borrowed into Middle English by way of Anglo-Norman. Middle English *cokewold,* the ancestor of Modern English *cuckold,* is first recorded in a work written around 1250.

curfew

A curfew was originally a medieval regulation requiring that fires be put out or covered at a certain hour at night. *Curfew* comes from the Anglo-Norman word *coeverfu*, from the Old French phrase *Couvre feu!* "Cover the fire!" containing an imperative of the verb *couvrir*, "to cover," and the noun *feu*, "fire." The rule of curfew was probably instituted as a public safety measure to minimize the risk of a general conflagration. A bell was rung at the prescribed hour, and as a result the word *curfew* has extended its meaning to denote the bell, the hour, and the regulation. *Curfew* did not enter English until the thirteenth century. Anglo-Norman was England's language of law after the Norman Conquest and *curfew* was simply a naturalized form of *coeverfu*, originally a legal term.

cushy

Since *cushy* has a breezy American ring, it is difficult to believe that it is an import, as some etymologists claim. Members of the British army in India are supposed to have picked up the Anglo-Indian version of the Hindi word *khuś*, meaning "pleasant," to which the suffix -y, as in *empty* and *sexy*, was added to form a new English word. *Cushy*, however, was first recorded in a letter from the European battlefront during World War I. This fact, in conjunction with our inability to find an Anglo-Indian source, casts some doubt on the Hindi or Anglo-Indian origin of *cushy*. Two other possibilities are that *cushy* is a shortening of *cushion* with the -y suffix or that it is a borrowing of French *couchée*, "lying down; a bed."

cute

Cute is a good example of how a shortened form of a word can take on a life of its own, developing a sense that dissociates it from the longer word from which it was derived. *Cute* was originally a shortened form of *acute* in the sense "keenly perceptive or discerning, shrewd." In this sense *cute* is first recorded in a dictionary published in 1731. Probably *cute* came to be used as a term of approbation for things demonstrating acuteness, and so it went on to develop its own sense of "pretty, fetching."

cynic

A cynic may be pardoned for thinking that this is a dog's life. The Greek word *kunikos,* from which *cynic* comes, was originally an adjective meaning "doglike," from *kuōn,* "dog." The word was probably applied to the Cynic philosophers because of the nickname *kuōn* given to Diogenes of Sinope, the prototypical Cynic. He is reported to have been seen barking in public, urinating on the leg of a table, and engaging in other unacceptable behaviors in the middle of the street. The first use of the word recorded in English, in a work published from 1547 to 1564, is in the plural for members of this philosophical sect. In 1596 we find the first instance of *cynic* meaning "faultfinder," a sense that was to develop into our modern sense. The meaning "faultfinder" came naturally from the behavior of countless Cynics, who in their pursuit of virtue pointed out the flaws in others. Such faultfinding could lead quite naturally to the belief associated with cynics of today that selfishness determines human behavior.

daisy

The word *daisy* contains more than meets the eye. So does the plant to which the name was originally applied. The European plant *Bellis perennis*, known in the United States as the *English daisy*, folds its petals at night, hiding its yellow center, and opens them in the morning with the sun, like an eye that sleeps and wakes. Because of this habit, the old English name for the plant was *dægesēage*, a compound word made up of *dæges*, "day's," and *ēage*, "eye," which gives us the Modern English word *daisy*. Folk names for flowers are frequently based on such metaphors, and names are often as delightful as the flowers themselves: Queen Anne's Lace, a folk name for the wild carrot, has a flower that looks like a doily; the tiger lily is orange with black mottling. *Dandelion*, another interesting word that was originally a compound, is discussed below. In the case of *daisy*, sound change has obscured the formerly distinct elements of the compound. For a similar change, see **hussy**.

dandelion

Dent-de-lioun, the Middle English form of *dandelion*, makes it easy to see that our word is a borrowing of Old French *dentdelion*, literally, "tooth of the lion," referring to the sharply indented leaves of the plant. Modern French *dent-de-lion*, unlike Modern English *dandelion*, reveals to anyone who knows French what the components of the word are. The English spelling reflects the pronunciation of the Old French word at the time it was borrowed into English. The earliest recorded instance of the word occurs in an herbal written in 1373, but we find an instance of *dandelion* used in a proper name, Willelmus Dawndelyon, in a document dated 1363.

common dandelion plant

debunk

One can readily see that *debunk* is constructed from the prefix *de-*, meaning "to remove," and the word *bunk.* But what is the origin of the word *bunk,* denoting the nonsense that is to be removed? *Bunk* came from a place where much bunk has originated, the United States Congress. During the 16th Congress (1819–1821) Felix Walker, a representative from western North Carolina whose district included Buncombe County, carried on with a dull speech in the face of protests by his colleagues. Walker later explained he had felt obligated "to make a speech for Buncombe." Such a masterful symbol for empty talk could not be ignored by the speakers of the language, and *Buncombe,* spelled *Bunkum* in its first recorded appearance in 1828 and later shortened to *bunk,* became synonymous with *claptrap.* The response to all this bunk seems to have been delayed, for *debunk* is not recorded until 1923.

deer

In various Middle English texts one finds a fish, an ant, or a fox called a *der,* the Middle English ancestor of our word *deer.* In its Old English form *dēor,* our word referred to any animal, including members of the deer family, and continued to do so in Middle English, although it also acquired the specific sense "a deer." By the end of the Middle English period, around 1500, the general sense had all but disappeared. *Deer* is a commonly cited example of a semantic process called *specialization,* by which the range of a word's meaning is narrowed or restricted. When Shakespeare uses the expression "mice and rats, and such small deer" for Edgar's diet in *King Lear,* probably written in 1605, we find a trace of the older meaning. It is interesting to note that the German word *Tier,* the cognate of English *deer,* still has the general sense of "animal."

delight

Delight, with its connotations of effervescence and brightness of spirit, would seem to have a natural connection with *light,* "not heavy," or *light,* "illumination," but the connection exists in form only. The Old French and Middle English form of the noun *delight* was *delit,* which was ultimately derived from the Latin verb *dēlectāre,* "to delight." Like many other Old French and Anglo-Norman words, *delit* was naturalized in

English in the thirteenth century. In Middle English, the verb *delit* appeared almost simultaneously with the noun. The spelling *delight* began to be used in the sixteenth century, a time when the spelling of English words was still unsettled. Several spellings could represent the same sound, and *delit* was respelled to resemble words that rhymed with it, like *light* and *night*. Another English adjective, *delectable,* also entered English from Old French, ultimately from the same Latin origin, in the fourteenth century. *Delightful* emerged in the sixteenth century, and suddenly there were more words than one needed to describe the same attribute. English retained both words, but the two have come to have slightly different connotations. Since the eighteenth century, *delightful* has been the more general term, *delectable* the term more likely to describe sensual experience.

delta

A Greek letter sits at the mouth of many rivers. Noticing the resemblance between the island formed by sediment at the mouth of a river such as the Nile and the triangular shape of their letter delta (Δ), the Greeks gave the name *delta* to such an island. English borrowed this sense from Greek, although the word *delta* appeared first in English as the name of the letter, in a work written possibly around 1200. The sense "alluvial deposit" is not recorded until 1555, when *delta* is used with reference to the Nile River delta.

Democrat

A Democrat was once a Republican. The political party that elected Thomas Jefferson, James Madison, James Monroe, and John Quincy Adams as presidents was first called the *Republican* or *Democratic- Republican Party.* During the years 1825 to 1828 the party was reorganized. When Andrew Jackson was elected in 1828, the word *Republican* was dropped altogether, and the reconstituted party was renamed the *Democratic Party*—a name it has kept ever since. A Democrat, with an uppercase *D,* is a member of this party, which survives to this day. (A *democrat* with a lowercase *d* is simply one who supports democracy.) The Republican Party of today was organized in 1854, for the most part by Democrats and members of the older Whig Party who shared a common opposition to the institution of slavery.

Politically, the English and Americans owe a great deal to the French. *Democracy* entered English in the sixteenth century, adapted from French *démocratie.* The adjective *democratic,* borrowed from French *démocratique,* first appeared in the seventeenth century. The word *democrat* was borrowed from French during the French Revolution of 1789 to refer to one who espoused a democratic philosophy. The French formed *démocrate* by analogy with *aristocrate.* All these French words go back to the Greek *dēmokratia,* derived from *dēmos,* "people, free citizens," and the suffix *-kratia,* "power, rule."

The Greek word was forged in the city-states of ancient Greece such as Athens, where assemblies of eligible citizens made the laws themselves. There were systems of rotation and selection by lot that ensured that all citizens could have their turn in executive office or the judiciary. This was direct democracy, but by the standards of today, it would not seem very democratic. In Athens, for instance, most inhabitants were slaves or otherwise did not qualify as citizens, and they could not participate directly in governing the city. Women, too, were excluded from political activity. In the twenty-first century, we can be thankful to enjoy the rights won for us by those who have fought to widen the definition of *democracy* to include all people.

derrick

A grim presence hangs over our oil wells and construction projects, perceived dimly through the smoke and dust only by those who know etymology. A well-known hangman of around 1600, surnamed Derrick, has been immortalized in the name of contraptions far removed from his fatal business. Credited with a total of more than three thousand executions during his career as a hangman at Tyburn, near what is now Marble Arch in Hyde Park, London, Derrick was so famous that his name came to mean first "a hangman" and then, by association, "the gallows." Prior to our modern uses of the term, *derrick* was applied to the apparatus used on ships for lifting or moving heavy things. This machine apparently resembled a device that the hangman Derrick invented to execute as many as twenty-three condemned people simultaneously. The name, perhaps finally free of gallows humor, was then applied to devices on land as well as sea, such as the large cranes used at construction sites or the tall frameworks on top of oil wells that support boring equipment and that hoist and lower lengths of pipe.

dervish

The word *dervish* calls to mind the phrases *howling dervish* and *whirling dervish.* Certainly there are dervishes whose religious exercises include making loud howling noises or whirling rapidly to induce a dizzy, mystical state. But a dervish is really the Muslim equivalent of a monk or friar, for the Persian word *darvēsh,* the ultimate source of *dervish,* means "religious mendicant." The word is first recorded in English in 1585.

desert

When Shakespeare says in Sonnet 72, "Unless you would devise some virtuous lie,/To do more for me than mine own desert," he is using the word *desert* in the sense of "worthiness; merit," a word perhaps most familiar to us in the plural, meaning "something that is deserved," as in the phrase *just deserts.* This word goes back to the Latin word *dēservīre,* "to devote oneself to the service of," which in Vulgar Latin came to mean "to merit by service." *Dēservīre* is made up of *dē-,* meaning "thoroughly," and *servīre,* "to serve." Knowing this, we can distinguish this *desert* from *desert,* "a wasteland," and *desert,* "to abandon," both of which go back to Latin *dēserere,* "to forsake, leave uninhabited," which is made up of *dē-,* expressing the notion of undoing, and the verb *serere,* "to link together." We can also distinguish all three *deserts* from *dessert,* "a sweet course at the end of a meal," which is from the French word *desservir,* "to clear the table." *Desservir* is made up of *des-,* expressing the notion of reversal, and *servir* (from Latin *servīre*), "to serve," hence, "to unserve" or "to clear the table."

digitalis

The name of the plant genus *Digitalis*, whose member the foxglove provides an important drug used to treat heart disease, is associated with another part of the body, the finger. In *Digitalis*, which comes from the Latin word *digitālis*, meaning "relating to a finger," we recognize *digit*, which derives from Latin *digitus*, "finger, toe." In Modern Latin the genus name was chosen because the German name for the foxglove is *Fingerhut*, "thimble," or literally "finger hat." The second part of our word *foxglove* also refers to the similarity of the foxglove blossoms to the fingers of a glove. *Digitalis* is first recorded in English in a work published in 1664.

foxglove plant

dinner

Eating foods such as pizza and ice cream for breakfast may be justified etymologically. In Middle English *dinner* meant "breakfast," as did the Old French word *disner*, or *diner*, which was the source of our word. The Old French word came from the Vulgar Latin word **disiūnāre*, meaning "to break one's fast; to eat one's first meal," a notion also contained in our word *breakfast*. The Vulgar Latin word was derived from an earlier word, **disiēiūnāre*, the Latin elements of which are *dis-*, denoting reversal, and *iēiūnium*, "fast." Middle English *dinner* not only meant "breakfast" but, echoing usage of the Old French word *diner*, more commonly meant "the first big meal of the day, usually eaten between 9 A.M. and noon." Customs change, however, and over the years we have let the chief meal become the last meal of the day, by which time we have broken our fast more than once.

dirge

The history of the word *dirge* illustrates how a word with neutral connotations, such as *direct,* can become emotionally charged because of a specialized use. The Latin word *dīrige* is a form of the verb *dīrigere,* "to direct, guide," which is used in uttering commands. In the Office of the Dead *dīrige* is the first word in the opening of the antiphon for the first nocturn of Matins: *"Dirige, Domine, Deus meus, in conspectu tuo viam meam,"* (Direct, O Lord, my God, my way in thy sight). The part of the Office of the Dead that begins with this antiphon was named *Dīrige* in Ecclesiastical Latin. This word with this meaning was borrowed into English as *dirige,* first recorded in a work possibly written before 1200. *Dirige* was then extended to refer to the chanting or reading of the Office of the Dead as part of a funeral or memorial service. In Middle English the word was shortened to *dirge,* although it was pronounced as two syllables. After the Middle Ages the word took on its more general senses of "a funeral hymn or lament" and "a mournful poem or musical composition," and developed its one-syllable pronunciation.

disaster

A disaster, etymologically speaking, is a calamity brought about by the evil influence of a star or planet. *Disaster* is ultimately derived from Latin *dis-,* a pejorative prefix, and *astrum,* "star," itself from

Greek. The immediate source of the word *disaster* is not Latin but rather Italian, where the word *disastro* was first formed from these Latin elements. Although astrology was very important in ancient and medieval times, neither the French word *désastre* nor the English word *disaster* appeared before the sixteenth century. The meaning "evil celestial influence" did not survive the seventeenth century, and the more general sense "misfortune, calamity" has been current since the introduction of *disaster* as an English word in the late sixteenth century. Shakespeare uses both senses of the word in his works. He even plays on the double signification of the word in *King Lear,* as the treacherous character Edmund muses that it is his very nature to be evil, no matter what star he was born under:

This is the excellent foppery of the world,
that, when we are sick in fortune,—often the
surfeit of our own behavior,—we make guilty
of our disasters the sun, the moon, and the
stars: as if we were villains by necessity; fools
by heavenly compulsion . . .

dismal

The adjective *dismal* was originally an Anglo-Norman noun phrase—*dis mal*—meaning "evil days," from Latin *diēs malī.* In the medieval calendar two days each month were considered unlucky, for example, January 1 and 25 and February 4 and 26. A *dismal day* was one of these unlucky days. By the sixteenth century the phrase *dismal day* had become so common that *dismal* was interpreted as an adjective and came to mean "unlucky" and "causing dread" in general. In more recent times these senses have become obsolete or rare, have lost force, or have become associated with the sense "depressing, gloomy." Today the word does not connote disaster so much as boredom.

ditto

Ditto, which at first glance seems a handy but insignificant sort of word, actually has a Roman past, for it comes from *dictus,* "having been said," the past participle of the verb *dīcere,* "to say." In Italian *dīcere* became *dire* and *dictus* became *detto,* or in the Tuscan dialect *ditto.* Italian *detto* or *ditto* meant what *said* does in English, as in the locution "the said story." Thus the word could be used in certain constructions to mean "the same as what has been said"; for example, having given the date *December 22,* one could use *26 detto* or *ditto* for *26 December.* The first recorded use of *ditto* in English occurs in such a construction in 1625. The sense "copy" is an English development, first recorded in 1818. *Ditto* has even become a trademark for a duplicating machine.

dog

Although the dog was the first domesticated animal, the English word *dog* has an obscure history. The Old English ancestor of *dog* appears only once, as a translation of the Latin word *canis,* "dog." A number of other languages have a word similar to *dog,* but this is because they have more or less recently borrowed the word from English, especially with reference to stocky or powerful breeds. These words include French *dogue,* "mastiff," and Spanish *dogo,* "bulldog." However, the ultimate origins of the English word *dog* are completely unknown.

The usual word for "dog" in Old English was *hund,* the ancestor of our modern English word *hound,* which has cognates in the other Germanic languages such as German *Hund. Hound* is further related to the words for "dog" in many other Indo-European languages, including Latin *caniʃ* (source of the Italian word *cane* and French word *chien*) and Greek *kuōn* (see **cynic**). Another cognate is Welsh *ci,* seen in English *corgi,* which literally means "a dwarf dog" in Welsh. All of these words descend from the Proto-Indo-European word for "dog," **kwō,* whose stem was **kwon-.* The initial *h* of English *hound,* as opposed to the *k*-sound of the other languages, is a result of GRIMM'S LAW (see glossary).

During the Middle English period *dogge* supplanted Old English *hund* as the everyday word for a dog of any breed. At first Middle English *dogge* was often used with a connotation of "worthless cur." Since the rise of the word *dog, hound* has become specialized and now usually refers to hunting breeds.

dollar

Many countries in the world today call their unit of currency a *dollar,* and this word has been in use for various coins long before the birth of the United States. *Dollar* ultimately derives from German *Taler,* which is short for *Joachimʃtaler,* a silver coin minted in Joachimsthal (now Jáchymov in the northwestern Czech Republic) in the sixteenth century. The Low, or North, German and early Modern Dutch form of *taler* was *daler,* the form which eventually reached English as *dollar* in the sixteenth century as a result of trade. From the sixteenth to the eighteenth century, the English used *dollar* to refer to the Spanish *dólar,* a coin also known as a *piece of eight* or *peʃo,* which was the medium of exchange in Spain and the Spanish-

American colonies. The name of this Spanish coin, *dólar,* was also derived from the Low German and Dutch *daler.* Because the North American colonists were familiar with the Spanish coin, Thomas Jefferson proposed that the monetary unit of the newly independent United States be called a *dollar* and resemble the Spanish peso, and his proposal was adopted in 1785.

donkey

In the most common pronunciation of the word *donkey* heard nowadays, the first syllable has the vowel in *honk.* But some speakers still preserve another pronunciation and rhyme *donkey* with *monkey.* The etymology of this word remains unsure, but many have thought it represents a shortening of the name *Duncan,* Irish *Donncha.* The first part of this name, *donn,* means "brown" in Irish, and the new word may have had something to do with the typical color of the donkey. But it is no surprise to see a personal name become the word for an animal, since the female of the donkey is known as the *jenny,* probably from *Jennifer,* and the male of the donkey is also known as the *jackass.*

Up until the late eighteenth century, everyone called the animal by his ancient name, *ass,* the descendant of Old English *assa.* The Old English word may ultimately go back to the Latin word *asinus,* "donkey," source of our word *asinine,* "senselessly stupid," whose meaning draws upon the donkey's reputation for obstinacy. *Asinus* itself is probably the Latin version of a word that spread throughout western Eurasia by way of ancient trade networks—there is a word similar to *asinus* all the way back in Sumerian, the earliest language ever to be written down. The Sumerians had domesticated the onager as a draught and pack animal. (Nowadays we don't hear much about the onager, also known as the *half-ass.* It looks very much like a donkey, but with a shorter ears.) The Sumerian word for this animal was *anśe,* which has reminded many scholars of Latin *asinus.*

It is interesting that the word *donkey* appears out of nowhere and begins to replace *ass* in the late eighteenth century, just when some English dialects were beginning to "drop their *r*'s"—that is, the consonant *r* was being lost at the end of words and within words before another consonant. In some varieties of British English, for example, words like *father* and *farther* were becoming homophones, being pronounced something like *fah-thuh.* Some American dialects also underwent similar changes. At about the same time in some British dialects, the vowel *a* acquired an open pronunciation *ah* in many words, especially before *s.* For example, most Americans say *mask* with the same vowel as in *cat,* but many Bristish speakers say it with the vowel in *father.* This change put the word *ass* on a collision course with the word *arse,* and speakers may have resorted to the word *donkey* to avoid disaster.

But Americans, too, avoid the word *ass* in the meaning "donkey," for obvious reasons.

The American pronunciation of *ass,* meaning "buttocks," as *ass,* rather than as *arse,* with an *r,* is something of a linguistic curiosity. Historically *ass* and *arse* are the same word, descended through Middle English *ars* from Old English *ears.* *Arse* is still pronounced with its *r* in most dialects which do not drop their *r*'s, such as the Irish and Scottish varieties of English, to name but a few. American *ass* should still have its *r,* at least among those speakers who don't drop their *r*'s. There are, however, several other words in which an *r* has disappeared before *s* in British and other varieties of English. The fish *bass* was originally the *barse.* *Cussing* was originally *cursing,* and to *bust* one's head or arm originally meant to make it *burst.* The colorful American dialect word *passel,* "a large quantity or group," derives from *parcel.* Many of these changes probably took place much earlier than the eighteenth century, perhaps even during the Middle English period in some cases, long before the general dropping of *r*. Most of the variant pronunciations that resulted from this earlier loss of *r* have now disappeared or become non-standard, but in the case of *ass*, a taboo word, this pronunciation has persisted. The word *ass* referring to the part of the body and the word *ass* referring to the animal may have been a little too close for comfort in polite American conversation, and as in British English the new word *donkey* handily solved the dilemma.

drench

Drink and *drench* mean quite different things today, but in fact they share similar origins, and, historically, similar meanings. *Drink* comes from a prehistoric Germanic verb **drinkan,* from the Germanic root ** drink-,* meaning "drink." Another form of this root, **drank-,* could be combined with a suffix, **-jan,* that was used to form causative verbs, in this case **drankjan,* "to cause to drink." The descendant of the simple verb **drinkan* in Old English was *drincan* (virtually unchanged), while the causative verb **drankjan* was affected by certain sound shifts and became Old English *drencan* (in which *c* is pronounced *ch*) and, in Middle and Modern English, *drench*. In Middle English *drench* came to mean "to drown," a sense now obsolete; the sense "to steep, soak in liquid" and the current modern sense "to make thoroughly wet" developed by early Modern English times. *Drink* and *drench* are not the only such pairs in English, where one verb comes from a prehistoric Germanic causative; some others include *sit* and *set* ("to cause to sit"), *lie* and *lay* ("to cause to lie"), and *fall* and *fell* ("to cause to fall").

dress

A dress is such a common article of modern attire that it is difficult to imagine that the word *dress* has not always referred to this garment. The earliest noun sense of *dress*, recorded in a work written before 1450, was "speech, talk." This *dress* comes from the verb *dress*, which goes back through Old French *drecier*, "to arrange," and the assumed Vulgar Latin *dīrēctiāre* to Latin *dīrēctus*, a form of the verb *dīrigere*, "to direct." In accordance with its etymology, the verb *dress* has meant and still means "to place," "to arrange," and "to put in order." The sense "to clothe" is related to the notion of putting in order, specifically in regard to clothing. This verb sense then gave rise to the noun sense "personal attire" as well as to the specific garment sense. The earliest noun sense, "speech," comes from a verb sense having to do with addressing or directing words to other people.

dunce

The word *dunce* comes from the name of John Duns Scotus. Duns Scotus was no dunce, however, but one of the most eminent theologians of the thirteenth century, and he was known as *Doctor Subtilis*, "the subtle doctor (learned man)." In the early sixteenth century, the humanist scholars of classical Greek and Latin and religious reformers harshly criticized followers of Duns Scotus, or the *Dunses*, for their resistance to the new learning of the Renaissance and the new theology of the Reformation. *Dunce*, therefore, is a word that defines the difference between the medieval and the modern. By the end of the sixteenth century *dunse*, or *dunce*, had acquired its current meaning "a stupid person." *Dunce* is one of many English words derived from a personal name, like **boycott**, **chauvinism**, and **derrick**.

dungeon

The word *dungeon* may have gone down in the world quite literally, if one etymology of the word is correct. *Dungeon* may go back to a Medieval Latin word, *domniō,* meaning "the lord's tower," which came from Latin *dominus,* "master." In Middle English, in which our word is first recorded in a work composed around the beginning of the fourteenth century, it meant "a fortress, castle" and "the keep of a castle," as well as "a prison cell underneath the keep of the castle." *Dungeon* can still mean "keep," although the usual spelling for this sense is *donjon,* but the meaning most usually associated with it is certainly not elevated. It is also possible that *dungeon* goes back to a Germanic word related to our word *dung.* This assumed Germanic word would have meant "an underground house constructed of dung." If this etymology is correct, the word *dungeon* has ended up where it began.

easel

"**A** painter's ass" is not a phrase that immediately brings to mind an accessory to the artist's profession. But *easel* comes to us from the Dutch word *ezel*, meaning "ass, donkey." The Dutch word was eventually extended to mean "an upright frame for displaying or supporting something," in the same way that the English word *horse* has come to mean "a piece of gymnastic equipment with an upholstered body." Developments such as these illustrate the playfulness or wit sometimes introduced into language when speakers use perceived similarities between two objects to name one of them.

Easter

Although the word *Easter* is now the name of a Christian festival, it has a decidedly pagan past. The Old English ancestor of our word *Easter* was ēastre, which apparently came from the name of a pre-Christian festival that was celebrated during the spring. This festival was named for a Germanic and Indo-European dawn goddess whose holiday was apparently celebrated at the spring equinox. The Christian missionaries to England helped ease the transition from paganism to Christianity by adopting native words for Christian traditions; hence the use of a pagan name for a Christian festival. The word *Easter* is closely related to the Latin word *aurōra* and the Greek word *ēōs*, both meaning "dawn." They are all derived from the same Indo-European root, **aus-*, which is also the source of our word *east*, the direction of sunrise.

eavesdropper

One can be an eavesdropper without going near an eavesdrop. The word *eavesdropper* comes from the noun *eavesdrop*, the name for the space close to a building where water drips from the eaves. An eavesdropper was originally someone who stood in the eavesdrop to overhear private conversations taking place inside. We know that eavesdropping was a crime at least as early as 1487. A record of the English borough of Nottingham states that *"juratores ... dicunt ... quod Henricus Rowley ... est communis evysdropper"* (jurors ... say ... that Henry Rowley ... is a common ... eavesdropper). And a legal glossary of 1641 explains, "Evesdroppers are such as stand under wals or windows ... to heare news." Of course, eavesdropping has since moved beyond the confines of the eavesdrop, and the word has come to mean listening secretly to others almost anywhere, even remotely by means of electronic listening devices. *Eavesdrop* became a verb sometime in the seventeenth century. It is a back-formation from *eavesdropper*.

The development of the all-encompassing global economy is a frequent topic of debate nowadays, but the word *economy* itself has rather homely beginnings. The word *economy* can be traced back to the Greek word *oikonomos,* "one who manages a household," derived from *oikos,* "house," and *nemein,* "to manage." From *oikonomos* was derived *oikonomiā,* which had not only the sense "management of a houseold or family" but also senses such as "thrift," "direction," "administration," "arrangement," and "public revenue of a state." The first recorded sense of our word *economy,* found in a work possibly composed in 1440, is "the management of economic affairs," in this case, of a monastery. *Economy* is later recorded in other senses shared by *oikonomiā* in Greek, including "thrift" and "administration." What is probably our most frequently used current sense, "the economic system of a country or an area," seems not to have developed until the nineteenth or twentieth century.

electricity

The effects of electricity have been observed since ancient times, when it was noticed that amber, when rubbed, attracts small bits of straw, wood, and other light materials. These effects were first studied scientifically in the seventeenth century, and the words *electric* and *electricity* were coined then from the Latin word *ēlectrum,* "amber," a borrowing of Greek *ēlektron.* The English word *electron,* however, does not come directly from the Greek word; it has been formed in recent times from the word *electric* and the suffix *-on,* used in the names of subatomic particles. Already in the eighteenth century, even before the advent of electric lights, *electric* came to be used in a metaphorical sense, to describe thrilling experiences.

eleven

The decimal system of counting is well established in the English names for numbers. Both the suffix -*teen* (as in *fourteen*) and the suffix -*ty* (as in *forty*) are related to the word *ten.* But what about the anomalous *eleven* and *twelve?* Why do we not say *oneteen, twoteen* along the same pattern as *thirteen, fourteen, fifteen? Eleven* in Old English is *endleofan,* and related forms in the various Germanic languages point back to an original Germanic **ainlif,* "eleven." **Ainlif* is composed of **ain-,* "one," the same as our *one,* and the suffix **-lif* from the Germanic root **lib-,* "to adhere, remain, remain left over." Thus, *eleven* is literally "one-left" (over, that is, past ten), and *twelve* is "two-left" (over past ten).

empty

In Old English *Ic eom ǣmtig* could mean "I am empty," "I am unoccupied," or "I am unmarried." The sense "unoccupied, at leisure," which did not survive Old English, points to the derivation of *ǣmtig* from the Old English word *ǣmetta,* "leisure, rest." The word *ǣmetta* may in turn go back to the Germanic root **mōt-,* meaning "ability, leisure." In any case, Old English *ǣmtig* also meant "vacant," a sense that was destined to take over the meaning of the word. *Empty,* the Modern English descendant of Old English *ǣmtig,* has come to have the sense "idle," so that one can speak of empty leisure.

encyclopedia

The word *encyclopedia,* which to us usually means a large set of books, descends from a phrase that involved coming to grips with the contents of such books. The Greek phrase is *enkuklios paideia,* made up of *enkuklios,* "cyclical, periodic, ordinary," and *paideia,* "education," and meaning "general education." Copyists of Latin manuscripts took this phrase to be a single Greek word, *enkuklopaedia,* with the same meaning. This spurious Greek word became the New Latin word *encyclopaedia,* coming into English with the sense "general course of instruction," first recorded in 1531. The word was chosen as the title of a reference work covering all knowledge; the first such use in English is recorded in 1644.

English

English is derived from *England,* one would think. But in fact the language name is found long before the country name. The latter first appears as *Englaland* around the year 1000, and means "the land of the *Engle,*" that is, the Angles. The Angles, Saxons, and Jutes were the three Germanic tribes who emigrated from what is now Denmark and northern Germany and settled in England beginning about the fourth century A.D. Early on, the Angles enjoyed a rise to power that must have made them seem more important than the other two tribes, for all three tribes are indiscriminately referred to in early documents as Angles. The speech of the three tribes was conflated in the same way: they all spoke what would have been called **Anglisc,* or "Anglish," as it were. By the earliest recorded Old English, this had changed to *Englisc.* In Middle English, the first vowel had already changed further to the familiar (ĭ) of today, as reflected in the occasional spellings *Ingland* and *Inglish*. Thus the record shows that the Germanic residents of what Shakespeare called "this sceptered isle" called the language they spoke English long before they named the land England.

ennui

Were they alive today, users of Classical Latin might be surprised to find that centuries later a phrase of theirs still survives, although as a single word. The phrase *mihi in odiō est* (literally translated as "to me in a condition of dislike or hatred is"), meaning "I hate or dislike," gave rise to the Vulgar Latin verb **inodiāre*, "to make odious," the source of the Old French verb *ennuyer* or *anoier*, "to annoy, bore." This was borrowed into English by around 1275 as *anoien*, our *annoy*. From the Old French verb a noun meaning "worry, boredom" was derived, which became *ennui* in modern French. This noun, with the sense "boredom," was borrowed into English in the eighteenth century, perhaps filling a need in polite, cultivated society.

enthusiasm

"Nothing great was ever achieved without enthusiasm," said the very quotable Ralph Waldo Emerson, who also said, "Everywhere the history of religion betrays a tendency to enthusiasm." These two uses of the word *enthusiasm*—one positive and one negative—both derive from its source in Greek. *Enthusiasm* first appeared in English in 1603 with the meaning "possession by a god." The source of the word is the Greek *enthousiasmos*, which ultimately comes from the adjective *entheos,* "having the god within," formed from *en,* "in, within," and *theos,* "god." Over time the meaning of *enthusiasm* became extended to "rapturous inspiration like that caused by a god" to "an overly confident or delusory belief that one is inspired by God," to "ill-regulated religious fervor, religious extremism," and eventually to the familiar sense "craze, excitement, strong liking for something." Now one can have an enthusiasm for almost anything, from water skiing to fast food, without religion entering into it at all.

See also **fan** and **giddy.**

envelope

The word *envelope* was borrowed into English from French during the early eighteenth century, and the first syllable acquired the pronunciation similar to that of the preposition *on* as an approximation to the nasalized French pronunciation. Gradually the word has become anglicized further and is now most commonly pronounced with a first syllable that rhymes with *men.* The earlier pronunciation is still considered acceptable, however. Other similar words borrowed from French in the modern period include *envoy* (seventeenth century), *encore, ennui, ensemble, entree* (eighteenth century), *entourage,* and *entrepreneur* (nineteenth century). Most retain their pseudo-French pronunciations, with the exception of *envoy,* which, like *envelope,* is mainly pronounced with a first syllable that rhymes with *men* now.

ethnic

When it is said in a Middle English text written before 1400 that a part of a temple fell down and "mad a gret distruccione of ethnykis," one wonders why ethnics were singled out for death. The word *ethnic* in this context, however, means "gentile," coming as it does from the Greek adjective *ethnikos,* meaning "national, foreign, gentile." The adjective is derived from the noun *ethnos,* "people, nation, foreign people," that in the plural phrase *ta ethnē* meant "foreign nations." In translating the Hebrew Scriptures into Greek, this phrase was used for Hebrew *gōyīm,* "gentiles"; hence the sense of the noun in the Middle English quotation. The noun *ethnic* in this sense or the related sense "heathen" is not recorded after 1728, although the related adjective sense is still used. But probably under the influence of other words going back to Greek *ethnos,* such as *ethnography* and *ethnology,* the adjective *ethnic* broadened in meaning in the nineteenth century. After this broadening, the noun sense "a member of a particular ethnic group," first recorded in 1945, came into existence.

eureka

The classical world of the Greeks and the Romans continues to live in our own culture in a variety of surprising ways, as the history of the exclamation *eureka* illustrates. The story is told that Hiero II, the ruler of the rich Greek city of Syracuse in Sicily, asked the great scientist Archimedes (287?-212 B.C.) to determine if a certain crown had silver or another cheaper metal mixed in with the gold. Shortly afterward, Archimedes stepped into his bath, which was full of water, and slopped water onto the floor. Therefore, he concluded, a body displaces its own volume when immersed in water. Archimedes knew that gold is denser than silver—a given weight of silver would be bulkier than a given weight of gold and would displace more water. He leapt from his bath crying *"Heurēka!"*, which in Greek means "I have found (it)!" Not stopping to clothe himself, Archimedes dashed home to test his conclusion and soon discovered that the crown was not pure gold. We do not know what the unhappy Hiero exclaimed when he heard the news.

The first known appearance of Archimedes exclamation in an English text occurs in a translation from 1603 of the *Moralia,* a series of essays on general topics, by the Greek writer Plutarch (ca. 45–125 A.D.) It is there correctly spelled *heureca,* although it was later almost always spelled *eureka,* probably reflecting the dropping of *h* that occurred in the later stages of the Greek language. Since the eighteenth century the English word has been used to express delight at finding something. California chose *Eureka* as its state motto, in reference to the recent discovery of gold there in 1848, before it became a state in 1850. *Eureka* is also a remarkably popular American place-name, applied to towns, townships, and mountains from sea to shining sea. Eureka, Colorado, and Eureka, Nevada, are in rich mining areas, but Eureka, Kansas, was supposedly named after the discovery of a spring, as was Eureka Springs, Arkansas.

fan

Since some sports fans are disposed to wild acts and excessive partiality, it may not surprise their critics to learn that behind our word *fan* lies a history of lunacy, demonic possession, and religious zeal. *Fan* is short for *fanatic,* which goes back to the Latin word *fānāticus. Fānāticus* comes from *fānum,* "temple," and means "belonging to a temple," and by extension "inspired by orgiastic rites, furious, frantic." The earliest recorded English use of the noun *fanatic* refers to a lunatic, while *fanatic* as an adjective is first recorded with reference to behavior of the sort that might result from possession by a god or demon; hence, frantic or furious behavior. In the seventeenth century when religious controversy between Puritans and Royalists ran high in England, the noun and adjective were applied to religious zealots. The noun *fanatic* was used as a hostile epithet for those who refused to accept the doctrine and practices of the Church of England. The noun and adjective *fanatic* are still used to refer to religious zeal, but they have broadened their meaning to include other types of fervent devotion.

For interesting examples of similar developments of meaning in other words, see **enthusiasm** and **giddy**.

farm

The word *farm* has its origins in an Anglo-Norman legal term *ferme*, meaning "fixed payment." This is in turn derived from Medieval Latin *firma*, a form of the word *firmus*, "firm, steady," and the source of our word *firm*. Because Anglo-Norman was the language of English law during the Middle Ages, it was the source of many words of legal importance (such as **curfew**) in the history of English. The earliest sense of the English word *farm* is "a fixed yearly amount payable as a tax or rent," since it was a common practice to lease agricultural lands for a fixed annual rent rather than a percentage of the crop. The word *farm* was also applied to land occupied on such terms. Originally, a farmer was "one who collects tax or rent," not the one who paid it for the privilege of cultivating a given plot of land. The phrase *farm out* "to send out (work to be done elsewhere)" also derives from the use of this word in medieval systems of leasing land. From the sixteenth century on, *farm* was used to indicate any cultivated agricultural land, regardless of the circumstances of its tenancy or ownership, and *farmer* became the occupational name of the tenant or owner.

fascism

drawing of fasces

It is fitting that the name of an authoritarian political movement like Fascism, founded in 1919 by Benito Mussolini, should come from the name of a symbol of authority. The Italian name of the movement, *fascismo,* is derived from *fascio,* "bundle, (political) group," but also refers to the movement's emblem, the fasces, a bundle of rods bound around a projecting axe-head that was carried before an ancient Roman magistrate by an attendant as a symbol of authority and power. The name of Mussolini's group of revolutionaries was soon used for similar nationalistic movements in other countries that sought to gain power through violence and ruthlessness, such as Nazism.

fawn

The word *fawn,* "young deer," is a fascinating example of how a word can pass through various languages and end up looking very different from the way it began. This word's odyssey is particularly interesting because another descendant of the Latin word from which *fawn* comes also exists in English. If we track *fawn* backward, we find that it comes from the Old French word *feon,* also spelled *foun* and *faon,* meaning "the young of an animal," later undergoing specialization to "a young deer." This Old French word in turn goes back to the Vulgar Latin word **fētō,* "young of an animal." **Fētō* is derived from Latin *fētus,* "childbearing" or "offspring." This Latin word was also directly borrowed into English as *fētus,* "unborn young." The Latin word was derived from the Indo-European root *dhē-,* "to suck," which is found in several words relating to childbearing in Latin. See more at **female.**

fee

It is possible to see the idea of money taking hold of the human mind by studying a few words that express the notion of wealth or goods. The word *fee* now denotes money paid or received for a service rendered. *Fee* comes from Old English *feoh,* which has three meanings, all equally ancient: "cattle, livestock"; "goods, possessions, movable property"; "money." The Germanic form behind the Old English is **fehu,* which derives by GRIMM'S LAW (see glossary) from Indo-European **peku-,* "cattle." **Fehu* is therefore a cognate of Latin *pecu,* "cattle," also a direct descendant of Indo-European **peku-.* Latin *pecu* has several derivatives that ultimately were borrowed into English. One was *pecūnia,* "money," the source of our word *pecuniary.* Another was *pecūliāris,* "pertaining to one's *pecūlium,* or property," the source of our word *peculiar.* Finally, our word *peculator* comes from yet a third derivative, *pecūlātor,* "embezzler of public money, peculator."

fellow

A jolly good fellow might or might not be the ideal business associate, but the ancestor of our word *fellow* definitely referred to a business partner. *Fellow* was borrowed into English from Old Norse *fēlagi,* meaning "a partner or shareholder of any kind." Old Norse *fēlagi* is derived from *fēlag,* "partnership," a compound made up of *fē,* "livestock, property, money," and *lag,* "a laying in order" and "fellowship." The notion of putting one's property together lies behind the senses of *fēlagi* meaning "partner" and "consort." In Old Norse *fēlagi* also had the general sense "fellow, mate, comrade," which *fellow* has as well, indicating perhaps that most partnerships turned out all right for speakers of Old Norse.

female

Modern English speakers may at first suspect that the word *female* is derived from *male* by the addition of a prefix of some sort, but the word *female* is in fact originally unrelated to the word *male*. *Female* is a respelling of Middle English *femelle,* which is ultimately from the Latin word *fēmella,* a diminutive of *fēmina,* "woman." The Middle English word *femelle,* a borrowing from Old French, first appears in the early fourteenth century, and it originally sounded much less like the word *male* than it does today. In one poem of the time, *femelle* rhymes with the word *querele* (the ancestor of *quarrel*). However, since *femelle* and *male* share an *m* and an *l,* and since the two words belonged to the same sphere of meaning and occurred in close correlation in many contexts, *femelle* was soon altered under the influence of *male*. The spelling *female* began to appear by the end of the fourteenth century. This mistaken etymological association with *male* and the resultant change in spelling and pronunciation is continued in the now standard *female.*

The Latin word *fēmina,* "woman," the source of *female,* has given English several other words, such as *feminine.* The Latin word itself goes back to an Indo-European form **dhēmnā-,* "she who suckles," from the root **dhē-,* "to suck" and also "to suckle, nourish." In Latin, where the Proto-Indo-European sound *dh became *f* at the beginning of a word, this root served as the source of several other words having to do with childbearing that have been borrowed into English, such as *fetus* and *fecund*. See more at **fawn**.

The English word *male,* on the other hand, comes from Old French *maɑle,* itself the regular development of Latin *maɑculuɑ.* This Latin word is obviously the source of English *maɑculine.* In the spoken Latin of Spain, however, *maɑculuɑ* developed first into the unattested form **maɑcluɑ,* and then the cluster *-ɑcl-* became *ch,* giving Spanish *macho,* which was subsequently borrowed into English. *Male* and *macho* are thus in origin the same word, having reached English through two different routes.

fey

The history of the words *fey* and *fay* illustrates a rather fey coincidence. Our word *fay,* "fairy, elf," the descendant of Middle English *faie,* "a person or place possessed of magical properties," and first recorded around 1390, goes back to Old French *fae,* "fairy," the same word that has given us *fairy. Fae* in turn comes from Vulgar Latin *Fāta,* "the goddess of fate," from Latin *fātum,* "fate." If *fay* is connected to *fate,* so is *fey* in a manner of speaking, for its Old English ancestor *fǣge* meant "fated to die." The sense we are more familiar with, "magical or fairylike in quality," seems to have arisen partly because of the resemblance in sound between *fay* and *fey.*

filibuster

A *freebooter* and a *filibuɑter* may not share many attributes, but they do share a common linguistic ancestor: both come from the Dutch word *vrijbuiter,*

which is derived from *vrij,* "free," and *buit,* "booty."
Freebooter, first recorded in the sixteenth century,
was a direct borrowing of the Dutch word. *Filibuster,*
however, has had a more checkered career. French borrowed the Dutch word and passed it along to English
in the eighteenth century in the form *flibustier.*
French *flibustier* was also borrowed by the Spanish,
and the Spanish form *filibustero* has influenced the
Modern English form *filibuster.*

The development of the senses of *filibuster* also
reflects its Spanish origins. At first *flibustier* or *filibustero* meant "pirate," but in the nineteenth century
the word was used in the United States to denote an
adventurer who tried to foment revolution in the
Spanish colonies of Central America and the
Caribbean. It was also used as a verb to indicate the
activities of a filibuster. The obstreperous behavior of
such pirates was probably uppermost in the minds of
those who first applied the term *filibuster* to the
obstreperous course taken by legislators seeking to
delay or prevent legislative action.

film

One indication of the gulf between us and our Vic-
torian predecessors is that the *Oxford English
Dictionary* fascicle containing the word *film,* published in 1896, does not have the sense "a motion picture." The one hint of the future to be found among
still familiar older senses of the word, such as "a thin
skin or membranous coating" or "an abnormal thin
coating on the cornea," is the sense of *film* used in
photography referring to a coating of material, such
as gelatin, that could substitute for a photographic
plate or be used on a plate or on photographic paper.
Thus a word that has been with us since Old English
times took on this new use, first recorded in 1845,

which has since developed and now refers to an art form, a sense first recorded in 1920.

fire

Primitive Indo-European had pairs of words for some very common things, such as water or fire. Typically, one word in the pair was active, animate, and personified; the other, impersonal and neuter in grammatical gender. In the case of the pair of words for "fire," English has descendants of both, one inherited directly from Germanic, the other borrowed from Latin. Our word *fire* goes back to the neuter member of the pair. In Old English, "fire" was *fȳr*, from Germanic **fūr*. The Indo-European form behind **fūr* is **pūr*, whence also the Greek neuter noun *pūr*, the source of the prefix *pyro-*. The other Indo-European word for fire appears in *ignite*, which is derived from the Latin word *ignis*, "fire," from Indo-European **egnis*. The Russian word *ogon'* (stem form *ogn-*) and the Sanskrit *agni-*, "fire" (deified as Agni, the god of fire), also came from **egnis*, the active, animate, and personified word for fire.

flour

Since the words *flower* and *flour* are spelled differently and are nowadays used in quite different contexts, it is surprising to learn that the two are in origin the same word, Anglo-Norman *flur*. *Flour* is simply a specialized use of the word *flower*, which was the finest part of wheat meal left after the bran had been sifted out. As it still is today, the word *flower* is here being used metaphorically to mean "the best, the choicest part." In the *Canterbury Tales,* Geoffrey Chaucer plays delightfully on these two meanings when the Wife of Bath laments the passing of her youth and beauty but states her intention to keep enjoying the pleasures of this world: "The flour is goon, ther is namoore to telle / The bren as I best kan now moste I selle." (The flower is gone, there is no more to tell, I must sell the bran as best I can.) At first, *flower,* or *flour,* referred only to flour made from wheat; however, by the fourteenth century the word came to mean "powder produced by pulverizing any grain or other foodstuff." The distinction in spelling between *flour* and *flower* did not become standard until the nineteenth century. Anglo-Norman *flur* (modern French *fleur*) comes from the Latin word for "flower," *flōs,* whose stem was *flōr-.* The Latin word is derived from the Proto-Indo-European root **bhel-,* "bloom," which is also the source of the English word *blossom,* as well as *bloom* itself.

flunky

The word *flunky* entered into Standard English from Scots, in which the word meant "liveried manservant, footman," and came at least by the nineteenth century to be a term of contempt. The word is first recorded and defined in a work about Scots published in 1782. The definition states that a flunky is "literally a sidesman or attendant at your flank," which gives support to the suggestion that *flunky* is a derivative and alteration of *flanker,* "one who stands at a person's flank."

Fond is a word that has undergone melioration, or a shift in connotation from bad to neutral or good. *Fond* was originally *fanned,* meaning "foolish." In some dialects of Middle English, *fanned* also meant "insipid, tasteless," a sense that persisted in the East Anglian dialect of British English almost into the twentieth century. Later, the word came to mean "foolishly affectionate, doting," but the mild reproach conveyed by this sense is rarely present in the minds of those who currently use the word. *Fond* is now most frequently used simply to mean "having a strong liking for." The verb *fon,* "to be foolish," of which *fond* was originally a past participle, may be the source of our English word *fun.* By the thirteenth century, the verb *fon* could mean "to make a fool of (someone)" and, by the fourteenth century, "to be foolish." Around the same time, *fon* was also a noun meaning "fool." The noun *fun* for "practical joke" (as in "We had a bit of fun at his expense") isn't attested until the seventeenth century, and *fun,* "amusement" and the accompanying adjective *funny,* "amusing," don't develop until the eighteenth century. A wide chronological gap separates Middle English *fon* from Modern English *fun,* and the supposed development of one from the other has been lost in unrecorded dialectal forms. The modern senses of *fun* were frowned upon at first. Samuel Johnson recorded *fun* with disapproval in his *Dictionary* (1755): he called it "a low cant word," that is, one inappropriate for elevated discourse. Though one can barely believe it now, many common words were once considered "low." The characters in Jane Austen's *Northanger Abbey* (1817), for instance, debate the acceptability of the adjective *nice* in the sense "pleasing, agreeable," another usage that Johnson rejected. Eventually, though, like *fun,* it achieved respectability.

fool

The pejorative nature of the term *fool* is strengthened by a knowledge of its etymology. Its source, the Latin word *follis,* meant "a bag or sack, a large inflated ball, a pair of bellows." Users of the word in Late Latin, however, saw a resemblance between the bellows or the inflated ball and a person who was what we would call "a windbag" or "an airhead." The word, which passed into English by way of French, is first recorded in English in a work written around the beginning of the thirteenth century with the sense "a foolish, stupid, or ignorant person."

fornication

The word *fornication* had a lowly beginning suitable to what has long been the low moral status of the act to which it refers. The Latin word *fornix,* from which *fornicātiō,* the ancestor of *fornication,* is derived, meant "a vault, an arch." The term also referred to a vaulted cellar or similar place where prostitutes plied their trade. This sense of *fornix* in Late Latin yielded the verb *fornicārī,* "to commit fornication," from which is derived *fornicātiō,* "whoredom, fornication." Our word is first recorded in Middle English about 1303.

frank

The word *frank,* "straightforward, open," which originally meant "free, not a serf," goes back to the Late Latin word of Germanic origin, *Francus,* "Frank." The Franks were a West Germanic people that conquered Gaul in the fifth and sixth centuries A.D., and their name is still used today to designate the new lands they occupied, France. As the dominant group in the newly conquered territory, only the Franks possessed full freedom; eventually, their tribal name described their fortunate social and political status. The idea of political freedom originally conveyed by the English word *frank* was later extended to include freedom of expression as well. And while most of us pay postage on every letter we send, members of Congress and other high-ranking government officials have *franking* privileges—that is, their postage is free. The word *franchise* is related to *frank*; it comes from the same Latin word through Old French *franc*. Originally, *franchise* meant "the social status of a freeman" or "the sovereignty of a political entity (such as a city or the Church)," along with all the rights and privileges that went with this status. The various nature of these rights explains the multiple senses in which the word *franchise* is commonly used today. The current political sense of the word, "the right to vote in public elections," emerged in the eighteenth century. Another specialized use of the term, the "right to engage in certain commercial activities," is frequent today, as many fast food restaurants and retail stores operate on a *franchise* granted by the parent corporation.

freeze

Describing the landscape of Hell in Book II of *Paradise Lost,* Milton depicts "a frozen Continent . . . beat with perpetual storms . . . the parching Air Burns frore, and cold performs th' effect of Fire." It is evident from these lines that *frore* has some relationship to *frozen,* but what exactly is it? The Modern English paradigm for the verb *freeze* is *freeze, froze, frozen,* with a *z* throughout. However, in Old English, the principal parts were *frēoṡan, frēaṡ, froren.* The *r* in the past participle *froren* is from a prehistoric *ṡ* that became *r* by Verner's Law, a sound shift that changed *ṡ* in certain positions into *r.* (The effects of Verner's Law can also be seen in such Modern English pairs as *waṡ* and *were,* and *loṡe* and *(love-)lorn.*) During the Middle English period, a new past participle *froṡen* was created using the *ṡ* from the first two principal parts; this survives as *frozen* nowadays. The older participle, spelled *froren* or *frore* in Middle English, lived on as a poetic word for "cold," but well before Milton's day it had become archaic in the standard language.

Friday

Friday night is a time to meet friends, and it is the first taste of freedom after the long work week. It is only fitting that Frigg, the ancient Germanic goddess of love, should preside over this day, since the words *friend, free,* and *Friday* all derive from the same Germanic root, **frī-,* "love." This root developed from Proto-Indo-European **prī-* by the workings of GRIMM'S LAW (see glossary), which changes the original **p* to a Germanic **f.* The original **p* can be seen in words for "beloved" all over the Indo-European world, such as Hindi *priya,* "beloved," and Russian *prijatel',* "friend."

In English, too, a friend is a lover, etymologically. The relationship between Latin *amīcuṡ,* "friend," and *amō,* "I love," is clear, as is the relationship between Greek *philoṡ,* "friend," and *phileō,* "I love." In English, though, we have to go back a millennium before we see the verb related to *friend.* At that time, *frēond,* the Old English word for "friend," was simply the present participle of the verb *frēon,* "to love," from the Germanic root **frī-.* The Germanic protolanguage also made an adjective, **frija-,* from the same root. It meant "beloved, belonging to the circle of one's beloved friends and family." Thus by extension it came to mean "not in slavery"—that is, *free.*

The root also appears in the name of the Germanic deity called *Frigg* in Old Norse, the wife of Odin. Frigg's name comes from a Germanic word, **frijjō,* which meant "beloved, wife," and the English form of this word lives on today in *Friday,* from Old English *Frīgedæg.* The Old English in turn comes from a Germanic word, **frije-dagaz,* "day of Frigg," an ancient translation of Latin *Veneris diēs,* "day of Venus."

funky

When asked which words in the English language are the most difficult to define precisely, a lexicographer would surely mention *funky.* Linguist Geneva Smitherman has tried to capture the meaning of this word in *Talkin and Testifyin: The Language of Black America,* where she explains that *funky* means "[related to] the blue notes or blue mood created in jazz, blues, and soul music generally, down-to-earth soulfully expressed sounds; by extension [related to] the real nitty-gritty or fundamental essence of life, soul to the max." The first recorded use of *funky* is in 1784 in a reference to musty, old, moldy cheese. *Funky* then developed the sense "smelling strong or bad" and could be used to describe body odor. The application of *funky* to jazz was explained in 1959 by one F. Newton in *Jazz Scene:* "Critics are on the search for something a little more like the old, original, passion-laden blues: the trade-name which has been suggested for it is 'funky' (literally: 'smelly,' i.e. symbolizing the return from the upper atmosphere to the physical, down-to-earth reality)."

galore

Three Celtic languages are currently spoken in the British Isles: Irish, Scottish Gaelic, and Welsh. Although Irish and Scottish Gaelic, which are very closely related, have been losing ground to English over the last few centuries, they have still contributed a sizeable store of words to English vocabulary. In the case of *galore,* the word probably came from both languages at once. Irish has a phrase *go leór,* meaning "enough," from *go,* "to, until," and *leór,* "sufficiency." The Scottish Gaelic equivalent is *gu leòr.* On St. Patrick's Day, you can hear the same Irish preposition *go* being spoken in the popular phrase *Erin go bragh,* or in Irish itself *Éire go brách,* "Ireland until Doomsday!"

For other words from Irish, see **leprechaun** and **spree.**

gangplank

Although the element *gang-* in *gangplank* and *gangway* is the same as the word *gang*, "group, band," it preserves an older meaning of that word. In Old and Middle English, *gang* denoted the action of walking, with specific applications such as "way, passage" and "journey." A gangplank is simply a plank that provides passage between a ship and a landing place. The noun *gangway* denotes a gangplank as well as various other kinds of passageways, such as aisles. The element *gang-* in these words is related to the Old English verb *gangan*, "to walk, go," as well as to the Old Norse noun *gangr*, meaning "walking, going." However, as often happens, it is difficult to determine exactly which language contributed which words in the family of *gang*, since Old English and Old Norse are closely related. The verb *gang* meaning "to go" persists in Scotland, where borrowings from Old Norse are especially numerous. Robert Burns uses it in some of his most well-known verses:

> As fair art thou, my bonnie lass,
> So deep in luve am I,
> And I will luve thee still, my dear,
> Till a' the seas gang dry.

We also see the verb in Burns's proverbial verse: "The best laid schemes o' Mice an' Men, / Gang aft agley" (The best laid plans of mice and men go oft awry).

The use of the noun *gang* for a set of people, animals, or things that "go" together developed in the Middle English period. The newer noun *gangster*, for a member of a group of outlaws, was formed in the late nineteenth century. Within the past two decades or so, the spelling *gangsta*, representing a pronunciation of the word in African American Vernacular English, has taken on a life of its own in the genre of hip-hop music and culture called *gangsta rap,* which portrays the life of inner-city criminals in gritty detail. The enormous popularity of hip-hop music has begun to bring many words into the mainstream of American English, such as *bling-bling.* For words similar to *gangster* that has become differentiated in spelling and meaning into two words, see **flour** and **goatee.**

garage

It is difficult today to envision a world without garages or a language without the word *garage.* However, the word probably did not exist before the nineteenth century and certainly not before the eighteenth; possibly the thing itself did not exist before the end of the nineteenth century. Our word is a direct borrowing of French *garage,* which is first recorded in 1802 in the sense "place where one docks." The verb *garer,* from which *garage* was derived, originally meant "to put merchandise under shelter," then "to moor a boat," and then "to put a vehicle into a place for safekeeping," that is, a *garage,* a sense first recorded in French in 1901. English almost immediately borrowed this French word, the first instance being found in 1902.

garlic

Hidden in the word *garlic* is a figurative reference to its appearance. *Garlic* comes from the Old English word *gārlēac,* a compound composed of *gār,* "spear," and *lēac,* "leek, plant of the genus *Allium,* onion-like plant," which is the ancestor of the modern word *leek.* The compound may have been suggested by the similarity in shape between a clove of garlic and a spearhead. This element *gār* continues the Germanic word for "spear," **gaizaz,* which can also be found in many English names that are ultimately of Germanic origin, such as *Gerald,* "spear-power," or *Gerard,* "spear-hardy." The figurative expression originally present in Old English *gārlēac,* "spear-leek," has lost its point, if not its pungency, in Modern English *garlic.* For a word that has similarly developed from an old compound, see **hussy.**

gauntlet

The spelling *gauntlet* is acceptable for both *gauntlet* meaning "glove" or "challenge" and *gauntlet* meaning "a form of punishment in which lines of men beat a person forced to run between them"; but this has not always been the case. The story of the *gauntlet* used in "to throw down the gauntlet" is linguistically unexciting: it comes from the Old French word *gantelet,* a diminutive of *gant,* "glove." From the time of its appearance in Middle English (in a work composed in 1449), the word has been spelled with an *au* as well as an *a,* still a possible spelling. But the *gauntlet* used in "to run the gauntlet" is an alteration of the earlier English form *gantlope,* which came from the Swedish word *gatlopp,* a compound of *gata,* "lane," and *lopp,* "course." The earliest recorded form of the English word, found in 1646, is *gantelope,* showing that alteration of the Swedish word had already occurred. The English word was then influenced by the spelling of the word *gauntlet,* "glove," and in 1676 we find the first recorded instance of the spelling *gauntlet* for this word, although *gantelope* is found as late as 1836. From then on spellings with *au* and *a* are both found, but the *au* seems to have won out.

geezer

A relationship with a word we know well is disguised in the word *geezer.* A clue to this relationship is found in British dialect. The *English Dialect Dictionary* defines *geezer* as "a queer character, a strangely-acting person," and refers the reader to *guiser,* "a mummer, masquerader." The citations for *guiser* refer to practices such as the following: "People, usually children . . . go about on Christmas Eve, singing, wearing masks, or otherwise disguised," the last word of this passage being the one to which *geezer* is related.

giddy

The word *giddy* refers to fairly lightweight experiences or situations, but at one time it had to do with profundities. *Giddy* can be traced back to the same Germanic root, **gud-,* that has given us the word *God.* The Germanic word **gudigaz,* formed on this root, meant "possessed by a god." Such possession can be a rather unbalancing experience, and so it is not surprising that the Old English descendant of **gudigaz, gidig,* meant "mad, possessed by an evil spirit," or that Middle English *gidig,* or *gidi,* meant the same thing, as well as "foolish; mad (used of an animal); dizzy; uncertain, unstable." Our sense "lighthearted, frivolous" represents the ultimate secularization of *giddy.*

glamour

However unlikely it seems, the words *glamour* and *grammar* are related; both are descended from the Greek word *grammatike*, "grammar," through the Latin word *grammatica*. The Greek word *grammatike* is derived from *gramma*, "letter, written character," which itself is related to the verb *graphein*, "make a mark, draw, write," familiar from such English derivatives as *graphics* and *biography*. *Gramaire*, the Old French descendant of the Latin word *grammatica,* was borrowed into English and became our modern word *grammar*. Another English word derived from Latin *grammatica* in medieval times was *gramarye*, which denoted not just literacy but learning in general, including knowledge of occult sciences such as astrology and magic. In Medieval Latin, a variant *glomeria* developed as an alternative form of *grammatica*, perhaps by dissimilation of the first *r* to *l* under the influence of the second *r*. This Medieval Latin word may have been the source of an unattested Anglo-Norman word, **glomerie*, continued in the Scots word *glamour*. The Scots word is first recorded in the eighteenth century and preserved the sense "magic, magic spell" of *gramarye*. *Glamour* was introduced into literary English with the meaning "magic spell" by Sir Walter Scott early in the nineteenth century. Alfred, Lord Tennyson used *glamour* several times with this meaning in a long poem from 1859 belonging to his epic cycle about King Arthur, *Idylls of the King:* "That maiden in the tale / Whom Gwydion made by glamour out of flowers." The current sense of *glamour*, "alluring, and often illusory, charm," developed in English later in the nineteenth century.

glitch

Although *glitch* seems to be a word that people would always have found useful, it is first recorded in English in 1962 in the writing of John Glenn: "Another term we adopted to describe some of our problems was 'glitch.'" Glenn then gives the technical sense of the word the astronauts had adopted: "Literally, a glitch is a spike or change in voltage in an electrical current." It is easy to see why the astronauts, who were engaged in a highly technical endeavor, might have generalized a term from electronics to cover other technical problems. Since then *glitch* has passed beyond technical use and now covers a wide variety of malfunctions and mishaps. The ultimate origin of *glitch* is probably in Yiddish, where *glitsh* means "a slip, a lapse," from *glitshen,* "to slip." This in turn is an alteration of Middle High German *glīten,* "to glide," related to the English word *glide.*

goatee

When assessing American contributions to the English language and to fashion, let us not forget the *goatee.* Early comments on this style of beard appear first in American writings, making this word an Americanism. Although the style raises few eyebrows now, the early comments were not favorable: "One chap's . . . rigged out like a show monkey, with a little tag of hair hangin down under his chin jest like our old billy goat, that's a leetle too smart for this latitude, I think." This 1842 description, found in William Tappan Thompson's *Major Jones's Courtship,* also reveals the etymology of the word. The first recorded occurrence of the word itself, found in Daniel Lee and

Joseph H. Frost's *Ten Years in Oregon* (1844), also sounds disapproving: "A few individuals . . . leave what is called, by some of their politer neighbors, a 'goaty' under the chin."

god

English preserves several traces of the original Proto-Indo-European word for "god," *deiwos*. It can be seen in the word **Tuesday**, as well such words as *deity* and *divine* that are borrowed from Latin, where *deiwos* became *deus*. However, it is another reconstructed word, rather than *deiwos*, that is the source of the most fundamental religious term in English, *god*. The English word has exact cognates in all the other Germanic languages, allowing one to reconstruct a Germanic ancestral form, *gudam*. Traditionally, this is derived from the root *gheu(ə)-,* "to invoke," a god being "the one who is invoked." But there is an alternative view that derives *gudam* instead from the root *gheu-* "to pour," a root that also occupied a rather prominent role in religious terminology. It was used to refer to the making of a libation, or the pouring of a liquid sacrifice, as well as to the action of "pouring" (or heaping) earth to form a burial mound. Thus, Greek has the phrase *khutē gaia,* "poured earth," to refer to a burial mound. Greek *khutē* continues the Indo-European verbal adjective *ghu-to-,* "poured." If we take the neuter of this, *ghu-to-m,* and imagine what it would have become in prehistoric Germanic (applying the sound changes that we know occurred from Proto-Indo-European to Germanic), we would in fact get a form *gudam,* none other than our reconstructed word for "god." Given the Greek facts, the Germanic form may have referred in the first instance to the spirit immanent in a burial mound. Deriving *gudam* from *gheu-* rather than from *gheu(ə)-* would help to explain two odd facts. First of all, Germanic *gudam had neuter gender, not masculine, so that originally it might not have referred to a god, but rather to some inanimate object. Secondly, we would really expect *gudam to have a long vowel (*gūdam) if the word came from the root *gheu(ə)-, "to invoke." The sound written with a schwa *(ə)* in this root would have lengthened the vowel on the way to Germanic, and the English word would have ended up as something like *gowd,* rhyming with *loud.*

As it turns out, burial mounds are characteristic of the Kurgan peoples, who lived in the steppes north of the Black and Caspian seas between 5000–3000 B.C. Many archaeologists suspect that the Kurgan peoples spoke Indo-European languages, and it was the westward migrations of these peoples that gradually spread Indo-European languages, including Germanic, to the ends of Europe.

See also **Zeus.**

goodbye

No doubt more than one reader has wondered exactly how *goodbye* is derived from the phrase "God be with you." To understand this, it is helpful to see earlier forms of the expression, such as *God be wy you, god b'w'y, godbwye, god buy' ye,* and *good-b'wy.* The first word of the expression is now *good* and not *God,* for *good* replaced *God* by analogy with such expressions as *good day,* perhaps after people no longer had a clear idea of the original sense of the expression. A letter of 1573 written by Gabriel Harvey contains the first recorded use of *goodbye:* "To requite your gallonde [gallon] of godbwyes, I regive you a pottle of howdyes," recalling another contraction (of *how do ye,* or *howdy*) that is still used.

gorilla

Two traditions of exploration come together in the history of the word *gorilla,* which also illustrates how knowledge of the classics has influenced scientific terminology. Dr. Thomas S. Savage, an American missionary to western Africa, first described the gorilla scientifically in 1847, giving it the New Latin name *Troglodytes gorilla.* In doing so he was using his knowledge of Greek literature, in which there exists a fourth-century B.C. translation of a report written by Hanno, another visitor to western Africa. This Carthaginian navigator, who voyaged before 480 B.C., went as far as Sierra Leone in his explorations. In the Greek translation of his report he tells of seeing *Gorillai,* the name of which he allegedly learned from local informants and that he thought referred to members of a tribe of hairy women. In fact they were probably the same creatures that Thomas Savage described about twenty-four centuries later.

gossip

Calling someone a *gossip* in the Middle Ages was not derogatory at all. *Gossip* was originally an Old English compound of *god,* "God," and *sibb,* "blood relation," and meant "godparent." *Sib* is still used but is perhaps better known in the word *sibling* derived from it. Later in Middle English *gossip* could also mean "child of one's godparents" or "one's godparent's child." *Gossip* thus designated a relationship of peers as much as one between generations, and from such extended senses the meaning "friend, pal," evolved. This sense, first recorded in the fourteenth century, was likely in use from an earlier date. Given our tendency to chat idly about other people with our friends, we should not be surprised that the word came to refer to a person who engages in idle chatter and rumor-mongering, a sense first recorded in the sixteenth century. The verb *gossip* is first recorded in the sense "to engage in gossip" in the seventeenth century. The noun meaning "the conversation of a gossip," appears later, in the nineteenth century.

Gothic

The combination *Gothic romance* represents a union of two of the major influences in the development of European culture, the Roman Empire and the Germanic tribes that invaded it. The Roman origins of *romance* must be sought in the etymology of that word, but we can see clearly that *Gothic* is related to the name *Goth* used for one of those invading Germanic tribes. The word *Gothic*, first recorded in 1611 in a reference to the language of the Goths, was extended in sense in several ways, meaning "Germanic," "medieval, not classical," "barbarous," and also an architectural style that was not Greek or Roman. Horace Walpole applied the word *Gothic* to his novel *The Castle of Otranto, a Gothic Story* (1765) in the sense "medieval, not classical." From this novel, filled with scenes of terror and gloom in a medieval setting, descended a literary genre still popular today; from its subtitle descended the name for it.

gremlin

Elves, goblins, and trolls seem to be timeless creations of the distant past, but gremlins were born in the twentieth century. In fact, *gremlin* is first recorded only in the 1920s, as a Royal Air Force term for a low-ranking officer or enlisted man saddled with oppressive assignments. Said to have been invented by members of the Royal Naval Air Service in World War I, *gremlin* is used in works written in the 1940s for "an imaginary gnomelike creature who causes difficulties in aircraft." The word seems likely to have been influenced by *goblin,* but accounts of its origin are various and none are certain. One source cites Fremlin beer bottles to explain the word; another, the Irish Gaelic word *gruaimín,* "ill-humored little fellow." Whatever the word's origin, it is certain that gremlins have taken on a life of their own.

gringo

In Latin America the word *gringo* is an offensive term for a foreigner, particularly an American or English person. But the word existed in Spanish before this particular sense came into being. In fact, *gringo* may be an alteration of the word *griego,* the Spanish development of Latin *Graecus,* "Greek." *Griego* first meant "Greek, Grecian" as an adjective and "Greek, Greek language" as a noun. The saying "It's Greek to me" exists in Spanish as it does in English and helps us understand why *griego* came to mean "unintelligible language" and perhaps, by further extension of this idea, "stranger, " that is, "one who speaks a foreign language." The altered form *gringo* lost touch with the "Greek" sense but has the senses "unintelligible language," "foreigner, especially an English person," and, in Latin America, "North American or Britisher." Its first recorded English use (1849) is in John Woodhouse Audubon's *Western Journal*: "We were hooted and shouted at as we passed through, and called 'Gringoes.'"

grog

The words *grog* and *groggy* probably originated in an attempt by the Royal Navy to curb drunkenness more than two hundred years ago. In August 1740, Admiral Edward Vernon, wishing to practice economy and decrease the number of drunken brawls on his ships as well, ordered that all rations of rum were to be watered down and provided no more than twice a day, six hours apart. The irate but no doubt soberer sailors named this diluted mixture *grog*. *Grog* came from Vernon's nickname, *Old Grog*, an appellation he acquired because his boat cloak was made of a coarse fabric called *grogram,* developed from French *gros grain. Grog* and *groggy* are first recorded in English as part of a single statement in the *Gentlemen's Magazine* of 1770, in a glossary of terms for drunkenness: "Groggy; this is a West-Indian Phrase, Rum and Water, without sugar, being called Grogg."

guillotine

"At half past 12 the guillotine severed her head from her body." So reads the statement containing the first recorded use of *guillotine* in English, found in the *Annual Register* of 1793. Ironically, the guillotine, which became the most notable symbol of the excesses of the French Revolution, was named for a humanitarian physician, Joseph Ignace Guillotin. Guillotin, a member of the French Constituent Assembly, recommended in a speech to that body on October 10, 1789, that executions be performed by a beheading device rather than by hanging, the method used for commoners, or by the sword, reserved for the nobility. He argued that beheading by machine was quicker and less painful than the work of the rope and the sword. In 1791 the Assembly did indeed adopt beheading by machine as the state's preferred method of execution. A beheading device designed by Dr. Antoine Louis, secretary of the College of Surgeons, was first used on April 25, 1792, to execute a highwayman named Pelletier or Peletier. The device was called a *louisette* or *louison* after its inventor's name, but because of Guillotin's famous speech, his name became irrevocably associated with the machine. After Guillotin's death in 1814, his children tried unsuccessfully to get the device's name changed. When their efforts failed, they were allowed to change their name instead.

gun

The word *gun* originally referred to cannons and other instruments of war. The English word *gun* is shortened from a feminine name of Old Norse origin, *Gunilda,* a compound of two Old Norse words, *gunnr* and *hildr,* both meaning "battle." (*Hildr* was also the name of a Valkyrie, one of the Old Norse goddesses of battle who selected dead heroes from the battlefield and brought them to carouse in the hall of the god Odin.) A certain "Lady Gunilda" (in Latin, *Domina Gunilda*) is mentioned in a munitions inventory from Windsor Castle dated 1330-31. Lady Gunilda, however, was no lady, but the

a ballista

nickname of a missile-casting ballista, a siege engine in the form of a huge crossbow. Thus the Middle English word *gonnilde,* "cannon," seems to have developed from the principle of giving names to weapons. The use of feminine names for guns is more frequent than one might guess. In the late fifteenth century, James III of Scotland imported a state-of-the-art cannon from Mons, France, and installed it in Edinburgh Castle. The gun was called *Meg,* perhaps after James's consort, Margaret of Denmark. In World War I, the preeminent German arms manufacturer, Gustav Krupp, produced a large howitzer, which he named *Dicke Bertha,* "Big Bertha," after his wife.

guppy

R. J. Lechmere Guppy and his contributions to natural history are for the most part forgotten, but his name is more familiar than that of many a better-known naturalist. Guppy was a clergyman of Trinidad who delighted in ichthyology, the study of fish. In the mid-nineteenth century he sent to the British Museum a collection of New World fishes. Among them was a new species, discovered in 1850 and subsequently named after him, *Gemidinus guppyi.* The fish was later renamed *Poecilia reticulata,* or *Lebistes reticulatus,* but it still bears the common name *guppy.* When Charles Dickens named a character in *Bleak House* (1853) Mr. Guppy, he may simply have borrowed the surname—or he may have been on the cutting edge of English.

guy

The word *guy* is now extremely common in everyday conversation: good guys, bad guys, my guy, your guy. In the plural, *guys* is a handy word for a group of persons of either sex, as in the phrase *you guys,* which serves to make the plural of *you* in some dialects of

American English that don't use *y'all.* However, this commonest of words has the strangest of origins. *Guy* originally referred not just to any fellow but to an effigy of Guy Fawkes. Fawkes was a leader of the Gunpowder Plot, a scheme to blow up King James I and the Parliament during its ceremonial opening on November 5, 1605. The plot was foiled when Fawkes was arrested on the night of November 4, probably in the cellar of the House of Lords, where the gunpowder was stashed. Fawkes was tortured, signed a confession implicating the other members of the plot in a decidedly shaky hand, and was hanged with his fellow conspirators on January 31, 1606. That same year November 5 became a holiday, Guy Fawkes Day. On that day children wandered through the streets carrying figures dressed in old clothes, which they called *guys* after Guy Fawkes, lit bonfires, and set off fireworks (still a feature of Guy Fawkes Day). Because these figures were dressed in rags and clothes that did not match, *guy* came to mean "a person of odd appearance." Still current chiefly in British English, this sense is first found in Julia Charlotte Maitland's *Letters from Madras during the Years 1836-39 by a Lady:* "The gentlemen are all 'rigged Tropical' . . . grisly Guys some of them turn out!" The sense recorded in Maitland's *Letters* may have led to the more general and current sense, "a man, fellow," first recorded in a work called *Swell's Night Guide,* published in 1847: "I can't tonight, for I am going to be seduced by a rich old Guy."

The word *dude* shows a similar pattern in development of meaning. Although its ultimate origin is unknown, it is first recorded in the late nineteenth century in the sense of "dandy, fop, someone fastidious in dress," such as a city slicker from the East Coast of the United States roughing it out West, as at a *dude ranch.* Its further development to mean "man, fellow," seems to have taken place already by the early twentieth century.

hamburger

Because the world has eaten countless hamburgers, the origins of the name may be of interest to many. By the middle of the nineteenth century, people in the port city of Hamburg, Germany, enjoyed a form of pounded beef called *Hamburg steak.* The large numbers of Germans who migrated to North America during this time probably brought the dish and its name along with them. The entrée may have appeared on an American menu as early as 1836, although the first recorded use of *Hamburg steak* is not found until 1884. The variant form *hamburger steak,* using the German adjective *Hamburger,* meaning "from Hamburg," first appears in a Walla Walla, Washington, newspaper in 1889. By 1902 we find the first description of a Hamburg steak that is close to our conception of the hamburger, namely a recipe calling for ground beef mixed with onion and pepper. By then *hamburger* was on its way, to be followed—much later—by the shortened form *burger,* used in forming *cheeseburger* and the names of other variations on the basic burger, as well as on its own.

hangnail

At first sight, the etymology of *hangnail* seems obvious: the word is composed of the verb *hang* and the noun *nail,* as in *fingernail.* In actual fact, however, the word has a different origin. It has been reshaped by folk etymology, the tendency to break down words whose constituent elements are unfamiliar, reshape them, and make them resemble more familiar words in a way that makes sense. The Old English ancestor of *hangnail* was *angnæl,* a compound of *ange,* "troubled, sorrowful," and *næl,* "nail, peg." The element *ang-* comes from the Indo-European root **angh-,* "painful, constricted," which also shows up in borrowings of Latin and French origin, such as *anxiety* and *anguish.* The Old English word *angnæl* originally meant "corn; a painful, hard, rounded excrescence like a nail in the foot." In fact, the Latin name for a "corn" was *clāvus,* "a nail" (for hammering). Later on, the second element of the descendant of the Old English word was associated with the nails of the fingers and toes, and the word came to designate various kinds of painful fingernail and toenail conditions, including what is now called a *hangnail.* Because a hangnail consists of partially detached hanging skin, the unfamiliar element *ang-* was refashioned in modern times as *hang.* Another development of Old English *angnæl* is the rarer word *agnail,* meaning "hangnail."

harlot

The word *harlot* nowadays refers to a particular kind of woman, but, interestingly, it used to refer to a particular kind of man. The word, ultimately finding its origin in Old French *arlot,* or *herlot,* is first recorded in English in a work written around the beginning of the thirteenth century, meaning "a man of no fixed occupation, vagabond, beggar," and soon afterwards meant "male lecher." Already in the fourteenth century it appears as a deprecatory word for a woman, though exactly how this meaning developed from the male sense is not clear. For a time the word could also refer to a juggler or jester of either sex, but by the close of the seventeenth century its usage referring to males had disappeared.

The further origin of the Old French word *herlot* is uncertain. W. W. Skeat, a great scholar of the English language, offered the suggestion that it comes from a Germanic compound meaning "army-loafer" or "camp-follower." The first part of the compound would derive from Germanic **harjaz,* "army." This word is continued in Modern German *Heer,* "army." It is also the first element, *her-,* in the English word *herald,* a borrowing through Old French of a Germanic word meaning "commander of an army." The second element in *arlot,* or *herlot,* would be related to such words as Old High German *lotar,* "useless fellow."

hearse

The usual meaning of *hearse* today, "a vehicle for transporting the dead," was the latest to develop. The Latin word *hirpex,* the ancestor of *hearse,* meant "harrow," an agricultural implement that in one of its forms consists of a framework with teeth that is used to break up plowed land. The emergence of the sense "vehicle" occurred through an interesting series of steps. Latin *hirpex* had a variant form *hercia* in Medieval Latin. This developed into Old French *herce*, which also meant "harrow" but could be used more generally to mean simply "frame." It is in this sense, "a framework used for holding candles," that *hearse*, is recorded in Middle English during the thirteenth century. This framework was used at the Holy Week service of Tenebrae, a dramatic ceremony still performed today, during which all the candles but one in the church are extinguished in commemoration of Christ's death. The same *hearse* also held candles over a coffin at a funeral. Later extensions of the meaning of *hearse* preserved the idea of a framework and the funereal circumstances of its use. In the sixteenth century, the word came to denote a support for the funeral pall as well, and by the seventeenth century, it indicated the bier or coffin itself. Finally, late in the seventeenth century, *hearse* was used to describe the vehicle that carries the coffin at a funeral.

heart

Many of our most basic English terms for parts of the body have been inherited from Proto-Indo-European, including *eye* from **hokw-, ear* from **haws-, knee* from **genu, foot* from **ped-,* and even *ass* from **orsos.* The fundamental word *heart* is no exception. Using GRIMM'S LAW (see glossary), we can recover the Proto-Indo-European root meaning "heart" from the English word by starting with the Middle English spelling *hert.* Grimm's Law tells us that an Indo-European *k* will develop into an English *h,* and an Indo-European *d* will develop into an English *t.* If we take the Middle English word *hert* and undo the changes wrought by Grimm's Law, we get Proto-

Indo-European *kerd-. This root *kerd- is also the source of Greek *kardia* and Latin *cor,* both meaning "heart." The English medical term *cardiac* comes from the Greek form, while the stem of the Latin noun, *cord-,* can be seen in a multitude of English words used in all areas of life. *Concord* is ultimately derived from Latin *concors,* meaning literally "with the heart" (i.e, of the same mind), and *discord* comes from *discors,* "apart, away from the heart" (i.e., of a different mind). The word *courage* originates in Latin *cor* as well.

As these derivatives show, in English and Latin alike the word for "heart" has both a physical meaning, "the muscle that pumps blood," and a metaphorical meaning, "the organ of thought and feeling." This second meaning is familiar from such phrases as *half-hearted* or *a hearty (*that is, *cordial) welcome.* One of the most interesting results of studying the etymology of words is the discovery of fundamental similarities among different peoples widely separated in space, time, and culture—from prehistoric herdsmen to the so-called global citizens of the twenty-first century. Many different cultures, speaking both Indo-European and non-Indo-European languages, consider the heart to be the seat of the emotions. This idea lies behind the English words *creed* and *credo.* Both words come from Latin *credo,* "I believe," and this in turn comes from Proto-Indo-European *kred-dhē-,* literally "to put heart." (Here the Proto-Indo-European root *kerd-,* "heart," takes the form *kred-,* with *e* inserted after the *r* instead of before, as occasionally happens in other roots.) This was a Proto-Indo-European idiom, as is assured by related forms from the extreme western and eastern ends of the Indo-European world, Irish *creideann* and Sanskrit *śrad-dhā-,* both meaning "believe." The words *Credo in unum Deum,* "I believe in one God," begin the Latin version of the Nicene Creed, the affirmation of faith of millions of Christians worldwide, often simply called the "Credo." This phrase employs the ancient formula, *kred-dhē-, "to put heart," inherited from Indo-European times. After six thousand years, the descendants of Proto-Indo-European root *kerd- still expresses heartfelt belief.

heist

The language of crime novels and gangster movies bristles with wonderful words like *yegg* or *shamus* which lack assured etymologies despite the investigations of many word detectives. The whole point of having an argot, of course, is to keep a secret, and these words have kept their secrets very well. We do know the origin of the colorful word *heist,* however. *Heist* is simply a dialectal form of *hoist,* which has taken on life as a separate word. Since the early eighteenth century, *hoist* is attested in various senses related to crime. *Hoisting* was getting on someone's back to enter a shop through an open window or transom; a *hoister* was a shoplifter.

Heist preserves a dialectal pronunciation in which words such as *joint* have a diphthong similar to the one heard nowadays in the standard American pronunciation of *pint.* This pronunciation was once extremely widespread in the United States. It is still traditional in many parts of the country, including Appalachia and the Atlantic coast from Chesapeake Bay down to South Carolina. You may have heard another relic of this regional feature in the joking phrase "Name yer pizen," used when offering someone a drink. *Pizen* is also commonly heard in renditions of the classic American ballad "On Springfield Mountain": "Once he was angling by a creek, / A serpent bit him upon his cheek, / His girlie tried with gentle sips / To drain the pizen with her lips." Similarly, the dialect pronunciation of the word *join* as *jine* is sometimes encountered in songs from the nineteenth century, such as the camp-songs of the American Civil War. Folksongs and other traditional songs are in fact rich sources for the study of obsolete or old-fashioned speech, since the pleasing play with the sounds of words, which makes the songs so enjoyable, will often depend upon specific dialect pronunciations.

Words such as *heist* illustrate the phenomenon that linguists call *dialect borrowing,* or *dialect mixture,* in which words with features characteristic of one dialect are used in a dialect that does not usually show those features.

hell

ell comes to us directly from Old English *hel.* Because the Roman Catholic Church prevailed in England from an early date, the Roman—that is, Mediterranean—belief that hell was hot prevailed there too; in Old English *hel* is a black and fiery place of eternal torment for the damned. But because the Vikings were converted to Christianity centuries after the Anglo-Saxons, the Old Norse *hel,* from the same source as Old English *hel,* retained its earlier pagan senses as both a place and a person. As a place, *hel* is the abode of oathbreakers, other evil persons, and those unlucky enough not to have died in battle. It contrasts sharply with *Valhalla,* the hall of slain heroes. Unlike the Mediterranean hell, the Old Norse *hel* is very cold. *Hel* is also the name of the goddess or giantess who presides in *hel,* the half blue-black, half white daughter of Loki and the giantess Angrbotha. The Indo-European root behind these Germanic words is **kel-,* "to cover, conceal" (so *hell* means the "concealed place"); it also gives us *hall, hole, hollow,* and *helmet.*

hello

Every word can reveal fascinating facts when we take the time to trace its history. Take, for example, the banal word that is the first thing many people utter or mutter at the beginning of their day, *hello*. The common use of *Hello!* as a polite or neutral greeting is not even 150 years old—as old as the telephone. *Hello* began life as a variant of *hullo*, originally an exclamation calling attention to something. Exclamations similar to *Hello!* such as *Ho (there)!* and *Hey!* and *Hi!* can be found in many languages. In Old English, the exclamation *lá* was used to call attention to something, and Middle English *lo* is the regular continuation of this word. However, in *Antique Phonograph Monthly* 76 (1987), researcher Allen Koenigsberg revealed an unexpected twist in linguistic history. Among the many useful things that Thomas Edison invented, the many devices that make modern life possible, he also was instrumental in popularizing a greeting that is surely used many millions of times a day: *hello*. In 1877, the first word Edison ever recorded using his newly invented phonograph was a form of this word, *hullo*. The word, in the form *halloo*, was apparently used quite often in Edison's inventing workshop at Menlo Park, New Jersey. It was in this workshop that Edison and his workers made many improvements to the telephone, recently patented by Alexander Graham Bell in 1876. Again in a letter of 1877, Edison was apparently the first person ever to use the spelling variation *hello*. By 1880, the delegates to the National Convention of Telephone Companies were all wearing buttons saying "Hello!" signaling the unofficial adoption of the word as the standard telephone greeting that we still use today. From there it has spread all around the world to every possible social situation. Edison's choice *Hello!* replaced Alexander Graham Bell's own suggestion for the telephone greeting, now used only by 105-year-old nuclear-power mogul Montgomery Burns, Homer's boss on TV's *The Simpsons.* Burns continues to answer the telephone like Bell, with a hearty: *Ahoy-ahoy!*

hermetic

The adjective *hermetic,* "completely sealed, especially against the escape or entry of air," is derived from the name of the god Hermes, specifically Hermes Trismegistus, the designation in Greek and Roman antiquity for the Egyptian god Thoth, who was regarded as the originator of the science of alchemy. In New Latin, the adjective *hermēticus* was formed from the name of this god, and the English is borrowed from the New Latin. In the seventeenth century, English *hermetic* meant "pertaining to alchemy" and the occult sciences in general. Alchemy, and later chemistry, was itself known as the hermetic art, philosophy, or science. A hermetic seal was a kind of seal used by alchemists that involved melting closed an opening in a glass vessel. Since the resultant seal was airtight, any similar type of seal has come to be called *hermetic.*

hex

The word *hex* is a good example of the sort of borrowing from other languages that occurred in the English-speaking colonies of Great Britain. German and Swiss immigrants who settled in Pennsylvania in the late seventeenth and eighteenth centuries spoke a dialect of German known as Pennsylvania Dutch. In this dialect, *hexe* was the equivalent of the German verb *hexen,* "to practice sorcery." The English verb *hex,* first recorded in the sense "to practice witch-craft" in an 1830 work called *Annals of Philadelphia,* is borrowed from Pennsylvania Dutch, as is the noun.

high muckamuck

One might not immediately associate the word *high muckamuck* with fur traders and Native Americans, but it seems that English borrowed the term from Chinook Jargon, a pidgin language that combined words from English, French, Nootka, Chinook, and the Salishan languages and that was formerly used by traders in the Pacific Northwest. In this language *hayo makamak* meant "plenty to eat" and is recorded in that sense in English contexts, the first one dated 1853, in which the phrase is spelled *hiou muckamuck.* In 1856 we find the first recorded instance of the word meaning "pompous person, person of importance," in the *Democratic State Journal* published in Sacramento, California: "The professors—the high 'Muck-a-Mucks'—tried fusion, and produced confusion."

hobby

The modern word *hobby* goes back to Middle English word *hoby,* "a small horse." *Hobby* and a related word *Hobin* probably originated as alternate forms of *Robin.* The name *Hobin* was used by ploughmen for horses. *Hoby,* "a small horse," became part of the compound *hobbyhorse.* From the sixteenth century onwards one of the meanings of the word was "a model of a horse worn around the waist of a performer in a morris dance." Morris dances are English folk dances in which stories are enacted by costumed dancers. Soon after *hobbyhorse* is recorded in other senses, including "a toy horse for children to ride." This last meaning led to the development of a new sense for *hobbyhorse,* "pleasurable activity," in the seventeenth century, for which the shortened form *hobby* has become general.

hobnob

The verb *hobnob* originally meant "to drink together" and occurred as a varying phrase, *hob or nob, hob-a-nob,* or *hob and nob,* the first of which is recorded in 1763. This phrasal form reflects the origins of the verb in similar phrases that were used when two people toasted each other. The phrases were probably so used because *hob* is a variant of *hab* and *nob* of *nab,* which are probably forms of *have* and its negative. In Middle English, for example, one finds the forms *habbe,* "to have," and *nabbe,* "not to have." *Hab or nab,* or simply *hab nab,* thus meant "get or lose; hit or miss," and the variant *hob-nob* also meant "hit or miss." Used in the drinking phrase, *hob or nob* probably meant "give or take"; from a drinking situation *hob nob* spread to other forms of chumminess.

Another phrase that resembles *hobnob* in its derivation is *willy-nilly,* which come from an alteration of *will ye (or he or I), nill ye (or he or I),* "be you (or he or I) willing, be you (or he or I) unwilling." *Nabbe* and *nill* are survivals of an Old English construction in which the word for "not," *ne,* was contracted with a following verb, in the present cases with *habban,* "to have," and *willan,* "to want, be willing, will."

honcho

Honcho sounds like a word out of the American-West, keeping company with *sheriff* and *bandit*, but it actually comes from the Japanese word *hanchō*, "squad leader," a compound of *han*, "squad," and *chō*, "leader." American soldiers stationed in Japan during World War II and the subsequent American occupation returned to the United States with a new English vocabulary word. It is first recorded in James M. Bertram's *Shadow of a War*, published in 1947. Since then, *honcho* has become fully Americanized, especially in the alliterative phrase, *head honcho*.

hooker

In his *Personal Memoirs* Ulysses S. Grant described Maj. Gen. Joseph Hooker as "a dangerous man . . . not subordinate to his superiors." Hooker had his faults. He may indeed have been insubordinate; he was undoubtedly an erratic leader. But "Fighting Joe" Hooker is often accused of one thing he certainly did not do: he did not give his name to prostitutes. According to a popular story, the men under Hooker's command during the Civil War were a particularly wild bunch and would spend much of their time in brothels when on leave. For this reason, as the story goes, prostitutes came to be known as *hookers*. However neat this theory may be, it cannot be true. The word *hooker* with the sense "prostitute" is already recorded before the Civil War. As early as 1845 it is found in North Carolina, as reported in Norman Ellsworth Eliason's *Tarheel Talk; an Historical Study of the English Language in North Carolina to 1860*, published in 1956. It also appears in the second edition of John Russell Bartlett's *Dictionary of Americanisms*, published in

1859, where it is defined as "a strumpet, a sailor's trull." Etymologically, it is most likely that *hooker* is simply "one who hooks." The term portrays a prostitute as a person who hooks, or snares, clients.

humble pie

Humble pie originally had no connection with humility, although the spelling of the phrase has been influenced by the adjective *humble,* just as surely as its current meaning. *Humble pie* originally meant "a dish made of an animal's *numbles,*" that is, its entrails and other internal organs. *Numbles,* the original form of the first part of this compound, was borrowed from French in the fourteenth century. In the fifteenth century the variant form *umbles* appeared and existed alongside *numbles* through the eighteenth century, especially in the compound *umble pie.* The *n* may have been picked up by the indefinite article, so that one ate not *a numble pie* but *an umble pie,* much in the same way that *napron* and other English words lost their initial *n.* See **apron.**

The idiom *to eat humble pie* very possibly arose first in a dialect in which the *h* at the beginning of words was not pronounced. In such a dialect *umble* and the adjective *humble* would be pronounced alike, and the idiom would have arisen from the resulting semantic confusion, or perhaps from a deliberate pun. *Humble pie* is first recorded before 1648 with reference to the actual dish and in 1830 as part of the idiomatic phrase. The idiom is perhaps best preserved in the words of Charles Dickens's mean, crafty, malicious Uriah Heep, who says, in his *h*-dropping dialect, "When I was quite a young boy . . . I got to know what umbleness did, and I took to it. I ate umble pie with an appetite."

husband

The English word *husband,* even though it is a basic kinship term, is not a native English word. It comes ultimately from the Old Norse word *hūsbōndi,* meaning "master of a house," which was borrowed into Old English as *hūsbōnda.* The second element in *hūsbōndi, bōndi,* means "a man who has land and stock" and comes from the Old Norse verb *būa,* meaning "to live, dwell, have a household." The master of the house was usually a spouse as well, of course, and it would seem that the main modern sense of *husband* arises from this overlap. When the Norsemen settled in Anglo-Saxon England, they would often take Anglo-Saxon women as their wives; it was then natural to refer to the husband using the Norse word for the concept, and to refer to the wife with her Anglo-Saxon (Old English) designation, *wīf,* "woman, wife" (Modern English *wife*). Interestingly, Old English did have a feminine word related to Old Norse *hūsbōndi* that meant "mistress of a house," namely, *hūsbonde.* Had this word survived into Modern English, it would have sounded identical to *husband*—surely leading to ambiguities.

hussy

Hussy and *housewife* were originally the same word, meaning "mistress of a household." The word *hussy,* "a saucy or mischievous girl; an immoral woman," represents one normal phonetic development of the Middle English compound *houswif,* "housewife." Today we do not pronounce the vowels in *housewife* as they were pronounced in Middle English *houswif.* The long vowels *u* and *i* in *houswif* were pronounced as (ōo), the vowel in the modern pronunciation of *gooſe,* and (ē), the vowel in the modern pronunciation of *geeſe,* respectively. Already in the Middle English period, there is evidence for the shortening of these vowels, and through the loss of *w* and later the loss of *f* during the sixteenth century, *houſwif* developed into the familiar *huſſy.* Our Modern English word *houſewife* is a renewal of the Middle English word that restores the clarity of the elements *houſe* and *wife.* As the more phonetically evolved form *huſſy* acquired its pejorative semantic baggage in the seventeenth century, *houſewife* became restricted in meaning to the original sense of the word. A phonetic development similar to *huſſy* can be heard in *goody,* formerly used as a title of courtesy before the name of a married woman of lower social standing, where we would nowadays use *Mrſ.* The title *Goody* is a development of an original *goodwife.* It was in common use during the colonial era in New England. Goody Cole, for instance, is well known as one of the unfortunate victims of the persecution of women suspected of witchcraft that occurred in the colonies at that time.

iconoclast

16th-century Greek oil on wood icon depicting the Virgin and Child

An iconoclast can be unpleasant company, but at least the modern iconoclast only attacks such things as ideas and institutions. The original iconoclasts destroyed countless works of art. *Eikonoklastēs,* the ancestor of our word, was first formed in Medieval Greek from the elements *eikōn,* "image, likeness," and *-klastēs,* "breaker," from *klān,* "to break." The images referred to by the word are religious images, which were the subject of controversy among Christians of the Byzantine Empire in the eighth and ninth centuries, when iconoclasm was at its height. In addition to destroying many sculptures and paintings, those opposed to images attempted to have them barred from display and veneration. During the Protestant Reformation images in churches were again felt to be idolatrous and were once more banned and destroyed. It is around this time that *iconoclast,* the descendant of the Greek word, is first recorded in English (1641), with reference to the Byzantine iconoclasts. In the nineteenth century *iconoclast* took on the secular sense that it has today, as in "Kant was the great iconoclast" (James Martineau).

ignoramus

In Latin *ignōrāmus,* literally "we do not know," is the first person plural form of the verb *ignōrāre,* "to have no knowledge of." In its first known appearance in English, from before 1577, *ignoramus* is a legal term meaning "we take no notice of it," and it survived in this use until at least 1827. It served as the term for a grand jury's endorsement upon a bill of indictment when the evidence was deemed insufficient to send the case to a trial jury. *Ignoramus* also took on a general sense, "an answer that admits ignorance of the point in question," and a figurative sense, "a statement of ignorance."

Perhaps because of these senses, both the Latin one and the original English legal meaning, a play by George Ruggle (first performed in 1615 and published in 1630), "written to expose the ignorance and arrogance of the common lawyers," was titled *Ignoramus* and featured a lawyer so named. From this use or similar uses of *ignoramus* as a proper name, the word was generalized to mean "an ignorant person" soon afterwards.

In Latin, many nouns ending in *-us* made their plurals in *-ī,* and this way of forming the plural is kept when the word is borrowed into English, as, for example, in *alumnus, alumni.* However, since *ignoramus* was only a verb in Latin, the plural of the new English noun usually was, and has been, *ignoramuses.*

A plural *ignorami* is sometimes encountered, often in joking reference to the origin of the word that such a plural implies.

ilk

When one uses *ilk,* as in the phrase *men of his ilk,* one is using a word with an ancient pedigree even though the sense of *ilk,* "kind or sort," is actually quite recent, having been first recorded at the end of the eighteenth century. This sense grew out of an older use of *ilk* in the phrase *of that ilk,* meaning "of the same place, territorial designation, or name." This phrase was used chiefly in names of landed families, *Guthrie of that ilk* meaning "Guthrie of Guthrie." "Same" is the fundamental meaning of the word. The linguistic ancestors of the word *ilk,* Old English *ilca* and Middle English *ilke,* were common words, usually appearing with such words as *the* or *that,* but the word hardly survived the Middle Ages in those uses.

imp

We might at first associate the word *imp* with *impudent,* recalling the mischievous behavior characteristic of little demons and little children. But the word *imp* arose in an altogether different place: the orchard and the garden. Since ancient times farmers and gardeners have practiced the art of grafting, that is, joining a shoot to an established plant, which nourishes and supports it like a parent. Anglo-Saxon gardeners called the grafted sprig or shoot an *impa,* a noun derived from the Old English verb *impian,* "to graft." In time *impa* became *imp,* and the word came to mean "a child or offspring," as well as "a grafted shoot." By the late sixteenth century it was often used specifically for a demon, a scion or "child" of the Devil. Not surprisingly, the word *imp* eventually lost the neutral meaning "a child or offspring." If children are called *imps* today, it is usually because they are full of mischief.

impeach

Nothing hobbles a president so much as impeachment, and there is an etymological as well as a procedural reason for this. The word *impeach* can be traced back through Anglo-Norman *empecher* to Late Latin *impedicāre,* "to catch, entangle," from Latin *pedica,* "fetter for the ankle, snare." Thus we find that Middle English *empechen,* the ancestor of our word, means such things as "to cause to get stuck fast," "hinder or impede," "interfere with," and "criticize unfavorably." A legal sense of *empechen* is first recorded in 1384. This sense, which had previously developed in Old French, was "to accuse, bring charges against."

inch

Inches and *ounces,* though not interchangeable units of measure, both derive from the Latin word *uncia,* "a twelfth part." The word entered English twice at different times and from different sources, which resulted in the differences in form and meaning between the two words. First, Latin *uncia* was borrowed directly at a very early date by the ancestor of Old English, and it appears as Old English *ynce,* denoting a linear measure of one twelfth of a foot. The *c* in the Old English word represents a *ch* sound, and the word *ynce* develops regularly into Modern English *inch.* The Old

French word *unce* (modern French *once*), which is the natural development of Latin *uncia,* was then borrowed in the Middle English period as the name for a unit of weight equal to one twelfth of a pound—in effect, Modern English *ounce.* Today we weigh most solids according to the avoirdupois system, which gives sixteen ounces to the pound. However, the system of troy weight, still used for precious metals but used generally in the Middle Ages, is based on a twelve-ounce pound.

inkling

nkling has nothing to do with ink, but it may have something to do with niches. Our story begins with the Old French (and modern French) word *niche,* meaning "niche." It is possible that in Old French a variant form existed that was borrowed into Middle English as *nik,* meaning "a notch, tally." This word is probably related to the Middle English word *nikking,* meaning "a hint, slight indication," or possibly "a whisper, mention." *Nikking* appears only once, in a Middle English text composed around 1400. In another copy of the same text the word *ningkiling* appears, which may be a variant of *nikking.* This is essentially our word *inkling* already, the only major change being an instance of what is called *false splitting,* whereby people understood *a ningkiling* as *an ingkiling.* They did the same thing with *a napron,* getting *an apron.*

interloper

The word *interloper* has its origin in the time when England was embarking on the course that would lead to the British Empire. *Interloper,* first recorded in connection with the Muscovy Company, the earliest major English trading company (chartered in 1555), was soon being used in regard to the East India Company (chartered in 1600) as well. These companies were established as monopolies, and independent traders called *interlopers* were not welcome. The term is probably partly derived from Dutch, the language of one of the great trade rivals of the English at that time. The *inter-* is simply the prefix *inter-,* which English has borrowed from Latin, meaning "between, among." The element *-loper* is probably related to the same element in *landloper,* "vagabond," a word adopted from Dutch and composed of *land,* "land," and *loper,* from *lopen,* "to run, leap." The word *interloper,* first recorded around 1590, was too useful in a world of busybodies to be restricted to its original specialized sense and came to be used in the extended sense "busybody" in the seventeenth century.

internecine

When is a mistake not a mistake? In language at least, the answer to this question is "When everyone adopts it," and, on rare occasions, "When it's in the dictionary." The word *internecine* presents a case in point. Today, it usually has the meaning "relating to internal struggle," but in its first recorded use in English, in 1663, it meant "fought to the death." How it got from one sense to another is an interesting story in the history of English. The Latin source of the word, spelled both *internecīnus* and *internecīvus,* meant "fought to the death, murderous." It is a derivative of the verb *necāre,* "to kill." The prefix *inter-* was used here not in the usual sense "between, mutual" but rather as an intensifier meaning "all the way, to the death." This piece of knowledge was unknown to Samuel Johnson, however, when he was working on his great dictionary in the eighteenth century. He included *internecine* in his dictionary but misunderstood the prefix and defined the word as "endeavoring mutual destruction." Johnson was not taken to task for this error. On the contrary, his dictionary was so popular and considered so authoritative that this error became widely adopted as correct usage. The error was further compounded when *internecine* acquired the sense "relating to internal struggle." This story thus illustrates how dictionaries are often viewed as providing norms and how the ultimate arbiter in language, even for the dictionary itself, is popular usage.

island

It may seem hard to believe, but Latin *aqua*, "water," is related to *island*, which originally meant "watery land." *Aqua* comes almost unchanged from Indo-European **akwā-*, "water." **Akwā-* became **ahwō-* in Germanic by GRIMM'S LAW (see glossary) and other sound changes. From this was built the adjective **ahwjō-*, "watery." This then evolved to **awwjō-* or **auwi-*, which in pre-English became **ēaj-*, and finally *ēg* or *īeg* in Old English. *Island*, spelled *iland*, first appears in Old English in King Alfred's translation of Boethius about the year 888; the spellings *igland* and *ealond* appear in contemporary documents. This word is a compound of *īeg* and *land*. The *s* in *island* is due to a mistaken etymology, confusing English *iland* with French *isle*. *Isle* comes ultimately from Latin *īnsula*, "island," a component of *paenīnsula*, "almost-island," whence our *peninsula*.

"I told Anse it likely won't be no need." This quotation from William Faulkner's *As I Lay Dying* illustrates a use of *it* that occurs in some vernacular varieties of American speech. *It* is used instead of Standard English *there* when *there* indicates the mere existence of something rather than a physical location, as in *It was nothing I could do.* Existential *it* is hardly a recent innovation—it appears in Middle English and in Elizabethan English, as in Marlowe's *Edward II*: "Cousin, it is no dealing with him now." Although most British and American varieties no longer have this historical feature, it still occurs in some Southern-based dialects and in African American Vernacular English.

In some American vernacular dialects, particularly in the South (including the Appalachian and Ozark mountains), speakers may pronounce *it* as *hit* in stressed positions, especially at the beginning of a sentence, as in *Hit's cold out here!* This pronunciation is called a *relic dialect feature* because it represents the retention of an older English form. In fact, *hit* is the original form of the third person singular neuter pronoun and thus can be traced to the beginnings of the Old English period (c. 449-1100). Early in the history of English, speakers began to drop the *h* from *hit,* particularly in unaccented positions, as in *I saw it yesterday.* Gradually, *h* also came to be lost in accented positions, although *hit* persisted in socially prestigious speech well into the Elizabethan period. Some relatively isolated dialects in Great Britain and the United States have retained *h,* since linguistic innovations such as the dropping of *h* are often slow to reach isolated areas. But even in such places, *h* tends to be retained only in accented words. Thus, we might hear *Hit's the one I want* side by side with *I took it back to the store.* Nowadays, *hit* is fading even in the most isolated dialect communities and occurs primarily among older speakers. This loss of *h* reflects a long-standing tendency among speakers of English to omit *h*'s in unaccented words, particularly pronouns, such as *'er* and *'im* for *her* and *him,* as in *I told 'er to meet me outside.* This kind of *h*-loss is widespread in casual speech today, even though it is not reflected in spelling.

janitor

A holiday for janitors ought to take place in January, for both words are linked. In Latin, *iānus* was the word for "archway, gateway, or covered passage" and also for the god of gates, doorways, and beginnings in general. As many schoolchildren know, our month January–a month of beginnings–is named for the god. Latin *iānitor,* the source of our word *janitor* and ultimately also from *iānus,* meant "doorkeeper or gatekeeper." Probably because *iānitor* was common in Latin records and documents, it was adopted into English, first being recorded in the sense "doorkeeper" around 1567 in a Scots text. In an early quotation Saint Peter is called "the Janitor of heaven." The term can still mean "doorkeeper," but in Scots usage *janitor* also referred to a minor school official. Apparently this position at times involved maintenance duties and doorkeeping, but the maintenance duties prevailed, giving us the position of janitor as we know it today.

Japan

Stamp collectors know that *Nihon* and *Nippon* on Japanese stamps mean "Japan"; what they probably don't know is that *Nihon, Nippon,* and *Japan* are all ultimately the same word. In the early part of the Chinese Tang dynasty—in A.D. 670, to be precise—Japanese scholars who had studied Chinese created a new name for their country using the Chinese phrase for "origin of the sun, sunrise," because Japan is located east of China. In the Chinese of the time (called Middle Chinese), the phrase would have been pronounced something like *nyet-pun',* "sun-origin, land of the rising sun." (Linguists who work on the difficult problem of the sounds of Middle Chinese have slightly different systems of notation, which are approximated here. The final apostrophe represents glottalization, or a glottal stop, the sound between the two vowels in English *uh-oh.*) Later in the history of the Japanese language, this compound "sun-origin" came to be pronounced *Nip-pon,* a pronunciation which still survives in Japanese, as well as **Ni-pon.* This latter developed by regular sound change to Modern Japanese *Ni-hon.* Interestingly, the Chinese themselves took to calling Japan by the name that the Japanese had invented, and it is from the Chinese version of the name that English *Japan* is ultimately derived. In Mandarin Chinese, one of the forms of Chinese to develop from Middle Chinese, the phrase evolved to *Rìběnguó,* with the Middle Chinese word *-kwək,* "country," becoming Mandarin *guó,* added to the end. An early form of the Mandarin version was recorded by Marco Polo as *Chipangu.* The early Mandarin form was borrowed into Malay as *Japang,* which was encountered by Portuguese traders in Moluccas in the sixteenth century. These traders may have been the ones to bring the word to Europe; it is first recorded in English in 1577, spelled *Giapan.*

jaunty

French has not only given us hundreds of words, it has sometimes given us the same word more than once. A prime example is Old French *gentil,* "highborn, noble." In the early 1200s, this was borrowed into Middle English and spelled as *gentile,* which later developed to mean "having the character of a nobleman, courteous," and, by the 1500s, "soft, mild." After some changes in spelling, the result was Modern English *gentle.* French *gentil* was borrowed into English again at the end of the sixteenth century, also in the spelling *gentile* and meaning "well-bred, belonging to or appropriate to the gentry." In the ensuing century it also came to mean "courteous, elegant," and continues to do so today as the word *genteel.* Since the spelling *gentile* did not accurately represent the word's French pronunciation, in the seventeenth century some people wrote it *jantee* or *janty.* This word took on a life of its own: while it originally meant "well-bred," by the 1670s it meant "easy or unconcerned in manner," and thence "sprightly, lively, brisk." Thus was born *jaunty.* The French *gentil* that spawned these words comes from Latin *gentīlis,* which meant simply "belonging to (the same) *gēns* or family." It is from the original Latin meaning that we get the modern word *gentile,* borrowed in the fourteenth century (again through French) meaning, essentially, "belonging to the same family as all non-Jews."

jeans

Etymologically speaking, blue jeans are a product of the Italian fashion industry. Jeans are made of a twilled cotton cloth that was probably originally called *Gene fustian. Gene,* or *Geane,* was the Middle English name for the northern Italian city of Genoa, where a kind of cloth called *fustian,* made from cotton, flax, or wool, was produced. The shortened form, Modern English *jean,* eventually referred to the cloth, rather than to the city in which it was made. The plural form *jeans* then came to designate a kind of trousers made of cotton fabric. The first known use of the word in this sense of "cotton trousers," occurs in Robert Smith Surtees' 1843 novel *Handley Cross,* where jeans are not blue but white: "Septimus arrived flourishin' his cambric, with his white jeans strapped under his chammy leather opera boots."

jeopardy

The word *jeopardy* illustrates the human tendency to anticipate the worst in an uncertain situation. Its Old French source, *jeu parti,* "divided game, even game," originally denoted a problem in chess and then came to mean a position in any game in which the chances of winning or losing were even. *Jeu* is the French word for "game, sport" and is descended from Latin *jocus,* "game, sport, jest," also the source of the English word *joke.* Old French *parti* means "divided." In English *jeopardy* retained the senses of the French phrase but extended the meaning of the word to "an uncertain or undecided situation." By Chaucer's time in the late fourteenth century, *jeopardy* had acquired its modern sense of "peril, danger."

journeyman

A journeyman, or skilled craftsman, is not an itinerant worker—that is, one on a journey. Instead, *journeyman* preserves an older sense of the word *journey*, revealing the word's origins. By the fourteenth century, the word *journeyman* denoted "a daily worker," that is, one who worked for another for daily wages. He was distinguished from an apprentice, who was learning the trade, and a master artisan, who was in business for himself. *Journey* is derived from the Old French *jornee,* (Modern French *journée*) "a day, the length of the day" and "a day's work." *Jornee* also meant "a day's travel" and then "trip," whether the travel took a day or not.

jukebox

Gullah, the English-based creole language spoken by people of African ancestry off the coast of Georgia and South Carolina, retains a number of words from the West African languages brought over by slaves. One such word is *juke* or *joog,* "bad, wicked, disorderly," from a source word akin to Wolof *dzug,* "to live wickedly," and Bambara *dzugu,* "wicked." The Gullah word is the probable source of the English word *juke,* used originally in Florida and then chiefly in the Southeastern states as a term for a roadside drinking establishment that offers cheap liquor, food, and music for dancing and often doubles as a brothel. *To juke* is to dance, particularly at a *juke joint* or to the music of a *jukebox,* whose name, no longer regional and having lost the connotation of sleaziness, contains the same word.

We might suspect that the word *jungle* comes from a language of a tropical country where dense forests grow. The word does in fact originate in India, but the original meaning of the word was somewhat different. It goes back to the Sanskrit word *jaṅgalaḥ,* meaning "desert, wasteland, uncultivated land." *Jaṅgalaḥ* developed further in various Indian languages and passed from one or more of these languages into English in the eighteenth century. In the nineteenth century, *jungle* in English began to be used of land overgrown with rank vegetation.

junk

The word *junk* is an example of the change in meaning known as generalization, and very aptly too, since the amount of junk in the world seems to be generalizing and proliferating rapidly. The Middle English word *jonk,* ancestor of *junk,* originally had a very specific meaning restricted to nautical terminology. First recorded in 1353, the word meant "an old cable or rope." On a sailing ship it made little sense to throw away useful material since considerable time might pass before one could get new supplies. Old cable was used in a variety of ways, for example, to make fenders, material hung over the side of the ship to protect it from scraping other ships or wharves. The big leap in meaning taken by the word occurred when *junk* was applied to discarded but useful material in general. This extension may also have taken place in a nautical context, for the earliest, more generalized use of *junk* is found in the compound *junk shop,* referring to a store where old materials from ships were sold. *Junk* has gone on to mean "useless waste" as well.

kale

The names of the vegetables *cauliflower, collard greens, kale,* and *kohlrabi* are all ultimately derived from one of the Latin words for "cabbage," *caulis.* In fact, these four vegetables are all varieties of a single plant species, *Brassica oleracea,* which has been bred into a variety of forms since it was first cultivated at least 2,500 years ago. Many other common vegetables, such as broccoli, brussel sprouts, and both green and red cabbage, also belong to this species. The word *kale* is most commonly used nowadays to designate a variety of the plant with spreading, crinkled leaves that do not form a compact head like a cabbage's. *Kale* represents the natural phonetic development of Old English *cāl* in Scots (the dialect of English used in the Lowlands of Scotland). One of the most important features distinguishing Scots from the dialects of southern England (from which American dialects are for the most part ultimately descended) is the use of so-called long *a* where southern British English and American English have long *o.* By the twelfth and thirteenth centuries, Old English long *a* had become long *o* in most Middle English dialects of the south of England. For example, Old English *ꞩtāne,* "stone," became Middle English *ꞩtone,* and likewise *bāne* became *bone.* In northern dialects, such as Scots, this change did not occur, and the long *a* in these words instead ended up being pronounced with the sound it has today, as in *kale,* a word which has since spread into other dialects of English. The corresponding native outcome in the southern Middle English dialects, on the other hand, was *cole.* This is not a very common word nowadays, but it can still be found in *collardꞩ* or *collard greenꞩ,* an alteration of an earlier *colewort.* The word *cole* is also heard in *cole ꞩlaw,* from Dutch *koolꞩla,* "cabbage salad," in which the Dutch word for "cabbage," *kool,* is likewise a derivative of the original Latin word *cauliꞩ.* The dish was popularized in North America by Dutch settlers in what is now New York. *Cole ꞩlaw* was commonly spelled *cold ꞩlaw* until the middle of the nineteenth century, when it was eventually changed under the influence of the English word *cole.* The English word *kohlrabi* (naming a variety of vegetable with thick turnip-shaped stalks) has been borrowed from German, where it is a partial translation of Italian *cavoli rape,* itself a compound of words meaning "cabbage" and "turnips" in Italian. Both the German word *Kohl,* "cabbage," and the Italian word *cavolo* are ultimately descended from Latin *cauliꞩ* as well. The great diversity of the cabbage plant is almost matched by the diversity of the descendants of this Latin word, which has taken on four different forms in English.

kangaroo

A widelyheld belief has it that the word *kangaroo* comes from an Australian Aboriginal word meaning "I don't know." This is in fact untrue. The word was first recorded in 1770 by Captain James Cook when he landed to make repairs along the northeast coast of Australia. In 1820, while visiting the same area, one Captain Phillip K. King recorded a different word for the animal, written *mee-nuah.* As a result, it was assumed that Captain Cook had been mistaken, and the myth grew up that what he had heard was a word meaning "I don't know" (presumably as the answer to a question in English that had not been understood). Recent linguistic fieldwork, however, has confirmed the existence of a word *gaɲurru* in the northeast Aboriginal language of Guugu Yimidhirr, referring to a species of kangaroo. (The letter *ŋ* is called *aŋma* and has the sound of *ng* in the English word *ʌinger* without the addition of a pronounced *g,* as can be heard in *finger.*) What Captain King recorded as *mee-nuah* may have been the word *minha,* meaning "edible animal."

ketchup

The word *ketchup* exemplifies the types of changes that both words and things undergo when they cross over to a new culture. The source of our word *ketchup* may be the Malay word *kechap* (now spelled *kecap*), "fish sauce," which in turn is possibly from Chinese (Cantonese) *kē chap.* This Cantonese compound is the equivalent of Mandarin Chinese *qié zhī,* "juice, gravy," from *qié,* "eggplant," and *zhī,* "juice, gravy." *Kē chap,* like *ketchup,* was a sauce, but one without tomatoes; rather, it contained fish brine and spices. Sailors seem to have brought the sauce to Europe, where it was made with locally available ingredients such as the juice of mushrooms or walnuts. At some unknown point, the juice of tomatoes was used and ketchup as we know it was born. But it is important to realize that in the eighteenth and nineteenth centuries *ketchup* was a generic term for sauces whose only common ingredient was vinegar. Mushroom ketchup (without tomatoes) is still well known in Britain, and it is a common ingredient in the traditional cooking of the American South. The word *ketchup* is first recorded in English in 1690 in the form *catchup,* in 1711 in the form *ketchup,* and in 1730 in the form *catsup.* All three spelling variants of this foreign borrowing remain current.

kidnap

Appropriately enough, *kidnapper* seems to have originated among those who perpetrate this crime. We know this because *kid* and *napper,* the two parts of the compound, were slang of the sort that criminals used. *Kid,* which still has an informal air, was considered low slang when *kidnapper* was formed, and *napper* is obsolete slang for "a thief," coming from the verb *nap,* "to steal." *Nap* is possibly a variant of *nab,* which also still has a slangy ring. In 1678, the year in which the word is first recorded, kidnappers plied their trade to secure laborers for plantations in colonies such as the ones in North America. The term later took on the broader sense that it has today. The verb *kidnap* is recorded later (1682) than the noun and so is possibly a back-formation, that is, people assumed that a kidnapper kidnaps.

kiosk

The lowly kiosk, where newspapers are sold or advertisements are posted, is like a child in a fairy tale raised by humble parents but descended from kings. The word *kiosk* was originally taken into English from Turkish, in which its source, *köşk,* meant "pavilion." The open structures referred to by the Turkish word were used as summerhouses in Turkey and Persia. The first recorded use of *kiosk* in English (1625) refers to these Middle Eastern pavilions, which Europeans imitated in their own gardens and parks. In France and Belgium, where the Turkish word had also been borrowed, their word *kiosque* was applied to something lower on the architectural scale, structures resembling these pavilions but used as places to sell newspapers or as bandstands. England borrowed this lowly structure from France and reborrowed the word, which is first recorded in 1865 with reference to a place where newspapers are sold.

kith and kin

Kith is obsolete except in the alliterative phrase *kith and kin,* which originally meant "native land and people" and first appeared about 1377 in the allegorical poem *Piers Plowman. Kith* comes from the Old English noun *cÿth,* "knowledge; known, familiar country; acquaintances, friends." *Cÿth* in turn comes from the Germanic noun **kunthithō,* a derivative of **kunthaz,* "known." Germanic **kunthaz* was the past participle of a verb **kunnan,* "to know, know how," which became *cunnan* in Old English. The first person singular of this verb, *can,* is alive and well today, as is what was originally the verbal noun and adjective of *cunnan,* namely *cunning,* which first appeared in the fourteenth century. Germanic **kunthaz* itself survived in the Old English adjective *cūth,* "known, familiar," a word that became obsolete in southern English by 1600, but has survived in its negative, *uncouth.* Modern English *couth* is actually a jocular backformation introduced by the British Humorist Max Beerbohm in 1896.

laconic

The habit of stereotyping the speech of other regions or countries is as old as human history. American stereotypes of the linguistic habits of other English-speaking nations include the gift of the gab bestowed upon the Irish, the dry wit of the English, and the laconic speech of the Scots. The peoples of the various regions of Greece held similar opinions about one another, as the word *laconic* itself shows. The term comes to us via Latin from Greek *Lakōnikos*. The English word is first recorded in 1583 with the sense "of or relating to Laconia or its inhabitants." *Lakōnikos* is derived from *Lakōn*, "a Laconian, a person from Lacedaemon," the name for the region of Greece of which Sparta was the capital. The Spartans, noted for being warlike and disciplined, were also known for the brevity of their speech, and it is this quality that English writers still denote by the use of the adjective *laconic*, which is first found in this sense in 1589.

landscape

It would seem that in the word *landscape* we have an example of nature imitating art, at least insofar as sense development is concerned. *Landscape,* first recorded in 1598, was borrowed from Dutch during the sixteenth century, when Dutch artists were on the verge of becoming masters of the landscape genre. The Dutch word *landschap* had earlier meant simply "region, tract of land" but had acquired the artistic sense, which it brought over into English, of "a picture depicting scenery on land." Interestingly, thirty-four years pass after the first recorded use of *landscape* in English before the word is used of a view or vista of natural scenery. This delay suggests that people were first introduced to landscapes in paintings and then saw landscapes in real life.

larva

The word *larva,* referring to the newly hatched form of insects before they undergo metamorphosis, comes from the Latin word *lārva,* meaning "evil spirit, demon, devil." To understand why this should be so, we first need to know that the Latin word was also used for "a terrifying mask," and in Medieval Latin it could mean "mask or visor." *Larva* is therefore an appropriate term for that stage of an insect's life during which its final form is still hidden or masked. New Latin *lārva* was thus applied in 1691 by Carolus Linnaeus, the Swedish botanist who originated our system of classifying plants and animals. The word *larva* is first recorded in English in its scientific sense in 1768, although it had been used in its "spirit" sense in 1651 in a way that foreshadowed the usage by Linnaeus.

lava

Lava was appropriately named by people living near Mount Vesuvius in what is now southern Italy. The only active volcano on the European mainland, Vesuvius has erupted frequently since it buried Pompeii and Herculaneum in A.D. 79. The Neapolitans who lived in the vicinity took the Italian word *lava*, meaning "a stream caused suddenly by rain," and applied it to the streams of molten rock coming down the sides of Vesuvius. From the Neopolitans, the term was then taken into Standard Italian, where it came to mean the rock in both its molten and its solidified states. The Italian word in all its senses was borrowed into English around the middle of the eighteenth century (1750 being the earliest date of record).

lawn

The word *lawn*, which now denotes a carefully kept plot of closely mown grass, originated as a variant of *laund*, an obsolete word that meant "a woodland glade." From "woodland glade," *lawn* came to mean "a clearing between woods" by the sixteenth century and "a plot of mown grass" in the seventeenth century, influenced by the rise of ornamental gardening in England. *Laund* was borrowed from the Old French word *lande,* which probably entered Old French from a Celtic source related to Old Irish *land*, "open space." French *lande* of course bears more than a passing resemblance to the English word *land,* and indeed the two words are distant kin. Old English *land* developed from the Germanic word **landam.* Ultimately, all of these words descend from the Indo-European root **lendh-,* meaning "open land." *Land* and *lawn* provide another example of the numerous pairs of doublets which English has acquired as a result of borrowing from many languages over its history.

leap year

It is thought that this term for a 366-day year originated because adding an extra day to the year caused a "leap" in the Church calendar of festivals. In normal 365-day years, a fixed festival that in one year fell on a weekday, such as Tuesday, would fall on Wednesday the next year, but in a leap year—after the extra day had fallen—the festival would occur on Thursday, having leapt right over Wednesday. The term *leap year* first appears in the great English medieval encyclopedia *On the Properties of Things* (1398), translated by John Trevisa from the twelfth-century Latin original by Bartholomew the Englishman. But the word had probably been around for some time before that, as Old Norse seems to have borrowed it from Old or Middle English, in the form *hlaupár.*

lemon

Although it is not known for certain where the lemon was first grown or when it first came to Europe, we do know from its name that it reached England and English by way of the Middle East, since we can trace its etymological path. One of the earliest occurrences of our word is found in a Middle English customs document of 1420-1421. The word was originally spelled *limon* or *lymon,* and the more familiar modern spelling does not begin to appear until the sixteenth century. The Middle English word *limon* goes back to Old French *limon,* showing that yet another delicacy passed into England through France. The Old French word probably came from Italian *limone,* another step on the route that leads back to the Arabic word *laymūn* or *līmūn,* which comes from the Persian word *līmūn.*

The related word *lime* comes into English through another route but from the same ultimate source. Arabic *līma* or *līm,* "citrus fruit," also formed from Persian *līmūn,* was borrowed into Spanish as *lima.* From there it was borrowed into French and entered English in the seventeenth century.

See also **orange.**

lemur

A lemur, with its large eyes, soft fur, and foxlike muzzle, strikes some people as cute, but the eighteenth-century Swedish botanist Carolus Linnaeus saw a ghost. Linnaeus was a pioneer in the study of taxonomy, the systematic classification of living organisms according to their natural relations, and he was one of the first scientists to name species using the

black and white ruffed lemur

system of two Latin terms, the genus and species names. The word *lemur* comes from the Latin word that Linnaeus originally chose as the genus classification, *Lemur,* for members this group. Because of their noctural foraging and the ghostly reflective gleam of their eyes, Linnaeus associated lemurs with *lemurēs,* as the restless, malevolent spirits of the dead were called in ancient Rome. On the days that we would now call the ninth, eleventh, and thirteenth of May, the head of a Roman household would walk barefoot around the house at midnight while throwing black beans over his shoulder in order to exorcise these ghosts. The eeriness of some real-life lemurs may be illustrated by a species called the *aye-aye*. It has a long bony third finger that it uses to dig grubs out of trees, and some local traditions of Madagascar hold that if the aye-aye points this finger at someone, he or she will die.

Lent

Spring partially overlaps in time with Lent, the forty weekdays from Ash Wednesday until Holy Saturday observed by Christians as a season of fasting and penitence, an important fact for the development of the present meaning of the word. *Lent* is derived from the Old English word *lencten,* which meant both "the season of spring" and "the ecclesiastical season of Lent." *Lencten* is ultimately derived from the same root as the adjective *long,* and the meaning "spring" probably arose because spring is the time of year when the days grow longer. The ecclesiastical sense developed from the fact that Lent partly coincides with spring.

leprechaun

Nothing seems more Irish than the leprechaun; yet hiding within the word *leprechaun* is a word from another language entirely. If we look back beyond Modern Irish Gaelic *luprachán* and Middle Irish *luchrupán* to Old Irish *luchorpán,* we can see the connection. *Luchorpán* is a compound of Old Irish *lú,* meaning "small," and the Old Irish word *corp,* "body." *Corp* is borrowed from Latin *corpus* (which we know from *habeas corpus* and such words as *corporation,* "an independent legal body"). Here is a piece of evidence attesting to the deep influence of Latin on the Irish language. Although the word is old in Irish, it is fairly new in English, being first recorded in 1604.

lewd

A thousand years ago it was no disgrace to be a lewd person. The word *lewd,* from Old English *lǣwede,* originally meant "lay, not belonging to the clergy." As time passed and new senses of the word developed, each subsequent sense of *lewd* took on a worse connotation than the one before. Such a pattern of sense development is called *pejoration.* During Middle English times the word *lewd* ran the gamut of senses from "lay" through "unlearned," "low-class," "ignorant, ill-mannered," and "wicked" to "lascivious." The last sense is the only one that survives in Modern English.

liberal

The Latin adjective *līberālis,* from which *liberal* is derived, is formed from the adjective *līber,* which meant "free," especially in the sense "freeborn, not a slave." Many senses of *līberālis,* and therefore of *liberal,* reflect this derivation. The sense "generous" developed from the notion that generosity was an attribute characteristic of a freeman, who had a relatively high social status. The Latin word *līberālis* was then extended to mean "noble, gentlemanly." Although this sense is not recorded for our English word *liberal,* it survives in the phrase *liberal arts,* which originally designated those branches of learning that were suitable for persons of high social rank.

limbo

Our use of the word *limbo* to refer to states of oblivion, confinement, or transition is derived from the theological sense of *Limbo* as a place where souls remain that cannot enter heaven, for example, unbaptized infants. *Limbo* in Roman Catholic theology is located on the border of Hell, which explains the name chosen for it. The Latin word *limbus,* having meanings such as "an ornamental border to a fringe" and "a band or girdle," was chosen by Christian theologians of the Middle Ages to denote this border region. English borrowed the word *limbus* directly, but the form that caught on, *limbo,* first recorded in a work composed around 1378, is the ablative form of *limbus,* which would have been used in expressions such as *in limbō,* "in Limbo."

lingo

In many languages besides English, the word for "tongue" also doubles as a word for "language," from Arabic *lisān* to Greek *glōssa* to Russian *yazyk.* The English words *tongue* and *language,* as well as *lingo,* all go back to the Indo-European noun *dnghū-,* "tongue." *Tongue* is the native Germanic outcome in English, in which the *d* has been changed to *t* and the *gh* to plain *g* by GRIMM'S LAW (see glossary). In Latin, Indo-European *dnghū:-,* became *lingua,* the source of the English words *language* and *lingo.* The usual Middle English spelling of *language* was *langage,* reflecting its form in the language from which it was borrowed, Old French. Old French *langage* was in turn formed from the word *langue,* "tongue, language," the French descendant of Latin *lingua. Lingo,* on the other hand, entered English after the end of the Middle Ages, when Europe had opened itself to the larger world. We have probably borrowed *lingo* from *lingoa,* a Portuguese descendant of Latin *lingua.* The Portuguese were great traders before the English were, and the sense "foreign language" was likely strengthened as the Portuguese traveled around the world. Others have proposed that *lingo* comes from another descendant of Latin *lingua,* Provençal *lengo* or *lingo.* Interestingly enough, the first known attestation of *lingo* in English is in a text from the New World. The text dates from the year 1660, although it was not published until 1858, and makes reference to the "Dutch lingo." The development in sense to "unintelligible language" and "specialized language" is an obvious one.

lion

Old French *lion,* the source of English *lion,* comes from Latin *leō, leōnis.* After that the etymology is less clear. The Latin word is related somehow to Greek *leōn, leontos* (earlier **lewōn, *lewontos*), which appears in the name of the Spartan king *Leonidas,* "Lion's son," who perished at Thermopylae. The Greek word is somehow related to Coptic *labai, laboi,* "lioness." In turn, Coptic *labai* is borrowed from a Semitic source related to Hebrew *lābī'* and Akkadian *labbu.* There is also a native ancient Egyptian word, *rw* (where *r* could stand for either *r* or *l* and vowels were not indicated), which is surely related as well. Since lions were native to Africa, Asia, and Europe in ancient times (Aristotle tells us there were lions in Macedon in his day), we have no way of ascertaining who borrowed which word from whom.

Although litmus paper is familiar material to anyone who has spent time in a chemistry lab, the origin of the word *litmus* is probably not. This paper is treated with litmus, a blue powder derived from certain lichens that changes to red in acid solutions and becomes blue again in alkaline solutions. The word *litmus* goes back to a Scandinavian source akin to the Old Norse word *litmosi,* meaning "herbs used in dying." The compound *litmosi* was formed from the words *litr,* "color," or *lita,* "to dye," and *mosi,* "moss, lichen." In Middle English there also existed a competing form, *lykemose,* from Middle Dutch *lijkmoes,* a variant of *lēcmoes* from *lēken,* "to drip," and *moes,* "moss." Despite the somewhat Latin look of this scientific word, *litmus* is in fact entirely Germanic.

loaf

Loaf, *lord,* and *lady* are closely related words that testify to bread's fundamental importance in the Middle Ages. Curiously, though bread was a staple food in many Indo-European cultures, *loaf* and its cognates occur only in the Germanic languages, and *lord* and *lady* only in English. *Loaf* derives from Old English *hlāf,* "bread, loaf of bread," related to Gothic *hlaifs,* Old Norse *hleifr,* and Modern German *Laib,* all of which mean "loaf of bread." *Hlāf* survives in *Lammas,* originally *Hlāfmaesse,* "Loaf-Mass," the Christian Feast of the First Fruits, traditionally celebrated on August 1. Old English *hlāford,* "lord," was a compound meaning "loaf-ward, keeper of bread," because a lord maintains and feeds his household and offers hospitality. Similarly, *lady* derives from Old English *hlǣfdige,* which became *lady* by 1382. The *-dige* comes from *dæge,*

"kneader," and is related to our *dough.* A lady, therefore, is "a kneader of bread, a breadmaker." *Lord* and
lady both retain vestiges of their original meanings,
although England's aristocrats have not been elbow
deep in flour, let alone dough, for several centuries.

lobster

The lobster and the locust may share a common
source for their names, that is, the Latin word
locusta, which was used for the locust and also for a
crustacean that was probably a kind of lobster. We can
see that *locusta* would be the source of *locust,* but it
looks like an unlikely candidate as the source of *lobster.* It is thought, however, that Old English *loppestre,*
the ancestor of *lobster,* was formed from *locusta* and
the suffix *-ester,* used to make agent nouns (our *-ster*).
The change from Latin *locusta* to Old English
loppestre may have been influenced by Old English
loppe, meaning "spider."

long-lived

Some uncertainty exists as to the correct pronunciation of *long-lived.* Should the *i* be long (as in *hive*)
or short (*give*)? The answer depends in part on how
one looks at the word. Historically, the first pronunciation is the more accurate. The word was formed in
Middle English as a compound of *long* and the noun
life, plus the suffix *-ed.* This suffix, though identical
in form to the past tense suffix, has a different function: to form adjectives from nouns, as in the words
hook-nosed, ruddy-faced, and *round-shouldered.* (Note
that English has no verbs such as "to hook-nose" and
"to ruddy-face" that would have formed participial

adjectives ending in -*ed*.) In Middle English, the suffix -*ed* was always pronounced as a full syllable, so *long-lifed* (as it was then spelled) had three syllables. The *f* occurring between two vowels, by a rule of earlier English phonology, was voiced (became pronounced like *v*); eventually, the spelling became *long-lived* to reflect the pronunciation. (We see the same alternation in *life* and *lives;* in Middle English, *lives* had two syllables just like -*lived*.) However, this new spelling introduced an ambiguity; it was no longer clear from the spelling that the word came from the noun *life,* but rather looked as though it came from the verb *live.* In this way a second pronunciation, with a short vowel, was introduced.

lucre

W hen William Tyndale translated Greek *aiskhron kerdos,* "shameful gain" (Titus 1:11), as *filthy lucre* in his edition of the Bible, he was tarring the word *lucre* for the rest of its existence. But we cannot lay the pejorative sense of *lucre* completely at Tyndale's door. He was merely a link, albeit a strong one, in a process that had begun long before with respect to the ancestor of our word, the Latin word *lucrum,* "material gain, profit." This process was probably controlled by the inevitable conjunction of profit, especially monetary profit, with evils such as greed. In Latin *lucrum* also meant "avarice," and in Middle English *lucre,* besides meaning "monetary gain, profit," meant "illicit gain." Furthermore, many of the contexts in which the neutral sense of the word appeared were not wholly neutral, as in "It is a wofull thyng . . . ffor lucre of goode . . . A man to fals his othe" (It is a sad thing for a man to betray his oath for monetary gain). Tyndale thus merely helped the process along when he gave us the phrase *filthy lucre.*

maharajah

The element *maha* is familiar to English speakers from several words of Indian origin, such as *maharajah* and *mahatma*. *Maharajah* is from a Sanskrit word, *mahārājaḥ*, that means "great king." Similarly, *mahatma* is a compound of Sanskrit *mahā-*, "great," and *ātmā*, "soul." The element *mahā-* is related to Greek *mega-* and Latin *magnus*, both meaning the same thing as the Sanskrit. All three forms derive from Indo-European **meg-*, "great." This root became **mik-* in Germanic, where an adjective, **mikila-*, "great," was formed from it. This became *mikils* in Gothic, and *micel*, pronounced (mĭ′chəl), in Old English. The Old English word survives today in *much*, shortened from Middle English *muchel*.

Mail, "material handled by the post office," is a survivor of the days when the few letters and dispatches that were exchanged were carried by horsemen in their traveling bags. From the thirteenth century, the English word *mail,* borrowed from the Old French term *male,* simply meant "bag," especially one carried by a traveler for provisions. Such bags were also used to carry letters, and the word *mail* eventually came to designate the contents rather than the container.

early American woodcut of a mail courier on horseback

malaprop

"She's as headstrong as an allegory on the banks of the Nile" and "He is the very pineapple of politeness" are two of the absurd pronouncements from Mrs. Malaprop that explain why her name became synonymous with ludicrous misuse of language. A character in Richard Brinsley Sheridan's play *The Rivals* (1775), Mrs. Malaprop consistently uses language malapropos, that is, inappropriately. The word *malapropos* comes from the French phrase *mal à propos,* made up of *mal,* "badly," *à,* "to," and *propos,* "purpose, subject," and means "inappropriate." *The Rivals* was a popular play, and Mrs. Malaprop became enshrined in a common noun, first in the form *mala-*

prop and later in *malapropism,* which is first recorded in 1849. Perhaps that is what Mrs. Malaprop feared when she said, "If I reprehend any thing in this world, it is the use of my oracular tongue, and a nice derangement of epitaphs!"

malaria

Within the word *malaria* is a reference to an outmoded notion of how such an illness was caused. *Malaria* comes from the Italian word *malaria,* which is derived from *mala,* "bad," and *aria,* "air." It was thought that the illness called *malaria* was caused by the unwholesome state of the air in marshy districts. When it was discovered in the late 1800s that the anopheles mosquito carried the disease, *malaria* was medically redefined with greater precision, but the original name of the malady remained.

mantis

Although the female mantis has the habit of eating the male after mating, its name suggests a more benign activity. *Mantis* is from the Greek word *mantis,* meaning "prophet, seer." The Greeks, who made the connection between the upraised front legs of a mantis waiting for its prey and the hands of a prophet in prayer, used the name *mantis* to mean "the praying mantis." This word and sense were picked up in Modern Latin and from there came into English, being first recorded in 1658. Once we know the origin of the term *mantis,* we realize that the species names *praying mantis* and *Mantis religiosa* are a bit redundant.

marshal

Images of hard-riding marshals of the Wild West in pursuit of criminals reemphasize the relationship of the word *marshal* horses. The Germanic ancestor of our word *marshal* is a compound made up of **marhaz,* "horse" (related to the source of our word *mare*), and **skalkaz,* "servant," meaning as a whole literally "horse servant," hence "groom." The Frankish descendant of this Germanic word, **marahskalk,* came to designate a high royal official and also a high military commander—not surprising given the importance of the horse in medieval warfare. Along with many other Frankish words, **marahskalk* was borrowed into Old French by about 800; some centuries later, when the Normans established a French-speaking official class in England, the Old French word came with them. In English, *marshal* is first recorded in 1218 as a surname (still surviving in the spelling Marshall); its first appearance as a common noun was in 1258, in the sense "high officer of the royal court." The word was also applied to this high royal official's deputies, who were officers of courts of law, and it continued to designate various officials involved with courts of law and law enforcement, including the horseback-riding marshals we are familiar with in the United States.

mascot

A giant strutting bird leading a cheer at the homecoming game may seem a far cry from a witch fashioning a charm or spell, but these two figures are related historically in the development of the word *mascot. Mascot* came into English as a borrowing of the French word *mascotte,* meaning "mascot, charm."

The English word is first recorded in 1881 shortly after the French word, itself first recorded in 1867, was popularized by the opera *La Mascotte,* performed in December 1880. The French word in turn came from the Provençal word *mascoto,* "piece of witchcraft, charm, amulet," a feminine diminutive of *masco,* "witch." This word can probably be traced back to Medieval Latin *masca,* "witch, specter." Thus for all their apparent differences, yesterday's witches and today's cuddly mascots can be seen in the same light, as agents working their respective magic to bring about a desired outcome.

mattress

The history of the word *mattress* is a small lesson in the way amenities have come to Europe from the Middle East. During the earlier part of the Middle Ages, Arabic culture was more advanced than that of Europe. One of the amenities of life enjoyed by the Arabs was sleeping on cushions thrown on the floor. Derived from the Arabic word *ṭaraḥa,* "to throw," the word *maṭraḥ* meant "place where something is thrown" and "mat, cushion." This kind of sleeping surface was adopted by the Europeans during the Crusades, and the Arabic word was taken into Old Italian (*materasso*) and then into Old French (*materas*), from which comes the Middle English word *materas,* first recorded in a work written around 1300. The Arabic word also became Medieval Latin *matracium,* another source of our word.

maudlin

Mary Magdalene at Jesus's feet in a detail of The Deposition by Pietro Lorenzetti (c. 1280-1348), a fresco in the Basilica of St. Francis of Assisi, Assisi, Italy

The word *maudlin* is an English development of the second part of the name of Mary Magdalene, a woman mentioned in the Gospels. In Middle English her name took various forms, such as *Maudelaine* and *Madelin*. These are all descended from Latin *Magdalēna,* itself from Greek *Magdalēnē,* meaning "from Magdala," a fishing village on the western shore of the Sea of Galilee. Mary of Magdala is one of the women who witnessed the crucifixion and later the announcement of the resurrection of Christ by angels at his tomb. Tradition identifies this figure in the Gospels with certain other unnamed women in the New Testament, especially the sinful woman who washed Jesus's feet with her tears (Luke 7:36-50). From these and other fragments of Scripture evolved the popular legend of Mary Magdalene as a reformed prostitute who became one of Jesus's most devoted and favored female disciples. She was frequently depicted in art as weeping copiously for her sins, and it is this attribute of hers that gave rise to the current sense of the adjective *maudlin,* "effusively or tearfully sentimental." The word was used to mean "weeping" as early as the fourteenth century and came to mean "weak, sentimental" in the seventeenth century, prior to which (mainly in the sixteenth century) it sometimes meant "drunk," since those deep in their cups were prone to weep, though that sense has since fallen out of use.

mayday

"**M**ayday, mayday!" comes the international distress signal over the radio, and nobody stops to ask why the usually joyous first day of May is being mentioned at this time of crisis. *Mayday* in fact has nothing to do with the first of May. Instead, it is a spelling that represents the pronunciation of French *m'aider,* "help me," the latter part of the phrase *venez m'aider,* "come help me." *Mayday* is first recorded from 1927, between World War I and World War II; as one might expect, the term became known generally during World War II.

meat

Meat is an example of a word whose meaning has become narrower in the course of its development. In Old English the word *mete* denoted whatever was edible. This is the sense of meat in compounds such as *sweetmeat,* "a piece of candy," and *nutmeat,* "the edible part of a nut," as opposed to the shell. In the fourteenth century, *meat* came to signify animal flesh in contrast to fish, and at times in contrast to poultry as well, but the general sense persisted into the seventeenth century. A hint of the older meaning can perhaps still be perceived in the proverb, "One man's meat is another man's poison."

An enormous menu might be considered an oxy-moron if one were to restrict the word etymologi-cally. *Menu* can be traced back to the Latin word *minūtus,* meaning "small in size, amount, or degree" and also "possessing or involving minute knowledge." Latin *minūtus* became Old French *menut* and modern French *menu,* "small, fine, trifling, minute." The French adjective came to be used as a noun with the sense of "detail, details collectively" and "detailed list." As such, it was used in the phrase *menu de repas,* "list of items of a meal," which was shortened to *menu.* This word was borrowed into English, being first recorded in 1837. The French word had been bor-rowed before, perhaps only briefly, as a shortening of the French phrase *menu peuple,* "the common people." This usage, however, is recorded in only one text, in 1658.

mesmerize

When the members of an audience sit mesmerized by a speaker, their reactions do not take the form of dancing, sleeping, or falling into convulsions. But if Friedrich Anton Mesmer (1734-1815) were addressing the audience, such behavior could be expected. Mesmer, a visionary eighteenth-century physician, believed that cures could be effected by having patients do things such as sit with their feet in a fountain of magnetized water while holding cables attached to magnetized trees. Mesmer then came to believe that magnetic powers resided in himself, and during highly fashionable curative sessions in Paris he caused his patients to have reactions ranging from dancing or sleeping to convulsions. These reactions were actually brought about by hypnotic powers that Mesmer was unaware he possessed. One of his pupils, named Puységur, first used the term *Mesmerism* for Mesmer's practices, and the term appears in English in 1802. The related word *mesmerize,* having shed its reference to the hypnotic doctor, lives on in the sense "to enthrall."

mess

*M*ess has been in the English language since the fourteenth century, but its meanings "a disorderly jumble" and "an untidy condition" did not develop until as late as the nineteenth century. *Mess* (derived from the Latin word *missus,* "course of a meal," from the verb *mittere,* "to place") originally meant "a quantity of food" or simply "food." The word was used without disparagement, as it still is, for example, in the phrase "a mess of peas." In the nineteenth century *mess* was also used to refer to an unpalatable mixture of food, and it is likely that this usage gave rise to the modern meanings, which have been extended beyond references to food. In the sixteenth century, *mess* extended from "a portion of food" to mean "a group of persons who usually eat together," a sense preserved in expressions like *mess hall* and *officers' mess* that identify places at which such groups eat.

metal

In Modern English, *metal* and *mettle* are pronounced the same, and they are in fact both related. Middle English borrowed *metal* from Old French in the fourteenth century; Old French *metal,* also spelled *metail,* came from Latin *metallum,* from Greek *metallon,* "mine, quarry, ore, metal." By the sixteenth century, *metal* had also come to mean "the stuff one is made of, one's character," but there was no difference in spelling between the literal and figurative senses until about 1700, when the spelling *mettle,* originally just a variant of *metal,* was fixed for the sense "fortitude." The history of English has numerous examples of pairs of words, like *metal* and *mettle,* that are (historically speaking) spelling variants of the same word. Two other such pairs are *trump/triumph* and *through/thorough.*

methinks

The archaic expression *methinks,* "it seems to me," may seem puzzling and ungrammatical to speakers of Modern English. The expression is in fact a sort of linguistic fossil, preserving a turn of phrase that was common throughout the Middle English period, *me thinketh.* The verb *thinketh* in this expression means "seems" not "thinks," and the pronoun *me,* "me," is here the indirect object of the verb. The construction dates back to Old English times, where the equivalent is *mē þyncþ.* The Middle English verb *thinken,* "to seem," from Old English *þyncan,* has not survived as such into Modern English. (The letter *þ* is called *thorn* and was used in Old and Middle English to write the sounds that are now spelled in Modern English with the letters *th.* There are two such sounds, the voiceless *th* in *breath* and the voiced *th* in *breathe.*) However, this Old English verb *þyncan* is related to another verb, *þencan,* "to think, consider," from which the modern verb *think* has developed.

The Middle English grammatical construction with the verb *thinken,* "to seem," and the equivalent Old English constructions were not confined to using the pronoun *mē*. For example, the scholar Orrm (who lived around 1200) wrote the following perfectly normal Middle English sentence: "itt himm þuhhte swiþe god," meaning "it seemed very good to him." The form *þuhhte* here is the past tense of *thinken*.

midwife

The word *midwife* is the sort of word whose etymology seems perfectly clear until one tries to figure it out. *Wife* would seem to refer to the woman giving birth, who is usually a wife, but *mid-*? A knowledge of older senses of words helps us with this puzzle. *Wife* in its earlier history meant "woman," as it still did when the compound *midwife* was formed in Middle English (first recorded around 1300). *Mid* is probably a preposition, meaning "together with." Thus a *midwife* was literally a "with woman" or "a woman who assists other women in childbirth." The etymology of *obstetric* is rather similar, going back to the Latin word *obstetrīx*, "a midwife," from the verb *obstāre*, "to stand in front of," and the feminine suffix *-trīx*. The *obstetrīx* would thus literally stand in front of the baby.

migraine

Those afflicted with migraine headaches will not be surprised to learn that the word *migraine* goes back to a Greek word, *hēmikrānia*, derived from *hēmi-*, "half," and *krānion*, "upper part of the head, skull." Actually, the term in Greek meant "pain on one side of the head or face," as *migraine* usually does today. The Greek word was borrowed into Latin, where it developed into Old French *migraine,* which was adapted in Middle English as *megrim* in the fourteenth century. In the eighteenth century, learned speakers "corrected" the English form by reintroducing French *migraine,* the form of the word that persists to this day.

milquetoast

An indication of the effect on the English language of popular culture is the adoption of names from the comic strips as English words. Casper Milquetoast, created by Harold Webster in 1924, was a timid and retiring man named for a bland food. The first instance of *milquetoast* as a common noun is found in the mid-1930s. *Milquetoast* thus joins the ranks of other such words, including *sad sack,* from a blundering army private invented by George Baker in 1942, and *Wimpy,* from J. Wellington Wimpy in the *Popeye* comic strip, which became a trade name for a hamburger. If we look to a related form of popular culture, the animated cartoon, we must of course acknowledge *Mickey Mouse,* which has become a slang term for something that is easy, insignificant, small-time, worthless, or petty.

miniature

The idea of smallness was not originally part of the meaning of *miniature.* The word is derived from Latin *minium,* "red lead," a compound of lead used as a pigment. In medieval times chapter headings and other important divisions of a text were distinguished by being written in red, while the rest of the book was written in black. Sections of a manuscript were also marked off with large ornate initial capital letters, which were often decorated with small paintings. The Latin verb *miniāre,* derived from *minium,* meant "to color red." From this word the Italian *miniatura,* "illumination, small picture in a manuscript," was derived. Since the paintings were necessarily very tiny, *miniatura* was associated with Latin words denoting smallness, such as *minūtus,* "tiny, minute," and *minimum,* "least," and this association has influenced the development of the meaning of the word in the languages into which it was borrowed. The Italian word was borrowed as *miniature* into English, where it first appears in the sixteenth century.

Mississippi

In a letter dated August 27, 1863, Abraham Lincoln wrote, "the Father of Waters again goes unvexed to the sea," referring to General Grant's capture of Vicksburg, Mississippi. The sentence has all the simplicity and nobility of Lincoln's style, but *Mississippi* doesn't mean "Father of Waters." This colorful but false phrase first appeared in print in 1812, was repeated by James Fenimore Cooper in his novel *The Prairie* (1827), and thereafter was in common circulation. Our name for the river has a different source. In 1666 French explorers somewhere in the western Great Lakes region recorded *Messipi* as their rendering of the Ojibwa name for the river they had come upon, *misi-sipi,* "big river." The French took the name with them as they went down the river to its delta, and it superseded all the other names for "Big River" used by local Indian tribes and by earlier Spanish explorers. In 1798 Congress applied the Ojibwa name of the river to the territory of Mississippi, newly organized from lands inhabited by the Natchez, Choctaws, and Chickasaws. Still, *Father of Waters* is a happy error: "The

Big River again goes unvexed to the sea" just doesn't have the right Lincolnian ring.

mob

Every age has its linguistic fads and ephemeral coinages, some of which survive and become part of the standard vocabulary. Since the seventeenth century, the abbreviation of long words or phrases to one or two syllables has been a constant feature of slang and other colloquial English, much deplored by self-appointed literary watchdogs. *Mob* is one such abbreviation that caught on. It is short for *mobile,* used in the early seventeenth century to mean "the masses." In this usage *mobile* was itself a shortening of the Latin phrase *mobile vulgus,* "the fickle masses, the excitable common people." The shortened form *mob* was well established by the beginning of the eighteenth century. The note of contempt inherent in the English word *mob* was also found in the Latin phrase.

modern

The word *modern,* first recorded in 1585 in the sense "of present or recent times," has traveled through the centuries designating things that inevitably must become old-fashioned as the word itself goes on to be applied to the next modern thing. We have now invented the word *postmodern,* as if we could finally fix *modern* in time, but even *postmodern* (first recorded in 1949) will seem fusty in the end, perhaps sooner than *modern* will. Going back to Late Latin *modernus,* "modern," which is derived from Latin *modo* in the sense "just now," the English word *modern* (first recorded at the beginning of the sixteenth century) was not originally concerned with anything that could later be considered old-fashioned. It simply meant "being at this time, now existing," an obsolete sense today. In the later sixteenth century, however, we begin to see the word contrasted with the word *ancient* and also used of technology in a way that is clearly related to our own modern way of using the word. *Modern* was being applied specifically to what pertained to present times and also to what was new and not old-fashioned. Thus in the nineteenth and twentieth centuries the word could be used to designate a movement in art, *modernism,* which is now being followed by *postmodernism.*

Monday

Monday begins the work week for many and brings an unwelcome reminder of the passage of time. *Monday* was once literally "the Moon's day" and derives from Old English *Mōnandaeg.* The *mōnan* in this word is the genitive (possessive) case of the Old English word for the moon, *mōna.* This word goes back to a Germanic **mēnōn-,* which contains the Proto-Indo-European root *mē-,* "to measure." From the Indo-European point of view, the moon measured out time in *months,* as it still does in the many parts of the world that use lunar calendars. The word *month* and its near relatives, such as German *Monat,* go back to Germanic *mēnēth-,* derived from the same root *mē-.* Many other Indo-European languages have words for "moon" or "month" containing an element **mēn-* built from the root **mē-,* such as Latin *mēnsis,* "month." From the Latin phrase *cursus sēmēstris,* "a course of six months" (from *sex,* "six," and *mēnsis*) English obtained the word *semester.*

The root *mē-* can also be seen in many other words, including *measure* itself, which comes from Latin *mēnsūra* through Old French *mesure.*

T*he love of money is the root of all evil.*

—I Timothy 6:7

Money may be the root of all evil, but the root of the word *money* is a mysterious divine epithet. One of the titles of the Roman goddess Juno was *Monēta,* an epithet whose exact meaning is not known. *Monēta* is perhaps derived from the same root as the verb *monēre,* "to remind, admonish, warn." Money was coined in the temple of Juno Moneta in Rome, and the name *Monēta* became a word meaning "the mint" and by extension "coined money." *Monēta* developed into the Old French word *moneie* with the sense "coined money," which was borrowed into English in the thirteenth century. The Latin term *monēta,* meaning "mint, a place where money is coined," was also borrowed into the Germanic languages before Old English times and descended into Old English as *mynet,* whose modern form is *mint.*

mortgage

T he great jurist Sir Edward Coke, who lived from 1552 to 1634, explained why the term *mortgage* comes from the Old French words *mort,* "dead," and *gage,* "pledge." It seemed to him that it has to do with the doubtfulness of whether or not the mortgagor will pay the debt. If the mortgagor does not, then the land pledged to the mortgagee as security for the debt "is taken from him for ever, and so dead to him upon condition, &c. And if he doth pay the money, then the pledge is dead as to the [mortgagee]." This etymology, as understood by seventeenth-century attorneys, of the Old French term *morgage,* which we adopted, may well be correct. The term has been in English much longer than the seventeenth century, being first recorded in Middle English with the form *morgage* and the figurative sense "pledge" in a work written before 1393.

mosquito

Though flies may be unpopular, we cannot escape the fact that they are everywhere. Two examples of the fly's influence on our lives can be found in the etymologies of the words *mosquito* and *musket,* both of which can be traced back to *musca,* the Latin word for fly. This Latin word became *mosca* in Spanish and Portuguese, Romance languages that developed from Vulgar Latin. *Mosquito,* the diminutive of *mosca,* was borrowed into English (first recorded around 1583) with the same sense "mosquito" that it had in Spanish and Portuguese. The Romance language French was the source of our word *musket* (first recorded around 1587), which came from French *mousquet,* which in turn entered French from yet another Romance language, Italian. From Italian *mosca,* another descendant of Latin *musca,* was formed the diminutive *moschetta,* with the senses "bolt for a catapult" and "small artillery piece." From *moschetta* came *moschetto,* "musket," the source of French *mousquet.* The use of *moschetta,* literally "little fly," to mean "bolt from a crossbow" can be ascribed to the fact that both bolt and insect fly through the air and buzz and sting.

muscle

The word *muscle* goes back to the Latin word *mūsculus,* which is derived from Latin *mūs,* "mouse." *Musculus* meant both "a little mouse" and "muscle," from the resemblance of a flexing muscle, such as the biceps, under the skin to the movements of a mouse. The Greek word *mūs* also meant both "mouse" and "muscle." Many English medical words are derived from this Greek word, including *myocardium*, "the muscular tissue of the heart." The resemblance between the Greek and Latin words and the English word *mouse*, from Old English *mūs*, is no accident, and words cognate with English *mouse* are found in most branches of the Indo-European language family. We can reconstruct the Proto-Indo-European word for "mouse" as **mūs* and be sure that these humble creatures skittered around the dwellings of the speakers of Proto-Indo-European six thousand years ago —especially since we cannot reconstruct any Proto-Indo-European word for the cat that would catch them.

mutt

The clipping not of sheep but of a word having to do with sheep has given us our term *mutt* for "a mongrel dog." Clipping or abbreviating words, a standard process of word formation, sheared *mutt* from *muttonhead*, a pejorative term meaning "a stupid person" based on the notion that sheep are stupid. *Mutt* in its first recorded use in 1901 is used in the same sense as *muttonhead*, but it is soon recorded (1904) as a term of contempt for a horse and then (1906) for a dog. *Mutton* itself is from French *mouton*, "sheep."

namby-pamby

We are being very literary when we call someone a *namby-pamby*, a word derived from the name of Ambrose Philips, a little-known eighteenth-century poet whose verse incurred the sharp ridicule of his contemporaries Alexander Pope and Henry Carey. Their ridicule, inspired by political differences and literary rivalry, had little to do with the quality of Philips's poetry. In poking fun at some children's verse written by Philips, Carey used the nickname *Namby Pamby*: "So the Nurses get by Heart Namby Pamby's Little Rhimes." Pope then used the name in the 1733 edition of his satirical epic *The Dunciad.* The first part of Carey's coinage came from *Amby,* or *Ambroje. Pamby* repeated the sound and form but added the initial of Philips's last name. Such a process of repetition is called *reduplication.* After being popularized by Pope, *namby-pamby* went on to be used generally for people or things that are insipid, sentimental, or weak.

nap

The famous fourth verse of Psalm 121, rendered in the King James version of the Bible as "Behold, he that keepeth Israel shall neither slumber nor sleep," is rendered in an earlier Middle English translation as "Loo, ha shal not nappen ne slepen that kepeth ireal." The word *nappen* is indeed the Middle English ancestor of our word *nap*. Lest it be thought undignified to say that God could nap, it must be realized that our word *nap* was at one time not associated only with the younger and older members of society nor simply with short periods of rest. The ancestors of our word, Old English *hnappian* and its Middle English descendant, *nappen,* could both refer to prolonged periods of sleep as well as short ones and also, as in the quotation from Psalm 121, to sleepiness. But these senses have been lost. Since the word has become less dignified, we would not find *nap* used in a modern translation of Psalm 121.

naughty

The word *naughty* at one time was an all-purpose word similar to *bad.* During the sixteenth century one could use *naughty* to mean "unhealthy, unpleasant, bad" (with respect to weather), "vicious" (of an animal), "inferior, or bad in quality" (one could say "very naughtie figes" or "naughty corrupt water"). All of these senses have disappeared, however, and *naughty* is now used mainly in contexts involving mischief or indecency. This recalls its early days in Middle English (with the form *noughti*), when the word was restricted to the senses "evil, hostile, ineffectual, and needy." Middle English *noughti,* first recorded in the last quarter of the fourteenth century, was derived from *nought,* which primarily meant "nothing" but was also used as a noun meaning "evil" and as an adjective meaning "immoral, weak, useless." Thus *naughty,* in a sense, has risen from nothing, but its fortunes used to be better than they are at present.

nausea

Nausea goes back to the Greek word *nausia,* ultimately derived from *naus,* "ship." *Nausia* meant "seasickness" and more generally "stomach disturbances characterized by the need to vomit." Although English mariners and many others must have suffered nausea much earlier, the word *nausea* enters the English lexicon in the sixteenth century. The Greek word *naus,* came from the Proto-Indo-European word for "ship," **nāu-.* In Latin, this word developed into *nāvis,* "ship," which is the source of such English words as *naval* and *navigate.*
See also **noise.**

neighbor

Loving one's neighbor as oneself would be much easier, or perhaps much more difficult, if the word *neighbor* had kept to its etymological meaning. The source of our word, the assumed West Germanic form **nāhgabūr,* was a compound of the words **nēhwiz,* "near," and **būram,* "dweller, especially a farmer." A neighbor, then, was a near dweller. *Nēahgebūr,* the Old English descendant of this West Germanic word, and its descendant in Middle English, *neighebor,* and our Modern English *neighbor* have all retained the literal notion, even though one can now have many neighbors whom one does not know, a situation that would have been highly unlikely in earlier times. The extension of this word to mean "fellow" is probably attributable to the Christian concern with the treatment of one's fellow humans, as in the passage in Matthew 19:19 that urges love of one's neighbor.

nerd

The word *nerd,* undefined but illustrated, first appeared in 1950 in Dr. Seuss's *If I Ran the Zoo:* "And then, just to show them, I'll sail to Ka-Troo And Bring Back an It-Kutch a Preep and a Proo a Nerkle a Nerd and a Seersucker, too!" (The nerd is a small humanoid creature looking comically angry, like a thin, cross Chester A. Arthur.) *Nerd* next appears, with a gloss, in the February 10, 1957, issue of the Glasgow, Scotland, *Sunday Mail* in a regular column entitled "ABC for SQUARES": "Nerd—a square, any explanation needed?" Many of the terms defined in this "ABC" are unmistakable Americanisms, such as *hep, ick,* and *jazzy,* as is the gloss "square," the current meaning of *nerd.* The third appearance of *nerd* in print is back in the United States in 1970 in *Current Slang:* "Nurd [sic], someone with objectionable habits or traits . . . An uninteresting person, a 'dud.'" Authorities disagree on whether the two nerds—Dr. Seuss's small creature and the teenage slang term in the *Glasgow Sunday Mail*—are the same word. Some experts claim there is no semantic connection and the identity of the words is fortuitous. Others maintain that Dr. Seuss is the true originator of *nerd* and that the word *nerd* ("comically unpleasant creature") was picked up by the five- and six-year-olds of 1950 and passed on to their older siblings, who by 1957, as teenagers, had restricted and specified the meaning to the most comically obnoxious creature of their own class, a "square."

nest

nest is an ancient word, derived from Indo-European *nizdos*, which was composed of the prefix *ni-*, "down," plus a form of the verbal root *sed-*, "to sit," followed by a suffix used to form nouns, *-os*. The verbal root *sed-* is the ultimate source of the English verb *sit*, in fact. Thus a *ni-zd-os* literally means "(place where the bird) sits down." In Germanic, an old *zd* became *st*. Thus *nizdos* became *nistaz*, which further changed in Old English to *nest*. Latin also inherited the word *nizdos* from Indo-European, and in Latin it eventually changed to *nīdus*. This word has been borrowed into English as a scientific term, and it can be seen in such words as *nidifugous*, "leaving the nest shortly after hatching," and *nidicolous*, "remaining in the nest until nearly fully grown." The prefix *ni-* survives elsewhere in English, too, in the words *beneath* and *nether*.

nice

Since its adoption from Old French in the thirteenth century, the word *nice* has developed from a term of abuse into a term of praise, a process called *melioration*. *Nice* is derived from the Latin word *nescius*, "ignorant," and was used in Middle English, as in Old French, to mean "foolish; without sense." By the fifteenth century *nice* had acquired the sense "elegant" in conduct and dress, but not in a complimentary way: *nice* meant "overrefined, overdelicate." This sense survives in the meanings "fastidious" and "precise, subtle." In the eighteenth century, *nice* was first used as a vague term of approval, as in "He's a nice man" and "Have a nice day." Some commentators on the language thought that in the case of *nice* melioration had gone too far, and that *nice* had developed senses that fastidious speakers of English should reject. Samuel Johnson, the great English writer and author of the influential *Dictionary* (1755), disapproved of vague *nice,* just as he disapproved of the word *fun.* Characters in Jane Austen's *Northanger Abbey,* a novel from 1817, debate the acceptability of the word *nice* after one of them, Catherine, has used it in the sense "fine, great." Eventually Catherine is led to exclaim: "I am sure . . . I did not mean to say anything wrong; but it is a nice book, and why should not I call it so?"

nickel

Copper has been known and worked since ancient times, but nickel was isolated and identified only in the eighteenth century. Nickel is found in an ore that resembles copper ore; the German name for the ore is *Kupfernickel,* literally "copper demon." The ore was so named because although it produces no copper it can be mistaken for copper ore, just as fool's gold looks deceptively like gold. Baron Axel Frederic Cronstedt, the mineralogist who first isolated nickel in 1751, took its name from the second element of the word *Kupfernickel.* The word *nickel,* "demon, rascal," is derived from the name *Nikolaus,* "Nicholas." Similarly, *Old Nick* is used as a name for the devil in English.

nicotine

While serving as French ambassador to Portugal in the late 1550s, Jacques Nicot cultivated plants from tobacco seeds that Portuguese explorers had brought back from the New World. Nicot first introduced tobacco to the French nobility and then grew a crop that he sold for a profit in Paris. Nicot has been remembered in several ways for his enterprise. The Swedish botanist Linnaeus named the genus that includes the common tobacco plant *Nicotiana* in his honor. French *nicotiane* and English *nicotian* were both names for tobacco used in the sixteenth and seventeenth centuries, until *tobacco* (French *tabac*) superseded them. *Tobacco* entered English as early as 1577 from Spanish. This Spanish word is ultimately from Arabic, where *ṭabbāq,* or *ṭubbāq,* was used to designate certain medicinal herbs. We are most familiar with another word containing Nicot's name, *nicotine,* which was formed in French after *Nicotiana.* This new word was the name given to the oily substance found in tobacco leaves when it was first isolated in 1818.

nightmare

If you have ever had a nightmare in which you felt you were suffocating, read on. In Old and Middle English, *mare* was a word denoting an evil spirit. Although the spirit was imagined to be female, the word *mare* is unrelated to the modern word *mare,* "female horse." *Nightmare* is a compound of *night* (from Old English *niht*) and *mare*; it designated an evil spirit thought to afflict sleeping persons by sitting on them and causing a feeling of suffocation. In the sense "evil spirit," *nightmare* is first recorded in the thirteenth century, but in the sense "disturbing dream" it does not appear until the sixteenth century. Modern English *mare,* meaning "female horse," derives from Old English *mȳre* or *mēre,* influenced by forms of the related word *mearh,* "steed, horse."

niobium

Chemistry is a serious science, but it has its fanciful moments, which are revealed, for example, in the names of some of the elements. The word *niobium* is derived from *Niobe,* the personification of grief in Greek mythology. She was the daughter of the legendary king Tantalus, who gave his name to the mineral ore tantalite. Because the element niobium is extracted from tantalite, it was named after Tantalus's offspring, Niobe. Originally, the element was called *columbium,* but Heinrich Rose rediscovered it in tantalite in 1845, made the mythological connection, and renamed it. See also **tantalize.**

noise

Those who find that too much noise makes them ill will not be surprised that the word *noise* can possibly be traced back to the Latin word *nausea,* "seasickness, feeling of sickness." Our words *nausea* and *noise* are doublets, that is, words borrowed in different forms from the same word. *Nausea,* first recorded probably before 1425, was borrowed directly from Latin. *Noise,* first recorded around the beginning of the thirteenth century, came to us through Old French, which explains its change in form. Old French *nois* probably also came from Latin *nausea,* if, as seems possible, there was a change of sense during the Vulgar Latin period, whereby the meaning "seasickness" changed to a more general sense of "discomfort." Word meanings can sometimes change for the better, and nowadays, of course, a noise does not have to be something unpleasant, as in the sentence "The only noise was the wind in the pines."

nonchalant

A nonchalant person is not likely to become warm or heated about anything, a fact that is underscored by the etymology of the word *nonchalant*. It stems from Old French, where it was formed from the negative prefix *non-* plus *chalant,* the present participle of the verb *chaloir,* "to be concerned." This in turn came from the Latin word *calēre,* which from its concrete sense "to be hot or warm" developed the figurative sense "to be roused or fired with hope, zeal, or anger." French formed a noun, *nonchalance,* from the adjective *nonchalant,* that was borrowed into English by 1678; the adjective itself was borrowed later, as it is not attested for another half-century.

numb

Old English had many strong verbs—verbs that form their past tenses according to patterns such as *ride, rode, ridden* or *sing, sang, sung* —that did not survive into Modern English. One such was the verb *niman,* "to take," later replaced by *take,* a borrowing from Old Norse. The verb had a past tense *nam* and a past participle *numen,* and if the verb had survived, it would likely have become *nim, nam, num,* like *swim, swam, swum.* Although we do not have the verb as such anymore, its past participle is alive and well, now spelled *numb,* literally "taken, seized," as by cold or grief. (The older spelling without the *b* is still seen in the compound *numskull.*) The verb also lives on indirectly in the word *nimble,* which used to mean "quick to take" and then later "light, quick on one's feet."

O

obvious

The word *obvious* is derived ultimately from the Latin phrase *ob viam,* literally "in the way." The Latin word *via,* "road, way," is familiar to English speakers as a preposition meaning "by way of, by means of." Metaphorical senses of the Latin phrase (often written as one word, *obviam*) and of the Latin adjective *obvius* derived from it were "within reach, at hand." The English word *obvious,* a borrowing from Latin, preserved these senses at first, beginning in the seventeenth century, but they are now obsolete. The current sense, "evident, easily perceived," has developed since.

October

The Roman year originally began in March. Consequently, October was the eighth month, as its name suggests, for the word *October* is derived from Latin *octō,* "eight." The names of other months are also derived from the Latin names of numbers. *September,* the seventh month of the Roman calendar, is from *septem,* "seven"; *November,* the ninth month, is from *novem,* "nine"; and *December,* the tenth month, is from *decem,* "ten." The months now known as July and August were originally named, respectively, *Quintīlis,* "fifth month," and *Sextīlis,* "sixth month." They were later renamed by the Roman Senate to honor Julius Caesar and the emperor Augustus. Other emperors also made attempts to rename the months of the Roman calendar. The debauched emperor Nero had the month of April (*Aprīlis*) renamed *Nerōnēus* in his own honor, but after the end of his disastrous reign the Senate of Rome condemned his memory and changed it back.

oil

The word *oil* goes back to the Latin word *oleum* (notice that this is part of *petroleum,* derived from *petra,* "rock," and *oleum,* "oil"). *Oleum* comes from the Greek word *elaion,* both words meaning "olive oil" or "another oily substance." *Elaion,* in turn, is related to the Greek word *elaia,* "olive tree, olive," which is also the source of English *olive* through Latin *olīva.* The word *oil* is first recorded in English in the early thirteenth century. We find no clear uses of the word for any oil besides olive oil (and a miracle-working oil obtained from saints' bones) until the fourteenth century. It is difficult to say when *oil* came to mean "petroleum," but this is clearly an important meaning of the word today.

OK is a quintessentially American term that has spread from English to many other languages. Its origin was the subject of scholarly debate for many years until Allen Walker Read showed that *OK* is based on a joke of sorts. *OK* is first recorded in 1839 but was probably in circulation before that date. During the 1830s there was a humorous fashion in Boston newspapers to reduce a phrase to initials and supply an explanation in parentheses. Sometimes the abbreviations were misspelled to add to the humor. *OK* was used in March 1839 as an abbreviation for *all correct,* the joke being that neither the *O* nor the *K* was correct. Originally spelled with periods, this term outlived most similar abbreviations owing to its use in President Martin Van Buren's 1840 campaign for reelection. Because he was born in Kinderhook, New York, Van Buren was nicknamed *Old Kinderhook,* and the abbreviation proved eminently suitable for political slogans. That same year, an editorial referring to the receipt of a pin with the slogan *O.K.* had this comment: "frightful letters . . . significant of the birthplace of Martin Van Buren, old Kinderhook, as also the rallying word of the Democracy of the late election, 'all correct' . . . Those who wear them should bear in mind that it will require their most strenuous exertions . . . to make all things O.K."

ombudsman

The word *ombudsman* has one familiar element, *man,* but it is difficult to think of what *ombuds* could mean. *Ombudsman* is from Swedish, a Germanic language in the same family as English, and *man* in

Swedish corresponds to our word *man. Ombud* means "commissioner, agent," coming from Old Norse *umbodh,* "charge, commission, administration by a delegacy," *umbodh* being made up of *um,* "regarding," and *bodh,* "command." In Old Norse an *umbodhsmadhr* was a "trusty manager, commissary." In Swedish an *ombudsman* was a deputy who looked after the interests and legal affairs of a group such as a trade union or business. In 1809 the office of *riksdagens justitieombudsman* was created to act as an agent of justice, that is, to see after the interests of justice in affairs between the government and its citizens. This office of ombudsman and the word *ombudsman* have been adopted elsewhere, as in individual states in the United States. The term has also been expanded in sense to include people who perform the same function for business corporations or newspapers.

one

Why do we pronounce *one* (wŭn) and *once* (wŭns) while other words derived from *one,* like *only, alone,* and *atone,* are pronounced with a long *o* sound? Over time, stressed vowels commonly become diphthongs, as when Latin *bona* became *buona* in Italian and *buena* in Spanish. A similar diphthongization of *one* and *once* began in the late Middle Ages in the west of England and in Wales and is first recorded around 1400. The vowel sound underwent a series of changes. The pronunciation of the word started out in Middle English as (ōn), with the vowel (ō) found in Modern English *boat,* and then it developed to (ōoōn), with two syllables, the first having the vowel (ōo) in *boot.* From there it became (wōn), and then (wōon), and then (wŏon) with the vowel (ŏo) in *foot.* Finally it developed into (wŭn) with the vowel (ŭ) in *bun.* In southwest England, this diphthongization happened to other words beginning with the long *o* sound, such as *oats,* pronounced there now as (wŭts). Only in *one* and *once* did this diphthongal pronunciation gain widespread usage.

opossum

The word *opossum* takes us back to the earliest days of the American colonies. The settlement of Jamestown, Virginia, was founded in 1607 by the London Company, chartered for the planting of colonies. Even though the first years were difficult, promotional literature was glowing. In one such piece, *A True Declaration of the Estate of the Colonie in Virginia,* published in 1610, we find this passage: "There are . . . Apossouns, in shape like to pigges." This is the first recorded use of *opossum,* although in a spelling that differs from the one later settled on to reproduce the sound of the Virginia Algonquian word from which our word came. The word *opossum* and its shortened form *possum,* first recorded in 1613 in more promotional literature, remind us of a time when the New World was still very new, settlers were few, and the inhabitants for whom the New World was not new were plentiful.

orange

Oranges imported to China from the United States reflect a journey come full circle, for the orange had worked its way westward for centuries, originating in China, then being introduced to India, and traveling on to the Middle East, into Europe, and finally to the New World. The history of the word *orange* keeps step with this journey only part of the way. The word is possibly ultimately from Dravidian, a family of languages spoken in southern India and northern Sri Lanka. The Dravidian word or words were adopted into the Indo-European language Sanskrit with the form *nāraṅgaḥ.* As the fruit passed westward, so did the word, as evidenced by Persian *nārang* and Arabic *nāranj.* Arabs brought the first oranges to Spain, and the fruit rapidly spread throughout Europe. The important word for the development of our term is Old Italian *melarancio,* derived from *mela,* "fruit," and *arancio,* "orange tree," from Arabic *nāranj.* Old Italian *melarancio* was translated into Old French as *pume orenge,* the *o* replacing the *a* because of the influence of the name of the town of Orange, from which oranges reached the northern part of France. The final stage of the odyssey of the word was its borrowing into English from the Old French form *orenge.* Our word is first recorded in Middle English in a text probably composed around 1380, a time preceding the arrival of the orange in the New World.

orgy

The word *orgy* has become connected in the minds of many of us with unrestrained sexual activity, but its origins are much less licentious. We can trace the word as far back as the Indo-European root *werg-,* meaning "to do," also the source of our word *work.* Greek *orgia,* "secret rites, worship," comes from *worg-,* one form of this root. The Greek word was used with reference to the rites practiced in the worship of various deities, such as Orpheus and Dionysus. The word in Greek did not denote sexual activity, although this was a part of some rites. The rites of Dionysus, for example, included only music, dancing, drinking, and the eating of animal sacrifices. Having passed through Latin and Old French into English, the word *orgy* is first recorded in English (1589) with reference to the secret rites of the Greek and Roman religions. It is interesting to note that the word is first recorded with its modern sense in eighteenth-century English and perhaps in seventeenth-century French. Whether this speaks to a greater licentiousness in society or not must be left to the historian, but certainly the religious nature of the word has gone into eclipse.

oscillate

The rather dry word *oscillate* may become a bit less dry when we learn its story. It is possible that it goes back to the Latin word *ōscillum*, a diminutive of *ōs*, "mouth," meaning "small mouth." In a passage in the *Georgics*, the Roman poet Virgil applies the word to a small mask of Bacchus hung from trees to move back and forth in the breeze. From this word *ōscillum* may have come another word *ōscillum*, meaning "something, such as a swing, that moves up and down or back and forth." And this *ōscillum* was the source of the verb *ōscillāre*, "to ride in a swing," and the noun (from the verb) *ōscillātiō*, "the action of swinging or oscillating." The words have given us, respectively, our verb *oscillate*, first recorded in 1726, and our noun *oscillation*, first recorded in 1658. The next time one sees something oscillating, one might think of that small mask of Bacchus swinging from a pine tree in the Roman countryside.

outlaw

The word *outlaw* brings to mind the cattle rustlers and gunslingers of the Wild West, but it comes to us from a much earlier time, when guns were not yet invented but cattle stealing was. *Outlaw* can be traced back to the Old Norse word *ūtlagr,* "outlawed, banished," made up of *ūt,* "out," and *lög,* "law." An *ūtlagi* (derived from *ūtlagr*) was someone outside the protection of the law. The Scandinavians, who invaded and settled in England during the eighth through the eleventh century, gave us the Old English word *ūtlaga,* which designated someone who because of criminal acts had to give up his property to the crown and could be killed without recrimination. The legal status of the outlaw became less severe over the course of the Middle Ages. However, the looser use of the word to designate criminals in general, which arose in Middle English, lives on in tales of the Wild West.

oxygen

One of the most important substances on earth is misnamed. The word *oxygen* is the Anglicized form of French *oxygène,* coined in French by a collaborative of chemists in *Le Méthode de nomenclature chimique* (1787). The chemists responsible included Antoine Laurent Lavoisier, Louis Bernard de Guyton de Morveau, Claude Louis Berthollet, and Antoine François de Fourcroy soon after they isolated that element and others. (Oxygen had been discovered a few years before by Joseph Priestly in 1774.) The same publication also introduced the parent term of English *hydrogen* and *sodium chloride* (common salt), among others. The French word *oxygène* was intended to mean "acid-producing," from the Greek word *oxus,* "sharp," used in the sense "acid," and the Greek suffix *-genēs,* "born," misinterpreted as "producing." At the time oxygen was thought to be an essential component of an acid. Although this is not the case, the name *oxygen* has persisted for the element.

oyez

The courtroom cry "Oyez, oyez, oyez," has probably puzzled more than one auditor, especially if pronounced "O yes." (Many people have thought that the words were in fact *O yes.*) This cry serves to remind us that up until the eighteenth century, speaking English in a British court of law was not required and one could instead use Law French, a form of French that evolved after the Norman Conquest, when Anglo-Norman became the language of the official class in England. *Oyez* descends from the Anglo-Norman *oyez,* the plural imperative form of *oyer,* "to hear"; thus *oyez* means "hear ye" and was used as a call for silence and attention. Although it would have been much heard in medieval England, it is first recorded as an English word fairly late in the Middle English period, in a work composed around 1425.

pal

Pal, like *buddy* and *chum*, has an informal, thoroughly American ring to it. Its source, though, is rather unusual—Romany, the Indic language of the people called the Roma or Gypsies. First recorded in English in the seventeenth century, *pal* was borrowed from a Romany word meaning "brother, comrade," which occurs as *phal* in the Romany spoken in England and *phral* in the Romany spoken in Europe. The Indic languages are Indo-European languages of India. Gypsies speak an Indic language because they originally migrated to Europe from the border region between Iran and India. In other Indic languages we find related words meaning "brother," such as Hindi *bhāī.* They all come from Sanskrit *bhrātā,* which in turn traces its ancestry to the same Indo-European word that our word *brother* does.

palace

*O*ur word *palace* goes back to the name of one of the seven hills of Rome, the Palatine Hill, known in Latin as *Palātium.* From at least 330 B.C. the hill was the site of many grand houses, among them the residence of the emperor Augustus. Subsequent emperors, including Tiberius and Nero, also built houses on the Palatine Hill, and as a result *palātium* came to mean "one of the imperial residences on the Palatine." The word then began to denote other royal residences. *Palātium* passed into various languages, entering English by way of Old French *palais.*

pan out

*P*an out* comes from the noun *pan* in the sense "a shallow circular metal vessel used in washing gold from gravel." The expression *pan out* was used in a variety of senses, including "to wash gold-bearing earth in a pan," "to obtain gold by washing ore in a miner's pan," and, with reference to a mine or mineral-bearing soil, "to produce gold or minerals." All of these senses developed in mid-nineteenth century America, where everyone was looking for something to pan out, inspired by the California Gold Rush of 1849. From such

vintage photograph of a prospector panning for gold

literal usages *pan out* was transferred to other situations. In Frederick Whymper's *Travel and Adventure in the Territory of Alaska,* published in 1868, we are told that "it panned out well" means that "it gave good returns." All these uses occurred first in American English, making the expression a true Americanism.

pander

The word *pander* illustrates some of the unexpected ways that later Europeans developed the myths inherited from ancient Greece and Rome. Chaucer's *Troilus and Criseyde,* probably written about 1380, introduced the character Pandarus, a literary reincarnation of Pandaro from Boccaccio's *Il Filostrato* (circa 1340), the basis for Chaucer's poem. This character—the cousin of Criseida in *Il Filostrato* and Criseyde's uncle in Chaucer's poem—acts as the successful go-between for the two lovers in both works. Originally, Pandarus was a Lycian archer in the Trojan War, elevated by medieval legendary reinterpretations of epic to the status given him in Boccaccio and Chaucer. Our word *pander* comes directly to us from *Pandare,* the name Chaucer used in *Troilus and Criseyde.* This word was first a noun, an early sense of which was "a go-between in sexual intrigues, procurer," first recorded in 1530. Around 1600 Shakespeare played an anachronistic game with this sense in his own *Troilus and Cressida.* Shakespeare's Pandarus, supposedly speaking to the lovers during the Trojan War, says, "If ever you prove false one to another, since I have taken such pains to bring you together, let all pitiful goers-between be called to the world's end after my name; call them all Panders." *Pander* went on to develop the sense "one who caters to the low tastes and desires of others."

pants

One would not expect a word for a modern article of clothing to come ultimately from the name of a fourth-century Roman Catholic saint, but that is the case with the word *pants.* It can be traced back to *Pantaleon,* the patron saint of Venice. He became so closely associated with the inhabitants of that city that the Venetians were popularly known as *Pantaloni.* Consequently, among the stock characters of the commedia dell'arte the representative Venetian (a stereotypically wealthy but miserly merchant) was called *Pantalone,* or *Pantalon* in French. In the mid-seventeenth century the French came to identify him with one particular style of trousers, a style which became known as *pantaloons* in English. *Pantaloons* was later applied to another style that came into fashion in the late eighteenth century, tight-fitting garments that had begun to replace knee breeches. After that *pantaloons* was used to refer to trousers in general. The abbreviation of *pantaloons* to *pants* met with some resistance at first; it was considered vulgar and, as Oliver Wendell Holmes put it, "a word not made for gentlemen, but 'gents.'" First found in the writings of Edgar Allan Poe in 1840, *pants* has replaced the "gentleman's word" in American English and has lost all obvious connection to Saint Pantaleon.

parachute

Leonardo da Vinci sketched a design for the parachute over five hundred years ago, although it was not until 1797 that André Garnerin made the first parachute jump involving a long descent, in this case from a hot-air balloon. The English word *parachute* is of French origin, reflecting the important role of late-eighteenth-century aeronauts in its development. The second element of the word is *chute*, which in French means "fall." Obviously, skydivers hope that the *para-* part of the word will be more helpful. French *parachute* is modeled on the French words *parapluie*, "rain umbrella" *(pluie* meaning "rain"), and *parasol*, "a sunshade." French *parasol* comes from the Italian word *parasole*, "sunshade," the ultimate model for words like these, in which *sole* means "sun" and *para-* comes from the Italian verb *parare*, "to prepare, ward off." A parachute, then, is a device to ward off or protect one from a fall.

paradise

The history of *paradise* is an extreme example of melioration, the process by which a word comes to refer to something better than what it used to refer to. The old Iranian language Avestan had a noun *pairidaēza-*, "a wall enclosing a garden or orchard," which is composed of *pairi-*, "around," and *daēza-*, "wall." The adverb and preposition *pairi* is related to the equivalent Greek form *peri*, as in *perimeter. Daēza-* comes from the Indo-European root **dheigh-*, "to mold, form, shape." Zoroastrian religion encouraged maintaining arbors, orchards, and gardens, and even the kings of austere Sparta were edified by seeing the Great King of Persia planting and maintaining his own trees in his own garden. Xenophon, a Greek mercenary soldier who spent some time in the Persian army and later wrote histories, recorded the *pairidaēza-* surrounding the orchard as *paradeisos*, using it not to refer to the wall itself but to the huge parks that Persian nobles loved to build and hunt in. This Greek word was used in the Septuagint translation of Genesis to refer to the Garden of Eden, whence Old English eventually borrowed it around 1200.

pariah

The word *pariah*, which in English is now used of any social outcast, has its origin in southern India. English *pariah*, which has been extended in meaning, comes from Tamil *paṟaiyar*, the plural of *paṟaiyan*, the name of a certain low caste. The name literally means "(hereditary) drummer" and comes from the word *paṟai*, the name of a drum used at certain festivals in which the caste participated. The word is first recorded in English in 1613. In English it was extended to mean "outcaste" in general.

pasta

A meal featuring foods with etymologically interesting names might well include pasties, pasta, paté, and hamburger patties. The noun *pasty* (pronounced like *past* plus -*ee*), "a meat pie," was borrowed in the fourteenth century from the Old French word *pasté* or *pastée*. *Pastée* is derived from the Vulgar Latin word **pastāta*, "a meat dish wrapped in dough." Medieval Latin *pastāta* in turn goes back to the Latin word *pasta*, "paste," also the source of Italian *pasta*. *Pâté* is the modern French form of *paste*. Borrowed into English in the eighteenth century as a synonym for *pasty*, *paté* now usually means a meat paste or meat loaf without a pastry crust. *Patty* comes from English or French *pâté* by association with *pasty*. The word *pastry*, another food item made with dough, also belongs to this family. In the United States, pasties remain popular in the Northern Great Lakes region. Originally they were dough-wrapped meals carried to the mines. A pasty well-sealed in the morning would still be warm at lunchtime. Though the pasties of northern Michigan and Wisconsin sometimes included meat among their ingredients, they were often filled with root vegetables, like rutabaga or turnip, whether meat was available or not. The Great Lakes mines are closed now, but one can still buy pasties at diners and roadside stalls.

patter

Stand-up comics and musicians will probably be surprised to know that patter was originally a prayer. The word *patter* goes back to *pater,* a shortened form of *paternoster,* the Latin designation for the Lord's Prayer, from *pater,* "father," and *noster,* "our," the first two words of the prayer in Latin. Until the Reformation, most Christian prayers in western Europe were recited in Latin. Sometimes the prayers were recited rapidly, with little apparent regard for the actual sense of the words. From this practice, the Middle English verb *pateren,* with the senses "to say the paternoster," "pray," and "mutter prayers rapidly and insincerely," arose in the fourteenth century. In "We, harke, he jangelis like a jay . . . Me thynke he patris like a py" (Listen, he chatters like a jay-bird, it seems to me he patters like a magpie) from the *York Mystery Plays* (circa 1450), *patter* has taken on the sense "to chatter," from which developed our Modern English noun *patter.* Indeed, *patter* may have developed by analogy with *chatter,* recorded in English a century earlier.

pawn

Pawns are the peons of chess and with good reason. The words *pawn,* "one of the pieces used in chess," and *peon,* "unskilled laborer," are both derived from the Medieval Latin word *pedō* or *pedōn-,* "foot soldier," from a classical Latin word meaning "one who has broad feet." *Pawn* can be traced back to *pedō* by way of Old French *peon* or *paon* and Anglo-Norman *poun*, "foot soldier" and "pawn in chess." Apparently, *pawn* was never used in English to mean "foot soldier," but was used of the chess piece as early as the fourteenth century. The English word *peon* goes back to *pedō* by way of words in various languages, such as the Old French *peon* in the sense "soldier" or "domestic on foot," Spanish *peón* and Portuguese *peão,* both meaning "pedestrian," "pawn in chess," "foot soldier," or "day laborer." Another Old French word derived from Medieval Latin *pedō, pionnier,* entered English as *pioneer,* meaning "a foot soldier," and later developed its own connotations on the American frontier. French *pionnier* and English *pioneer* originally referred to a soldier whose task was to prepare the way, as by digging ditches and building earthworks and roads, for the main body of troops marching to a new area. From this use the word was applied in English, as in French, to anyone who ventures into an unknown region and opens the way for others to follow, like the pioneers who opened North America progressively to settlement in the eighteenth and nineteenth centuries.

The other English word *pawn,* meaning "pledge, security," is unrelated. Today the word is used in this sense as a verb more often than as a noun. *Pawn* entered English in the fifteenth century and derives from Old French *pan,* "pledge, security," ultimately of Germanic origin. The two English *pawns* of different origin are sometimes confused, because enemy foot soldiers and other peons were sometimes held for security in war.

pay

Given the unpeaceful feelings one often has in pay-
ing bills or income taxes, it is difficult to believe
that the word *pay* ultimately derives from the Latin
word *pāx,* "peace." However, it is not the peace of the
one who pays that is involved in this development of
meaning. From *pāx,* meaning "peace" and also "a settlement of hostilities," was derived the word *pācāre,*
"to impose a settlement on peoples or territories." In
Late Latin *pācāre* was extended in sense to mean "to
appease." The Old French word *paiier* that developed
from Latin *pācāre* came to have the specific application "to pacify or satisfy a creditor," a sense that came
into Middle English along with the word *paien* (first
recorded around the beginning of the thirteenth century), the ancestor of our word *pay.*

pea

Pease-porridge hot,
Pease-porridge cold,
Pease-porridge in the pot,
Nine days old.

The need for contrast between singular and plural
forms of nouns is so important in English that very
few nouns now have identical singular and plural
forms. Those that do tend to be long-term survivors
rather than borrowings or new formations: *sheep* and
deer are as old as English itself. Many words originally having identical forms for the singular and plural
eventually developed new plurals ending with the regular English plural suffix -*s:* the word *daughter,* for
instance, now has the plural *daughters,* although it
once had a plural *dohtor,* which was the same as the

singular in Old English. Still other words developed new singular forms, and the word *pea* is an example of this reverse process. The Old English word for "a pea" was *piѕe* or *pioѕe.* The regular plural of this word had the ending -*an.* In Middle English the plural suffix changed to -*en* and new plural forms were developed, such as *peѕe* and *peaѕe,* forms identical to the singular, so that one could request one *peaѕe,* or two *peaѕe.* In the sixteenth century people began to interpret the sound represented by ѕ as a plural ending, and a new singular, spelled *pea* in Modern English, was developed to conform to the usual pattern of English nouns. A similar development also took place in the history of the word *cherry,* in which the final ѕ-sound of the original Anglo-Norman *cheriѕe* was reinterprented as a plural ending and a new singular *cherry* formed.

pedigree

The word *pedigree* derives from the name of a symbol looking something like a fork or Greek letter Ψ turned upside-down, at least according to the accepted hypothesis for the origin of the word. The Old French name for this symbol was *pied de grue,* meaning literally "foot of a crane," because that is what it looked like to those responsible for the Old French word. Anglo-Norman *pe de grue* is the immediate source of our word *pedigree.* The word for the symbol, which was used in genealogical charts to indicate succession, took on the broader meaning "a genealogical chart, genealogical relationship; genealogy."

pen

Is the feather mightier than the sword? The English word *pen*, "a writing implement," is derived from the Latin word *penna*, which originally meant only "feather." The Latin word for a writing implement was *stilus*, which meant "a stake." Since the ancient Romans wrote on wax tablets, any pointed instrument would do and ink was unnecessary. However, the subsequent use of paper or parchment required ink, which was applied with the shaft of a large feather sharpened and split for that purpose. In later Latin times *penna* acquired the meaning "a feather used to write with; pen." *Penna* descended into Old French as *penne,* which English borrowed with both senses, "feather" and "pen," the former of which is now obsolete.

penicillin

In the rest of this article allusion will constantly be made to experiments with filtrates of a broth culture of this mould, so for convenience and to avoid the repetition of the rather cumbersome phrase "Mould broth filtrate," the name "penicillin" will be used. This will denote the filtrate of a broth culture of the particular penicillium with which we are concerned.
—Alexander Fleming, *The British Journal of Experimental Pathology,* 1929

In this quotation from the writings of the discoverer of penicillin we view the word *penicillin* almost at its moment of birth. Fleming derived the name *penicillin* from the genus name of the mold *Penicillium notatam,* from which he originally obtained the antibiotic. The name has since been applied to other antibiotics obtained naturally from other molds or made synthetically from them. The New Latin name of the genus, *Pēnicillium*, comes from the Latin word *pēnicilluṡ*, "paintbrush," to which our word *pencil* can also be traced. The mold *Penicillium* was so named because of its brushlike sporangia, or spore-bearing structures. The Latin word *pēnicilluṡ* in turn can be traced back to the Latin word *pēniṡ*, "tail, penis," also borrowed directly into English.

peninsula

Floridians and Michiganders may be interested to learn more about the origin of the word describing the land formation of their states. The word *peninṡula* is borrowed from the Latin word *pæninṡula*, which in turn is derived from *pæne īnṡula*, meaning literally "almost an island." Since the sixteenth century, English *peninṡula* has referred not only to land almost surrounded by water but also to a piece of land of which three of four sides are coastline.

penthouse

The word *penthouṡe* goes back to Latin *appendere*, "to cause to be suspended." In Medieval Latin *appendere* developed the sense "to belong, depend," a sense that passed into *apendre*, the Old French development of *appendere*. From *apent*, the past participle of *apendre*, came the derivative *apentiz*, "low building behind or beside a house," and the Anglo-Norman plural form *pentiz*. The form without the *a-* was then borrowed into Middle English, giving us *pentiṡ* (first recorded about 1300), which was applied to sheds or lean-tos added on to buildings. Because these structures often had sloping roofs, the word was connected with the French word *pente,* "slope," and the second part of the word changed by folk etymology to *house,* which could mean simply "a building for human use." The use of the term to refer to fancy rooftop apartments developed from its application to a structure built on a roof to cover such things as a stairway or an elevator shaft. *Penthouse* then came to mean an apartment built on a rooftop and finally the top floor of an apartment building.

period

Many may have wondered why the word *period* has the sense "punctuation mark (.)" as well as several senses having to do with time. The answer to this question lies in one of the senses of the Greek word *periodos* from which our word is descended. *Periodos,* made up of *peri-,* "around," and *hodos,* "way," in addition to meaning such things as "going around, way around; going around in a circle, circuit," and, with regard to time, "cycle or period of time," referred in rhetoric to "a group of words organically related in grammar and sense." The Greek word was adopted into Latin as *perihodos,* which in the Medieval Latin period acquired a new sense related to its use in rhetoric, "a punctuation mark used at the end of a rhetorical period." This sense is not recorded in English until 1609, but the word had already entered English as a borrowing from Old French in the sense "a cycle of recurrence of a disease," first being recorded in a work written around 1425.

petrel

Petrels are noted for flying so close to the water that they appear to be walking on it. Their name may have come from this behavior, although the origin of the word is not known for certain. The word is first attested in English as *pitterel* in the seventeenth century. Later, in Part I of his *Voyage to New Holland,* published in 1703, the English explorer and pirate William Dampier, a stormy petrel himself, gives the first recorded version of that explanation: "As they fly ... they pat the Water alternately with their Feet, as if they walkt upon it; tho' still upon the Wing. And from hence the Seamen give them the name of Petrels, in allusion to St. Peter's walking upon the [Sea of Galilee]."

pickle

Trade with the Low Countries across the North Sea was important to England in the later Middle Ages, and it is perhaps because of this trade that we have the word *pickle.* Middle English *pikel,* the ancestor of our word, is first recorded around 1400 with the meaning "a spicy sauce or gravy served with meat or fowl." This is a different sense from the one the word brings to mind now, but it is somewhat related to its possible Middle Dutch source *pekel,* a solution, such as spiced brine, for preserving and flavoring food. After coming into English, the word *pickle* expanded its sense range in several ways. It was applied, as it had been in Middle Dutch, to a pickling solution. Later *pickle* was used to refer to something so treated, such as a cucumber. The word also took on a figurative sense, "a troublesome situation," perhaps under the influence of a similar Dutch usage in the phrase *in de pekel zitten,* "sit in the pickle," and *iemand in de pekel laten zitten,* "let someone sit in the pickle."

plumber

A plumber works with water pipes, once made from lead, with lead solder for the joints. The Romans used lead pipes, and the word *plumber* comes from Old French *plomier,* from Latin *plumbārius,* "a lead worker," which is in turn from the Latin word for "lead," *plumbum.* The English verb *plumb* is from the same Latin source *plumbum,* since lead weights were used to plumb depths. There is no Latin, or even Indo-European, etymology for *plumbum,* but it bears a distant similarity to the Greek word for "lead," the standard form of which, *molubdos,* gives us the name of another element in the Periodic Table, *molybdenum.* Two nonstandard forms, *molibos* and especially *bolimos,* are even more similar to the Latin word.

poison

The phrase *poison potion,* besides being alliterative, also consists of doublets, that is, two words that go back ultimately to the same source in another language. The source for both words is Latin *pōtiō* (stem form *pōtiōn-*), which meant "the act of drinking, a drink, or a draft, as of a medicine or poison." Our word *potion,* which retains the sense "dose," passed through Old French (*pocion*) on its way to Middle English (*pocion*), first recorded in a work composed around 1300. In Old French *pocion* is a learned borrowing, one that was deliberately taken from Latin in a form corresponding to the Latin form. Our spelling *potion* is the result of a similar impulse toward

Latinization; in the late Renaissance and Enlightenment, numerous English words that had been borrowed from Old French were respelled according to
the shape of their Latin ancestors. *Pocion* thus was
changed to *potion* on the model of Latin *pōtiō.* But the
Latin word had also passed through Vulgar Latin into
Old French in the different form *poison.* This word
meant "beverage," "liquid dose," and also "poison beverage, poison." The word *poison* is first recorded in
Middle English in a work composed around 1200.

pompadour

The rock 'n' roll star's *pompadour* can be traced back to the eigh-teenth century, derived from the name of Madame de Pompadour, one of Louis XV's mis-tresses. Madame de Pom-padour, who may have been raised from an early age to fill such a post, occupied it well. She was pleasant to the king's wife, pleasing to the king, and in later years politi-cally indispensable to

*Elvis Presley and Judy Tyler in a publicity still
for the 1957 movie* Jailhouse Rock

him. Because she was the arbiter of fashion at that
time, *pompadour* has been used for such things as a
type of cloak, a fabric pattern covered with sprigs of
flowers, a pink or crimson color, a South American
bird with crimson-purple plumage, and several hair
styles, including the one worn by early rock 'n' roll
stars, in which the hair was brushed up and back from
the forehead. Though we associate the pompadour

with the 1950s, the word *pompadour* entered English in the nineteenth century to describe the hairstyles of both men and women.

poodle

When it rains cats and dogs, the dogs ought to be poodles. The word *poodle* comes from the German word *Pudel,* short for *Pudelhund,* both meaning "poodle." *Pudel* comes from Low German *pudeln,* "to splash in water." *Pudeln* in turn is derived from *pfudel,* "puddle," a term related to our word *puddle,* recorded in English from the fourteenth century and ultimately from Old English *pudd,* meaning "ditch, furrow," the very topographical features from which puddles are made. *Pudel* is part of the name of the *Pudelhund* because the dog was once used as a waterfowl retriever.

porpoise

The gracefully swimming animal known as the *porpoise* is also sometimes called by the ungraceful name *sea hog.* In fact, the word *porpoise* means "sea hog," from an etymological point of view. Old French *porpeis,* the source of Middle English *porpeis* and Modern English *porpoise,* is a compound of *porc,* "pig," and *peis,* "fish." The Old French word is in turn probably a translation of a Germanic compound meaning "sea-pig." An older German word for "porpoise" is *Meerschwein,* from *Meer,* "sea," and *Schwein,* which English speakers can recognize as a relative of the word *swine.* In modern French the word *porpeis* has not survived, being replaced by *marsouin,* a borrowing from a Scandinavian source related to the German word.

Although we do not know whether the speakers of Proto-Indo-European had a word for porpoises, they did have words for pigs and fish. Both of the Old French words in *porpoise*–*porc* and *peis*–are ancient. *Porc* descends from Latin *porcus,* which in turn directly continues the Indo-European word for "pig," **porko-.* The native Germanic outcome of this word in English is *farrow,* "a litter of pigs." The Old English ancestor of *farrow, fearh,* meant "little pig." The development of *fearh* from *porko-* illustrates the linguistic process called GRIMM'S LAW (see glossary), by which *p* changed to *f* and *k* changed to *h.* Proto-Indo-European **porko-* thus became Germanic **farha-,* which can also been seen in the word *aardvark.* This word is Afrikaans for "earth-pig," and the element –*vark* descends from *farha-.*

French *peis,* on the other hand, developed from Latin *piscis,* "fish," familiar from the name of the constellation *Pisces,* "the Fish." The Latin word continues Proto-Indo-European **pisk-.* Again, we can turn this Proto-Indo-European form into a Germanic word simply by applying Grimm's Law, which turns the initial *p* of this word into an *f.* We can see the results directly in a word borrowed from Norwegian, *lutefisk* (fish preserved in lye, a Scandinavian specialty still relished in Minnesota for instance). In English , the **-sk-* further developed into a *sh* sound, and we get *fish* out of it.

post

The meaning "mail" of the word *post* reflects the old systems of delivering mail. In the sixteenth century mounted couriers called *posts,* stationed at designated places along certain highways and byways, rode in relays with royal dispatches and other papers. As the system of mail delivery expanded during the next two centuries, *post* was applied to a delivery of mail and to the organization responsible for the entire system of mail delivery. The term was borrowed from French *poste,* ultimately from Italian *posta,* the word for one of the stations that formed part of the relay system. The Italian word comes from Latin *posita,* the feminine past participle of the verb *pōnere,* "to place, put in position."

posthumous

The word *posthumous* is associated with death, both in meaning and in form. Our word goes back to the Latin word *postumus,* meaning "last born," "born after the death of one's father," "born after the making of a will," and "last, final." *Postumus* was largely used with respect to events occurring after death but not exclusively so, since the word was simply one of the superlative forms of the adverb *post,* "subsequently, afterward." Because of its use in connection with death, however, later Latin writers decided that the last part of the word must have to do with *humus,* "earth," or *humāre,* "to bury," and began spelling the word *posthumus.* This form of the Latin word was borrowed into English and is first recorded in a work composed before 1464. Perhaps the most telling use of the word appears in the poet Robert Southey's comment on the rewards of an author: "It was well we should be contented with posthumous fame, but impossible to be so with posthumous bread and cheese."

prestige

Lest we be bamboozled into believing that the word *prestige* always connoted eminent, influential status, let us examine its early history. Strangely enough, *prestige* first meant "an illusion, conjuring trick, deception, imposture," a sense borrowed into English from French along with the word in the seventeenth century. The French word *prestige* derived from Latin *praestigiae,* "tricks." In French *prestige* developed a sense referring to influence achieved through such things as success, renown, or wealth, which was borrowed into English and first recorded in 1829. John Stuart Mill, writing in 1838, uses this sense of *prestige* while seeming to keep in mind its earlier sense. As he observed, "the *prestige* with which [Napoleon] overawed the world is . . . the effect of stage-trick." The word's more general sense, "inspiring admiration," does not appear in English until the twentieth century.

pretzel

The German word *Brezel* or *Pretzel,* which was borrowed into English (being first recorded in American English in 1856) goes back to the assumed Medieval Latin word **brāchitellum.* This would accord with the story that a monk living in France or northern Italy  first created the knotted shape of a pretzel, even though this type of biscuit had been enjoyed by the Romans. The monk wanted to symbolize arms folded in prayer, hence the name derived from Latin *brac-chiātus,* "having branches," itself from *bracchium,* "branch, arm."

priest

When John Milton in his sonnet "On the New Forcers of Conscience under the Long Parliament" denounced the elders, or presbyters, of the Presbyterian Church by saying *"New Presbyter is but Old Priest* writ large," he was aware of the etymological relationship between the two words. *Priest* and *presbyter* both descend from the Greek word *presbuteros,* which literally meant "elder," the comparative form of *presbus,* "old man." The Greek word was used in early Christian writing to denote one of the orders of ministers. *Presbuteros* was borrowed into Latin and from there into the Germanic languages, appearing in Old English as *prēost,* which became our modern word *priest.* Because Old English *prēost* and its descendants referred not only to Christian ministers but also to Jewish and pagan priests, *presbuteros* was re-borrowed as *presbyter* during the sixteenth-century Reformation to apply only to officials of the Christian church. Milton thus made an inspired pun, for *presbyter* was a longer word than *priest* when written, yet had the same etymological source and much the same meaning.

prize

Prize was at one time the same word as *price. Price* came from the Old French word *pris,* which derives from Latin *pretium,* "value, price, reward." *Pris* had a range of senses, including "money paid for something," "prize," and "esteem." Our word *price,* which came into English from French, is commonly used today only in the sense "sum of money, cost." *Price* also meant in Middle English, as it had in Old French, "reward, prize." During the past four hundred years this sense and related senses have broken off from *price,* becoming thought of as a separate word. From the sixteenth to the eighteenth century *prize,* our spelling for this word, was simply one of a number of possible spellings for *price.*

Procrustean

Procrustean is derived from the name of the legendary Greek robber Procrustes, who dwelt in Eleusis and was later killed by Theseus. According to one version of the legend, Procrustes would force strangers to lie down in one of his two beds—one bed being short; the other, long. If the unfortunate victim was longer than the short bed, Procrustes would cut the victim to fit. Victims shorter than the long bed were stretched out with weights in an early version of the rack. As a result, *Procrustean* came to mean "producing or designed to produce conformity by ruthless or arbitrary means" and "having merciless disregard for individual differences or special circumstances." The legend also led to the use of the phrase *bed of Procrustes* to refer to great inflexibility. The legend is old, but the English word is new, a product of the nineteenth century adaptation of mythological terms to present-day situations.

protean

Protean, "readily taking on varied forms," "exhibiting great variety," is another word whose origins lie in Greek myth. At the origin of *protean,* first recorded in English as early as the sixteenth century, is the name of the sea god Proteus. He had the power to change his shape, as well as the gift of prophecy, but those who wished to consult him had to bind him securely first. He would then change into various shapes: a lion, a dragon, a tiger, a wild boar, a tree, and water. But a questioner who could keep Proteus restrained until he returned to his original shape would receive an answer.

prude

Being called a prude is rarely considered a compliment, but if we dig into the history of the word *prude,* we find that it has a noble past. The change for the worse took place in French. French *prude* first had a good sense, "wise woman," but apparently a woman could be too wise or, in the eyes of some, too observant of decorum and propriety. Thus *prude* took on the sense in French that was brought into English along with the word, first recorded in 1704. The French word *prude* was a shortened form of *prude femme* (earlier in Old French *prode femme*), a word modeled on earlier *preudomme,* "a man of experience and integrity." The second part of this word is, of course, *homme,* "man." Old French *prod,* meaning "wise, prudent," is from Vulgar Latin *prōdis* with the same sense. *Prōdis* in turn comes from Late Latin *prōde,* "advantageous," derived from the verb *prōdesse,* "to be good." Despite this history filled with usefulness, profit, wisdom, and integrity, *prude* has become a term of reproach.

prune

The words *prune* and *plum* came into English by separate routes from the Latin word *prūnum,* "a plum." *Prūnum* was borrowed into the West Germanic languages at a very early date with the sound *l* instead of the sound *r*. The Old English form was *plūme,* which becomes *plum* in Modern English. In Old French, the Latin word *prūnum* became *prune*. English then borrowed *prune* from French with the specialized meaning "dried plum."

pupil

The pupil of the eye is so called because of the tiny image reflected in it. Our word *pupil* goes back to the Latin word *pūpilla,* meaning "a girl under the care of a guardian," "a little doll," and "the pupil of the eye." *Pūpilla* in turn was derived from *pūpa,* "a girl, doll." This use in Latin of *pūpilla* for "a doll" and "the pupil of the eye" was probably based on or parallel to the senses of the Greek word *korē,* which meant "girl;" "puppet, doll;" and "pupil of the eye." *Pupil* in the sense "a student" goes back to Latin *pūpilla,* too, and also to another word, *pūpillus,* "a minor under the care of a guardian," which was derived from *pūpus,* "a boy, child." English *pupil,* meaning "ward, orphan," entered English in the fourteenth century, but the sense "person under instruction" appeared much later, in the sixteenth century, as did the sense pertaining to the opening of the iris of the eye.

quahog

Quahogs and geoducks have nothing to do with mammals and birds in spite of the apparent similarity of their final elements—*hog* and *duck*—to the words *hog* and *duck*. Both *quahog* and *geoduck* were borrowed into English from Native American languages. The *quahog*, pronounced *coe-hog*, with the first syllable rhyming with *toe*, is an edible clam with a hard, rounded shell that is found abundantly from the Gulf of St. Lawrence to the Gulf of Mexico. Its name is from Narranganset *poquaûhock*, "quahog." Narraganset, a member of the Algonquin language family, was spoken by a people inhabiting the area of Rhode Island. The language is extinct, but some descendants of this group still live in Rhode Island today. *Geoduck*, (improbably pronounced like *gooey-duck*) is the name of a big clam weighing up to twelve pounds and found in coastal waters from British Columbia to southern California and especially in Puget Sound. Its name comes from the Puget Salish word *gwídaq*, meaning "geoduck." Puget Salish is a member of the Salishan language family, which also includes other languages of the Pacific Northwest such as Bella Coola and Squamish.

quaint

The adjective *quaint* is ultimately derived from the Latin word *cognitus,* "known," the past participle of *cognoscere,* "to know, learn." English did not borrow the word directly from Latin, but rather in the form of its Old French descendant *cointe* or *queinte,* which had developed senses of its own far removed from the meaning of the Latin word. The Old French term *queinte* basically meant "wise," "skilled," and "clever." From these senses *queinte* developed other meanings, such as "cleverly or ingeniously made or done" and "strange, curious." The usual modern sense of our English word *quaint* is "charmingly old-fashioned." *Quaint* declines in use during the eighteenth century. However, there was a revival in the use of *quaint* by writers of the romantic period. Many of these writers were interested in medieval customs, traditions, and literature, and they occasionally used obsolete and quaint words–such as *quaint*–when writing about antiquarian topics, as Edgar Allan Poe did in his famous lines: "Once upon a midnight dreary, while I pondered, weak and weary / Over many a quaint and curious volume of forgotten lore."

quark

"Three quarks for Muster Mark!/Sure he hasn't got much of a bark/And sure any he has it's all beside the mark." This passage from James Joyce's *Finnegans Wake,* part of a scurrilous thirteen-line poem directed against King Mark, the cuckolded husband in the Tristan legend, has left its mark on modern physics. The poem and the accompanying prose are packed with names of birds and words suggestive of birds, and the poem is a squawk against the king that suggests the cawing of a crow. The word *quark* comes from the Standard English verb *quark,* meaning "to caw, croak," and also from the dialectal verb *quawk,* meaning "to caw, screech like a bird." It is easy to see why Joyce chose the word, but why should it have become the name for a group of hypothetical subatomic particles proposed as the fundamental units of matter? Murray Gell-Mann, the physicist who proposed this name for these particles, said in a private letter of June 27, 1978, to the editor of the *Oxford English Dictionary* that he had been influenced by Joyce's words: "The allusion to three quarks seemed perfect" (originally there were only three subatomic quarks). Gell-Mann, however, wanted to pronounce the word with (ô) not (ä), as Joyce seemed to indicate by using rhyming words such as *Mark* in the vicinity. Gell-Mann got around that "by supposing that one ingredient of the line 'Three quarks for Muster Mark' was a cry of 'Three quarts for Mister . . .' heard in H.C. Earwicker's pub," a plausible suggestion given the complex punning in Joyce's novel. It seems appropriate that this perplexing and humorous novel should have supplied the term for particles that come in six "flavors" and three "colors."

queen

Queen and *quean* sound alike, are spelled almost identically, and both refer to women, but of wildly different kinds. *Queen* comes from Old English *cwēn,* with a long *ē*, "queen, wife of a king," which comes from Germanic **kwēn-iz,* "woman, wife, queen." *Quean* comes from Old English *cwene,* with a short *ĕ,* "woman, female, female serf"; from the eleventh century on it was also used to mean "prostitute." The Germanic source of *cwene* is **kwen-ōn-,* "woman, wife." Once established, the pejorative sense of *quean* drove out its neutral senses, and especially in the sixteenth and seventeenth centuries it was used almost solely to refer to prostitutes. Around the same time, in many English dialects the pronunciation of *queen* and *quean* became identical, leading to the obsolescence of the latter term except in some regions. The Germanic root for both words, **kwen-,* "woman," comes by GRIMM'S LAW (see glossary) from the Indo-European root **gʷen-,* "woman," which appears in at least two other English words borrowed from elsewhere in the Indo-European family. One is *gynecology,* from Greek *gunē,* "woman." Another, less obvious one is *banshee,* "woman of the fairies," the wailing female spirit attendant on a dying person, from Old Irish *ben,* "woman."

queue

When the British stand in queues (as they have been doing at least since 1837, when this meaning of the word is first recorded in English), they may not realize they form a tail. The French word *queue,* from which the English word is borrowed, is a descendant of Latin *cōda,* meaning "tail." French *queue* appeared in 1748 in English, referring to a plait of hair hanging down the back of the neck. By 1802 wearing a queue was a regulation in the British army, but by the mid-nineteenth century queues had disappeared along with cocked hats. Latin *cōda* is also the source of Italian *coda,* which was adopted into English as a musical term (like so many other English musical terms that come from Italian). A coda is thus literally the "tail end" of a movement or composition.

quibble

These lawiers have . . . such quite and quiddits [quibbles] that beggering their clients they purchase to themselves whole lordships.
—Robert Greene, *A Quip for an Upstart Courtier,* 1592

Quibble probably goes back to the Latin word *quibus,* a form of the Latin pronoun and adjective *quī,* meaning "who, which." *Quibus,* the plural form used to express the dative and ablative cases, meant such things as "to whom" and "from whom." This syntactic form appeared frequently in Latin legal documents; hence the word became associated with petty details and fine distinctions. From *quibus* we may have acquired the English word *quib,* meaning "an evasion of the point or a petty distinction," and thence probably the noun and verb *quibble.*

quiche

Quiche may seem to be a quintessentially French dish, but the word *quiche* is actually a Gallicized German word. *Quiche* was originally a specialty of Lorraine, a region in northeastern France bordering on Germany. Both French and German are spoken in Lorraine, which (along with Alsace) was claimed as territory by both countries at various times throughout history. The word *quiche* was borrowed into French from Alsatian German *Küche,* a diminutive of the German word *Kuchen,* "cake."

quicksilver

How is it that quicksilver is quick? The name *quicksilver* for the element mercury is a translation of the Latin phrase *argentum vīvum,* literally "living silver." Mercury was given this name because it is a silvery-colored metal that is free-flowing liquid at ordinary temperatures. In *quicksilver* the word *quick* preserves its original but now archaic sense "living, alive." We are familiar with this sense of *quick* in the phrase *the quick and the dead,* where *the quick* means "the living."

quiz

The origins of the word *quiz* are as difficult to pin down as the answers to some quizzes. We can say that its first recorded sense had to do with people, not tests. The term, first recorded in 1782, meant "an odd or eccentric person." From the noun in this sense came a verb meaning "to make sport or fun of" and "to regard mockingly." In English dialects and probably in American English the verb *quiz* acquired senses relating to interrogation and questioning. This presumably occurred because *quiz* was associated with *question, inquisitive,* or perhaps the English dialect verb *quiset,* "to question" (probably itself short for obsolete *inquisite,* "to investigate"). From this new area of meaning came the noun and verb senses all too familiar to students. The second recorded instance of the noun sense occurs in the writings of no less an educator than William James, who in a letter from 1867 proffers the hope that "perhaps giving 'quizzes' in anatomy and physiology . . . may help along."

racket

Racquetball and handball are quite different games, but from the point of view of etymology they should be the same. The word *racket* comes to us from the Old French term *raquette,* which meant "palm of the hand" and "sole of the foot," as well as "racket." This mixture of senses can be explained by the history of racket games. The ancestor of tennis, for example, was originally played with the hands, and in French this game was called *le jeu de paume,* "the game of the palm." The transition in meaning of the word *raquette* from "palm" to "racket" was a natural one, especially since the physical transition in the way the game was played was gradual, moving first from hand to glove, then to a glove with a binding of cords on its palm, then to boards, then to a short-handled paddle, and finally to a long-handled racket. The Old French word *raquette* is ultimately derived from Arabic *rāḥat,* a form of *rāḥa,* "palm."

raid

Few soldiers traveling a road to carry out a raid would connect the words *road* and *raid*. However, both descend from the same Old English word *rād.* Old English *rād* meant "the act of riding" and "the act of riding with a hostile intent, that is, a raid," senses that no longer exist for our word *road.* The *ai* in *raid* represents the standard development of Old English long *a* in the northern dialects, while the *oa* in *road* represents the standard development of Old English long *a* in the rest of the English dialects. It was left to Sir Walter Scott to revive the Scots form *raid* with the sense "a military expedition on horseback." The Scots were not the only ones conducting raids, however. We find these words in the Middle English *Coventry Leet Book:* "aftur a Rode . . . made uppon the Scottes at th'ende of this last somer." While *road* is not used in this way any more in English, a trace of this usage is still detectable in the compound *inroad,* literally "a riding or advance on or in."

rajah

Rajah is familiar to us from the Sanskrit *rājā,* "king," and *mahārājā,* "great king." The Sanskrit root *raj-,* "to rule," comes from the Indo-European root **reg-,* "to move in a straight line, direct, rule." The same Indo-European root appears in Italic (Latin) and Celtic. *Rēx* means "king" in Latin, coming from **reg-s,* whence our *regal* and, through French, *royal.* Two of the Gaulish kings familiar to us from Caesar, Dumnorix and Vercingetorix, incorporate the Celtic word *rīx,* "king," in their names. (*Rīx* also forms part of the name of that fictitious, indomitable Gaul *Asterix.*) Germanic at some time borrowed the Celtic word *rīx.*

It appeared as *reiks,* "ruler," in Gothic, as well as in older Germanic names ending in *-ric,* such as Alaric and Theodoric, the latter of whom had a name that is equivalent to German *Dietrich,* "people's king." A derivative of Celtic *rīx, *rīg-yo-,* meaning "rule, domain," was also borrowed into Germanic and is the source of German *Reich,* "rule, empire."

rankle

A persistent resentment, a festering sore, and a little snake are all coiled together in the history of the word *rankle.* "A little snake" is the sense of the Latin word *dracunculus* to which *rankle* can be traced, *dracunculus* being a diminutive of *dracō,* "snake." The Latin word passed into Old French as *draoncle,* having probably already developed the sense "festering sore," because some of these sores resembled little snakes in their shape or bite. The verb *draoncler,* "to fester," was then formed in Old French. The noun and verb developed alternate forms without the *d-,* and both were borrowed into Middle English, the noun *rancle* being recorded in a work written around 1190, the verb *ranclen,* in a work probably composed about 1300. Both words had literal senses having to do with festering sores. The noun is not recorded after the sixteenth century, but the verb went on to develop the figurative senses having to do with resentment and bitterness with which we are all too familiar.

read

English is the one of the few western European languages that does not derive its verb for "to read" from Latin *legere.* Compare, for example, *leggere* in

Italian, *lire* in French, and *lesen* in German. (Equally surprising is the fact that English is the only western European language not to derive its verb for "to write" from Latin *scrībere.) Read* comes from the Old English verb *rǣdan,* "to advise, interpret (something difficult), interpret (something written), read." *Rǣdan* is related to the German verb *raten,* "to advise" (as in *Rathaus,* "townhall"). The Old English noun *rǣd,* "counsel," survives in the rare noun *rede,* "counsel, advice," and in the name of the unfortunate King Ethelred the Unready, whose epithet is often misunderstood. *Unready* here does not have its current sense "unprepared"; it is a late sixteenth-century spelling of an earlier *unredy,* "ill advised, rash, foolish," from *rede.*

reindeer

Although Saint Nick uses reins on his reindeer, and reindeer are used to pull sleds in Lapland and northern Siberia, the word *reindeer* has nothing to do with reins. The element *-deer* is indeed our word *deer,* but the *rein-* part is borrowed from another language, specifically from the Scandinavian  languages spoken by the chiefly Danish and Norwegian invaders and settlers of England from the ninth to the eleventh century. Even though the Old Icelandic language in which much of Old Norse literature was written is not the same variety of Old Norse spoken by these settlers of England, it is close enough to give us an idea of the words that were borrowed into English.

Thus we can cite the Old Icelandic word *hreinn,* which means "reindeer," as the source of the first part of the English word. The word *reindeer* is first recorded in Middle English in a work composed before 1400.

revamp

The word *revamp* has to do with shoes, not seductive women. *Revamp* is formed from the English prefix *re-,* "again," and the verb *vamp,* "to refurbish." The verb *vamp* is derived from the noun *vamp,* from Old French *avantpie, a* compound of *avant,* "before," and *pie,* "foot." A *vamp* is the part of a shoe or boot covering the instep and sometimes extending over the toe. The verb originally meant "to provide a shoe with a new vamp" and was used figuratively to refer to any kind of restoration and refurbishing. Although the prefix *re-* in *revamp* means "again," it functions primarily as an intensifier. As for *vamp,* "an unscrupulous woman who seduces or exploits men with her charms," it is simply a shortening of the English word *vampire.*

rhinestone

Although rhinestones are inseparably associated with the costumes of country-and-western singers and Las Vegas dancers, the word originally had European associations. The *rhine* in *rhinestone* is the Rhine River, and *rhinestone* is a translation into English of the French phrase *caillou du Rhin.* Originally a rhinestone was a kind of rock crystal that was found in or near the Rhine. Other types of rock crystal, such as Cornish diamond, were given similar fancy names. Because rhinestones could be made to imitate diamonds, the name *rhinestone* was applied to artificial gems made from paste, glass, or gem quartz and as a result often carries a connotation of showbiz glitz.

right

The political sense of *right,* meaning "conservative" or "reactionary," has been taken over from French *droite,* which means both "right-hand side" and "the political right." The French usage dates from the French Revolution. In the French National Assembly of 1789 the nobles sat on the right of the president of the Assembly and the commoners sat on the left. The nobility as a group tended to be politically more conservative than the commoners. In later assemblies and parliaments, seating continued to be assigned on the basis of political views as established in the first assembly.

robot

Robot is a word that is both a coinage by an individual person and a borrowing. It has been in English since 1923 when the Czech writer Karel Čapek's play *R.U.R.* was translated into English and presented in London and New York. *R.U.R.,* published in 1921, is an abbreviation of *Rossum's Universal Robots; robot* itself comes from Czech *robota,* "servitude, forced labor," from *rab,* "slave." The Slavic root behind *robota* is *orb-,* from the Indo-European root **orbh-,* referring to separation from one's group or passing out of one sphere of ownership into another. This seems to be the sense that binds together its somewhat diverse group of derivatives, which includes Greek *orphanos,* "orphan," Latin *orbus,* "orphaned," and German *Erbe,* "inheritance," in addition to the Slavic word for "slave" mentioned above. Czech *robota* is also similar to another German derivative of this root, namely *Arbeit,* "work" (its Middle High German form *arabeit* is even more like the Czech word). *Arbeit* may be descended from a word that meant "slave labor" and was later generalized to just "labor."

rocket

Sophisticated rockets soaring into space have a rather prosaic origin, at least from an etymological standpoint. The etymological contrails of *rocket* lead us back to Italian, specifically to the Italian word *rocchetta,* which is a diminutive of *rocca,* meaning "rock." This particular *rock,* however, is not quite as down to earth as it sounds, for it means "distaff, a staff used in spinning to hold unspun material, such as wool." The cylindrical shape of the *rocca* led to the use of its diminutive *rocchetta* to mean "an apparatus consisting of a cylindrical case containing an inflammable mixture, which when ignited propels the apparatus."

Such devices, the invention of which is ascribed to the Chinese as early as A.D. 1000, were used as military weapons or as fireworks. In *The Generall Historie of Virginia, New-England and the Summer Isles,* published in 1624, Captain John Smith said that "in the evening we fired a few rackets, which flying in the ayre ... terrified the poore Salvages." Although modern rockets propelled by powerful engines can carry much heavier payloads to more distant targets, they are called *rockets* because they operate on the same basic principle that Captain Smith's projectiles did. The engine provides thrust by the ejection of gases produced when substances inside the device are burned. The word *rocket,* first recorded for the modern device in 1919, was used in this context by the American pioneer of rocketry Robert H. Goddard.

role

We all play many roles in life, such as parent or teacher, and it is not difficult to see how this sense of the word *role* is related to its meaning in the theater. *Role,* which is first recorded in English in 1606, came to us from French already having the sense "a part one has to play." The word *rôle* in its earlier history (Old French *rolle*) had meant "a roll, as of parchment," particularly with reference to a manuscript roll. The word could also mean "a legal document" or "a list or register." From such uses it also came to refer to the text from which an actor learned a part. This use brought the word into the world of the theater, where it has played an important role ever since. The theatrical meaning was then generalized to include parts played off the stage.

romance

Most users of the word *romance,* with its hints of passion and exotic climes, do not realize that it goes back to Rome, the great wellspring of organization and law. From the Latin name *Rōma,* "Rome," is derived Latin *Rōmānus,* "of Rome and its people," and from this word comes *Rōmānicus,* "of the Roman type or people." The Vulgar Latin word *Rōmānicē,* "in the Roman tongue," is hypothesized to be the next development, and from this comes Old French *romans,* "the French language," descended from Latin (the tongue of the Romans) but not Latin. Old French *romans* also meant "a work composed in French." The word *romans* first referred to any sort of work, but it narrowed in scope and came to mean a particular type of vernacular composition, "a chivalric tale in verse," a sense that we borrowed from French along with the word *romance*. Later, in the sixteenth and seventeenth centuries, *romance* meant "a long prose work in which the events were remote from everyday life." (The romance fiction of today, though somewhat changed from these earlier types, remains a lively genre, filled with heroes and heroines who no longer chase or flee dragons but rather each other.)

The sixteenth- and seventeenth-century sense of romance was influenced by the development of the word *romantic*. *Romantic,* with its foundation in the imaginative world of romances replete with heroes and ladies, went on to develop senses such as "chivalric, gallant," "exotic," and "imaginary, ideal." From 1728 onward, *romantic* is recorded in association with words such as *love, lover,* and *friendship and* used to express the idealistic quality of these relationships. Use of *romantic* in this way influenced the development of *romance* in the senses "a love affair," "the idealistic quality in a love affair," and "a love story." Now perhaps one can see why it would be appropriate to have a romance in Rome, etymologically at least.

roster

If we associate the roster of a football team with the word *gridiron,* it is not because the team's roster has the appearance of a football field. But etymologically at least a roster is a gridiron. Our word *roster* goes back to Dutch *rooster,* meaning "gridiron" (from the verb *roosten,* "to roast"), which was extended in sense to mean "a table, list." This extension was made because of the resemblance of a gridiron to a piece of paper divided by parallel lines that contains a list or table. (The application of *gridiron* to a football field is also based on similarity in appearance.) The earliest use in English (first recorded in 1727) for the word *roster* borrowed from Dutch was military, referring to a list or plan that outlined when officers, men, and bodies of troops should perform their turn of duty. *Roster* is no longer exclusively military in usage and can now be applied to members of a team scheduled to perform on the gridiron, baseball field, or other playing area.

rubber

The noun *rubber,* "a substance made from the sap of the rubber tree," is derived from the verb *rub.* Central American Indians are believed to have made rubber balls for their games, but one of the first uses of the substance was discovered by Europeans rubbing out pencil marks. Although many other uses have since been found, the name *rubber* has stuck.

rune

Among early peoples writing was a serious thing, full of magical power. In its only reference to writing, the *Iliad* calls it "baneful signs." The Germanic peoples had a runic alphabet as their form of writing, using it to identify combs or helmets, make calendars, encode secret messages, and mark funeral monuments. Runes were also employed in casting spells, as to gain a kiss from a sweetheart or to make an enemy's gut burst. In casting the spell the

common Germanic rune script, often called the "Elder Futhark"

writing of the runes was accompanied by a mumbled or chanted prayer or curse, also called a *rune,* to make the magic work. These two meanings also appear in Old English *rūn,* the ancestor of our word. The direct descendants of Old English *rūn* are the archaic verb *round,* "whisper, talk in secret," and the obsolete noun *roun,* "whispering, secret talk." The use of the word to refer to inscribed runic characters apparently disappeared in the late fourteenth or early fifteenth century but was revived by Danish writers on Germanic antiquities, who adopted it from Old Norse toward the end of the seventeenth century. Appropriately enough, this sense of *rune,* which had faded away like a whisper, reappeared from the mists of the past.

S

sack

The ordinary word *sack* carries within it a few thousand years of commercial history. *Sack,* which probably goes back to Middle Eastern antiquity, has a long history because it and its ancestors denoted an object used in trade between various peoples. Thus the Greeks got their word *sakkos,* "a bag made out of coarse cloth or hair," from the Phoenicians with whom they traded. We do not know the Phoenician word, but we know words that are akin to it, such as Hebrew *śaq* and Akkadian *saqqu.* The Greeks then passed the *sack,* as it were, to the Latin-speaking Romans, who transmitted their word *saccus,* "a large bag or sack," to the Germanic tribes with whom they traded, who gave it the form **sakkiz* (other peoples have also taken this word from Greek or Latin, including speakers of Welsh, Russian, Polish, and Albanian). The speakers of Old English, a Germanic language, used two forms of the word: *sæc,* from **sakkiz,* and *sacc,* directly from Latin; the second Old English form is the ancestor of our *sack.*

salad

Salt was and is such an important ingredient in salad dressings that the very word *salad* is based on the Latin word for "salt." Vulgar Latin had a verb **salāre,* "to salt," from Latin *sāl,* "salt," and the past participial form of this verb, **salāta,* "having been salted," came to mean "salad." The Vulgar Latin word passed into languages descending from it, such as Portuguese (*salada*) and Old Provençal (*salada*). Old French may have borrowed its word *salade* from Old Provençal. Medieval Latin also carried on the Vulgar Latin word in the form *salāta.* As in the case of so many culinary delights, the English borrowed the word and probably the dish from the French. The Middle English word *salade,* from Old French *salade* and Medieval Latin *salāta,* is first recorded in a recipe book composed before 1399.

Salt is of course an important ingredient of other foods and condiments besides salad dressings, as is evidenced by some other culinary word histories. The words *sauce* and *salsa,* borrowed into English from French and Spanish, respectively, both come ultimately from the Latin word *salsus,* meaning "salted." Another derivative of this word was the Late Latin adjective *salsīcius,* "prepared by salting," which eventually gave us the word *sausage.*

sandwich

Our name for "slices of bread with a filling" comes from the title of the English nobleman John Montagu, fourth Earl of Sandwich (1718-1792). An indefatigable gambler, he is reported to have instructed his servant to bring him this easily handled repast (the original filling is said to have been roast beef) so that he might eat without leaving the gaming table. Word of this incident circulated, and the happy meeting of meat and bread, dubbed *sandwich,* soon became a popular.

sanguine

The similarity in form between *sanguine,* "cheerfully optimistic," and *sanguinary,* "bloodthirsty," may prompt one to wonder how they have come to have such different meanings. The explanation lies in medieval physiology with its notion of the four humors or bodily fluids (blood, bile, phlegm, and black bile). The relative proportions of these fluids was thought to determine a person's temperament. If blood was the predominant humor, one had a ruddy face and a disposition marked by courage, hope, and a readiness to fall in love. Such a temperament was called *sanguine,* the Middle English ancestor of our word *sanguine.* The source of the Middle English word was Old French *sanguin,* itself from Latin *sanguineus.* Both the Old French and Latin words meant "bloody," "blood-colored," Old French *sanguin* having the sense "sanguine in temperament" as well. Latin *sanguineus* was in turn derived from *sanguis,* "blood," just as English *sanguinary* is. The English adjective *sanguine,* first recorded in Middle English before 1350, continues to refer to the cheerfulness and optimism that accompanied a sanguine temperament but no longer has any direct reference to medieval physiology.

sarcophagus

Sarcophagus, our term for a stone coffin located above ground and often decorated, has a macabre origin befitting a macabre thing. The word comes to us from Latin and Greek, having been derived in Greek from *ſarx,* "flesh," and *phagein,* "to eat." The Greek word *ſarkophagoſ* therefore meant "eating flesh," and in the phrase *lithoſ* ("stone") *ſarkophagoſ* it denoted a limestone that was thought to decompose the flesh of corpses placed in it. Used by itself as a noun, the Greek term came to mean "coffin." The term was carried over into Latin, where *ſarcophaguſ* was used in the phrase *lapiſ* ("stone") *ſarcophaguſ,* referring to the same stone as in Greek. *Sarcophaguſ* used as a noun in Latin meant "coffin of any material." This Latin word was borrowed into English, being recorded first in 1601 with reference to the flesh-consuming stone and then in 1705 with reference to a stone coffin.

satellite

Mars has two satellites, or moons, which are named *Deimoſ* and *Phoboſ,* literally "Terror" and "Fear," after the personifications of these emotions who attend the god when he drives his chariot out onto the battlefield in myth. Many of the other satellites of the planets have been named after the attendants of the gods, and the etymology of *ſatellite* is in keeping with this practice. The word goes back to Latin *ſatelleſ,* whose stem was *ſatellit-. Satelleſ* meant "one of a bodyguard or escort to a prince; attendant" and also in a bad sense, "henchman, accomplice." In English, the word is recorded with this meaning in the sixteenth century, but it was used infrequently until the eighteenth century, by which time it had already acquired an astronomical meaning. In 1611 the astronomer Johannes Kepler applied the Latin word *ſatellitēs,* the plural form of *ſatelleſ,* to the recently discovered bodies revolving around Jupiter because he thought these bodies surrounding the planet, which was still considered a heavenly personality, were like ever-hovering attendants. *Satellite* then took on the sense "a relatively small body orbiting a planet." Thus it was natural to use the word *satellite* for a man-made object orbiting a celestial body. This sense was prefigured in 1880 in an English translation of *The Begum's Fortune* by Jules Verne: "A projectile [that will] revolve perpetually round our globe . . . Two hundred thousand dollars is not too much to have paid for the pleasure of having endowed the planetary world with a new star, and the earth with a second satellite." The twentieth-century practice of calling countries that are subordinate to a more powerful one *satellite states* may mix the earlier senses, as often happens in the course of a word's semantic development: the dependent states may serve as "henchmen" to the superior state in international affairs, but they also figuratively orbit the master state, like planets around a sun.

satin

The term *satin* goes back through Old French to the Arabic word *zaytūnī,* which means "pertaining to the town of Zaitun." *Zaitun* is usually identified with Tsinkiang (Quanzhou) in China, a city described by Marco Polo as a thriving port during the thirteenth-century reign of Kublai Khan. The history of the word *satin* parallels the history of the importation of satin to the West: satin was carried to Europe by way of the Middle East from China, where it was first made. However, the road to England was a long one, and the term does not appear in English until sometime in the fourteenth century.

Saturday

Days and years are natural divisions of time based on the astronomical relation of the earth and the sun, but weeks and the names for the days of the week have their source in astrology. The practice of dividing the year into seven-day units is based on the ancient astrological notion that the seven celestial bodies (the sun, the moon, Mars, Mercury, Jupiter, Venus, and Saturn) influence what happens on earth and that each controls the first hour of the day named for it. This system was brought into Hellenistic Egypt from Mesopotamia, where astrology had been practiced for millennia and where seven had always been a propitious number. The ancient Romans did not divide their calendar into weeks; they named all the days of the month in relation to the ides, calends, and nones. In A.D. 321 Constantine the Great grafted the Hellenistic astrological system onto the Roman calendar, making the first day of the week a day of rest and worship and imposing the following sequence of names on the days: *Diēs Sōlis,* "Sun's Day"; *Diēs Lūnae,* "Moon's Day"; *Diēs Martis,* "Mars's Day"; *Diēs Mercuriī,* "Mercury's Day"; *Diēs Jovis,* "Jove's Day" or "Jupiter's Day"; *Diēs Veneris,* "Venus's Day"; and *Diēs Sāturnī,* "Saturn's Day." This new Roman system was adopted with modifications throughout most of western Europe. In the Germanic languages, such as Old English, the names of four of the Roman gods were converted into those of the corresponding Germanic gods. Therefore in Old English we have the following names (with their Modern English developments): *Sunnandaeg,* "Sunday"; *Mōnandaeg,* "Monday"; *Tīwesdaeg,* "Tuesday" (Tiu, like Mars, was a god of war); *Wōdnesdaeg,* "Wednesday" (Woden, like Mercury, was quick and eloquent); *Thunresdaeg,* "Thursday" (Thunor in Old English or Thor in Old Norse, like

Jupiter, was lord of the sky; Old Norse *Thōrᴣdagr* influenced the English form); *Frīgedaeg,* "Friday" (Frigg, like Venus, was the goddess of love); and *Saeterneᴣdaeg,* "Saturday." Saturn's Latin name *Sāturnuᴣ* is probably not Indo-European in origin, the only deity in the week names not to be so. Saturn was worshipped as a harvest god, since the Romans associated it with their word *ᴣatuᴣ,* "sown" (used of field or seeds), and indeed this word is related to English *ᴣeed* and *ᴣow* through the Indo-European root *ᴣē.* Many scholars think that Saturn is one of the gods inherited from the people who dominated Italy before the Romans, the Etruscans. Our understanding of the few Etruscan texts that have survived is limited, and no one has succeeding in definitely placing the Etruscan language in any known language family.

The names of the other days of the week are each the subject of a word history note in this book.

saw

One may at first suspect that an *old ᴣaw,* "a trite saying," originally referred to proverbs that just didn't cut it any longer, having been worn down from overuse. However, the noun *ᴣaw,* "a saying," is etymologically distinct from the noun *ᴣaw,* "toothed cutting instrument." *Saw,* "saying," goes back to the same Germanic ancestor as does the word *ᴣaga,* "a narrative." *Saw* is a native English word whose Old English form was *ᴣagu. Saga* was borrowed from Icelandic in the eighteenth century as the name of the historical legends of the Scandinavian peoples. In Old Norse and modern Scandinavian languages *ᴣaga* basically meant "a story or legend transmitted orally"; the narratives now called *ᴣagaᴣ* were written down several centuries after the events they recount. Both *ᴣaw* and *saga* are related to the verb *say*, from Old English *secgan.* All derive ultimately from the Indo-European root **sekw-*, "to say, utter."

scan

In the 1969 edition of *The American Heritage Dictionary* a dead issue was buried by our Usage Panel, 85 percent of whom thought it was acceptable to use *scan* in the sense "to look over quickly," though the note stated that this was less formal usage. The usage issue was raised because *scan* in an earlier sense meant "to examine closely." From a historical perspective it is easy to see how these two opposite senses of *scan* developed. The source of our word, Latin *scandere,* which meant "to climb," came to mean "to scan a verse of poetry," because one could beat the rhythm by lifting and putting down one's foot. The Middle English verb *scannen,* derived from *scandere,* came into the language in this sense (first recorded in a text composed before 1398). In the sixteenth century this highly specialized sense having to do with the close analysis of verse developed other senses, such as "to criticize, examine minutely, interpret, perceive." From these senses having to do with examination and perception, it was an easy step to the sense "to look at searchingly" (first recorded in 1798), perhaps harking back still to the careful, detailed work involved in analyzing prosody. The sense of looking something over to find a specific set of things was eventually broadened to include looking over the surface of something, with or without close scrutiny of the details. From this was born the modern usage of *scan* as a verb meaning "to look over quickly."

scarce

The words *scarce* and *excerpt* illustrate how two words with a common ancestor can diverge from one another in form while passing from one language to another over the centuries. Both words can be traced back to the Latin word *excerpere* (past participle stem *excerpt-*), meaning "to pick out," "to pick out mentally," and "to select a passage for quotation." The path is clear and direct from *excerpt-* to our noun *excerpt* (first recorded before 1638) and verb (first recorded around 1536), a past participle usage already being recorded in the fifteenth century. A more tangled path leads to our word *scarce*. It is assumed that side by side with Latin *excerpere* existed the Vulgar Latin form **excarpere*. **Excarpsus,* an adjective formed from the past participle of **excarpere* in Vulgar Latin, meant "narrow, cramped," and from this Vulgar Latin form came the Old French word *échars*, "insufficient, cramped" and "stingy." The Old French word, which existed in a variety of forms, including *scars* and the chiefly Old North French form *escarse*, was borrowed into Middle English as *scarse,* being first recorded in a manuscript written around 1300.

scold

A scold is not usually a poet, and a scolding rarely sounds like poetry to the one being scolded, but it seems that the word *scold* has a poetic background. It is probable that *scold,* first recorded in Middle English in a work probably composed around 1150, has a Scandinavian source related to the Old Icelandic word *skáld*, "poet." Middle English *scolde* may in fact have meant "a minstrel," but of that we are not sure. However, its Middle English meanings, "a ribald, abusive person" and "a shrewish, chiding woman," may be related to *ʃkāld,* as shown by the senses of some of the Old Icelandic words derived from *ʃkāld.* Old Icelandic *ʃkāldʃkapr,* for example, meant "poetry" in a good sense but also "a libel in verse," while *ʃkāld-ʃtöng* meant "a pole with imprecations or charms scratched on it." It would seem that libelous, cursing verse was a noted part of at least some poets' productions and that this association with poets passed firmly along with the Scandinavian borrowing into English.

scuba

Going *ʃcuba* diving sounds much more appealing than going *ʃelf-contained underwater breathing apparatuʃ* diving, and saying *ʃcuba* leaves more breath for swimming. The name for such an apparatus, first successfully tested in 1943, was formed by taking the first letter of each word in the phrase and putting them together to form a single word. *Scuba,* like other acronyms, has a vowel at a point that allows it to be pronounced like an English word. The word, first recorded in 1952, has been so widely adopted that people rarely think of it as a collection of initials and use it in forming other words, such as *ʃcuba-dive.* In fact, a verb *ʃcuba* was first recorded in 1973 and is still in use.

second

The noun *ʃecond,* meaning "a unit of time or of angular measure equal to 1/60 of a minute," is ultimately derived from the same Latin word as the adjective *ʃecond,* meaning "coming next after the first." The Latin word *ʃecunduʃ* was an adjective that meant "following" or "second." The sense of *secundus* referring to angular measure arose because of the method used to divide up degrees of a circle. Certain units, such as the degrees of a circle, were, as they still are, divided into equal parts, and those parts were further subdivided. The first subdivision was called *pars minuta prima,* or "first little part," and the subdivision of this unit was called *pars minuta secunda,* or "second little part." *Secunda* is the feminine singular form of the adjective *secundus,* agreeing with the feminine noun *pars. Secunda* alone was eventually used as a noun for the second subdivision of a degree and is the source of our word *second.* In the sense "coming after the first," *second* enters English in the thirteenth century, from Old French *second,* derived from the Latin word *secundus.*

seersucker

Through its etymology, *seersucker* gives us a glimpse into the history of India. The word came into English from Hindi *śīrsakar,* which had been borrowed from the Persian compound *shīroshakar,* meaning literally "milk and sugar" but used figuratively for a striped linen garment. The Persian word *shakar,* "sugar," in turn came from Sanskrit *śarkarā.* The linguistic borrowings here reflect a broader history of cultural borrowing. In the sixth century the Persians borrowed not only the word for "sugar" from India but sugar itself. During and after Tamerlane's invasion of India in the late fourteenth century, opportunities for borrowing Persian things and words such as *shīroshakar* were widespread, since Tamerlane incorporated Persia as well as India into his empire. It then remained for the English to borrow from an Indian language the material and its name *seersucker* (first recorded in 1722 in the form *Sea Sucker*) during the eighteenth century, when the East India Company and England were moving toward imperial supremacy in India.

sequoia

The giant sequoia acquired its name from a giant of another sort. George Guess (to most Americans of his time) or Sogwali (to his fellow Cherokees) was called *Sequoya* by missionaries. He devised a way of writing the Cherokee language, probably completing his work in 1821, and thus helped unify the members of his tribe. Stephan Ladislaus Endlicher, a nineteenth-century Hungarian ethnologist and botanist, probably knew of this achievement, and so used Sequoya's name for the genus of the redwood (*Sequoia sempervirens*). The scientific name of another large tree, the giant sequoia, is *Sequoiadendron giganteum*.

Sequoya's final writing system, known as a syllabary, consisted of eighty-five characters

serendipity

What do you call the faculty of making fortuitous and unexpected discoveries by accident? We are indebted to the English author Horace Walpole for coining the answer: *serendipity.* In a letter of January 28, 1754—one of the three thousand or more that he wrote and on which his literary reputation primarily rests—Walpole says that "this discovery, indeed, is almost of that kind which I call Serendipity, a very expressive word." Walpole formed the word on an old name for Sri Lanka, *Serendip.* (This designation derives from one of its names in Sanskrit, *Siṃhala-dvīpaḥ,* literally "Siṃhala-Island.") Walpole explained that this name was part of the title of "a silly fairy tale, called *The Three Princes of Serendip*: as their highnesses travelled, they were always making discoveries, by accidents and sagacity, of things which they were not in quest of . . . One of the most remarkable instances of this *accidental sagacity* (for you must observe that no discovery of a thing you *are* looking for, comes under this description) was of my Lord Shaftsbury [Anthony Ashley Cooper], who happening to dine at Lord Chancellor Clarendon's [Edward Hyde], found out the marriage of the Duke of York [later James II] and Mrs. Hyde [Anne Hyde, Clarendon's daughter], by the respect with which her mother [Frances Aylesbury Hyde] treated her at table."

shadow

Shade and *shadow* are not only related in meaning; historically they are the same word. In Old English, the ancestor of Modern English spoken a thousand years ago, nouns were inflected; that is, they had different forms depending on how they were used in a sentence. One of the inflected forms of the Old English noun *sceadu,* translatable as either "shade" or "shadow," was *sceaduwe*; this form was used when the word was preceded by a preposition (as in *in sceaduwe,* "in the shade, in shadow"). As time went on these two forms of the same word were interpreted as two separate words. The same thing happened to other Old English words, too: our *mead* and *meadow* come from two different case forms of the same Old English word for "meadow."

sherbet

Although the word ꜱherbet has been in the English language for several centuries (it was first recorded in 1603), it has not always referred to what one normally thinks of as sherbet. *Sherbet* came into English from Ottoman Turkish ꜱherbet or Persian ꜱharbat, both going back to Arabic ꜱarba, "drink." The Turkish and Persian words referred to a beverage of sweetened, diluted fruit juice that was popular in the Middle East and imitated in Europe. In Europe ꜱherbet eventually came to refer to a carbonated drink. Because the original Middle Eastern drink contained fruit and was often cooled with snow, ꜱherbet was applied to a frozen dessert (first recorded in 1891). It is distinguished slightly from ꜱorbet, which can also mean "a fruit-flavored ice served between courses of a meal." *Sorbet* (first recorded in English in 1585) goes back through French (ꜱorbet) and then Italian (ꜱorbetto) to the same Turkish ꜱherbet that gave us ꜱherbet.

short shrift

To be given short shrift is not the blessing it once was. The source of our verb ꜱhrive (ꜱhrove, ꜱhriven) and noun ꜱhrift, which have technical meanings from ecclesiastical Latin, is Classical Latin ꜱcrībere, "to write." The Old English form of the verb was ꜱcrīfan, "to decree, decree after judgment, impose a penance upon (a penitent), hear the confession of." The past participle of ꜱcrīfan is ꜱcrifen, our ꜱhriven. The noun ꜱhrift, "penance; absolution," comes from Old English ꜱcrift with the same meaning, which comes from ꜱcrīptuꜱ, the perfect passive participle of ꜱcrībere, and means "what is written," or, to use the Latin word, "what is prescribed." Theologians and confessors viewed the sacrament of penance as a prescription that cured a moral illness. In early medieval times penances were long and arduous—lengthy pilgrimages and even lifelong exile were not uncommon—and had to be performed *before* absolution, not after as today. However, less demanding penances could be given in extreme situations; *short shrift* was a brief penance given to a person condemned to death so that absolution could be granted before execution.

skirt

The relationship between a skirt and a shirt is not just a matter of fashion but also a matter of etymology. The connections between England and Scandinavia in peace and war during the Middle Ages were always close, and the interaction between them added greatly to the vocabulary of English. Some words borrowed from Scandinavian did not completely supplant the native words with which they shared a common Germanic ancestor, but existed alongside them. *Shirt* and *skirt* are one such pair. Both are descended from the Germanic word **skurtaz,* which became *scyrte* in Old English and *skyrta* in Old Icelandic, a dialect of Old Norse. *Skyrta* meant "a shirt or kind of knee-length tunic." Our word *skirt,* borrowed from Old Norse, came to denote the lower part of a garment or a lower garment by itself. Old English *scyrte* denoted a short garment of some sort, and its descendant *shirt* referred in Middle English to an undergarment worn on the upper part of the body. The downward drift of *skirt* and the upward hike of *shirt* fits with the fact that the original Germanic word denoted a short undergarment (wearable by itself in warm weather) that covered both parts of the body.

slave

The derivation of the word *slave* encapsulates a bit of European history and explains why the two words *slave* and *Slav* are so similar; they are, in fact, historically identical. The word *slave* first appeared in English around 1290, spelled *sclave*. The spelling was based on Old French *esclave* from Medieval Latin *sclavus*, "Slav, slave," first recorded around 800. *Sclavus* came from Byzantine Greek *sklabos*, pronounced (skläh-vos) and meaning "Slav," which appeared around 580. *Sklavos* approximated the Slavs' own name for themselves, the *Slověnci*, surviving in English *Slovene* and *Slovenian*. The spelling of English *slave*, closer to its original Slavic form, first appears in English in 1538. Slavs became slaves around the beginning of the ninth century when the Holy Roman Empire tried to stabilize a German-Slav frontier. By the twelfth century stabilization had given way to wars of expansion and extermination that did not end until the Poles crushed the Teutonic Knights at Grunwald in 1410.

As far as the Slavs' own self-designation goes, its meaning is, understandably, better than "slave"; it comes from the Indo-European root **kleu-*, whose basic meaning is "to hear" and which occurs in many derivatives meaning "renown, fame." The Slavs are thus "the famous people." Slavic names ending in *-slav* incorporate the same word, such as Czech Bohuslav, "God's fame," Russian Mstislav, "vengeful fame," and Polish Stanislaw, "famous for withstanding (enemies)."

sleuth

Tracking down the history of the word *sleuth* requires a bit of etymological sleuthing. The immediate ancestor of our word is the compound *sleuthhound,* "a dog, such as a bloodhound, used for tracking or pursuing." This term took on a figurative sense, "tracker, pursuer," which is closely related to the sense "detective." From *sleuthhound* came the shortened form *sleuth,* recorded in the sense "detective" as early as 1872. The first part of the term *sleuthhound* means "track, path, trail" and is first recorded in a Middle English work written probably around 1200. Sleuth is the Scots development of Middle English *sloth,* a borrowing of the Old Norse word *slōdh,* "a track or trail."

slogan

Advertising slogans declare the virtues of one or another product, reminiscent in a trivial way of the history of the once proud word *slogan. Slogan* is an adaptation of the Scots Gaelic word *sluagh-ghairm,* "war cry," from *sluagh,* "army," and *gairm,* "shout, cry." Our word was first used in Scots to denote such a cry. Sir George Mackenzie's *Science of Heraldry* (circa 1680), for example, states that "the Name of Hume have for their Slughorn (or Slogan, as our Southern Shires terme it) a *Hume, a Hume." Slogan* went on to develop the senses "a rallying cry; a word or phrase expressing the aims of a person or group."

smog

New phenomena require new words, so it is not surprising that *smog* is a relatively recent coinage. The word followed the phenomenon by perhaps half a century, for air pollution was first noticed during the Industrial Revolution. The word *smog* is first recorded in 1905 in a newspaper report of a meeting of the Public Health Congress. Dr. H. A. des Vœux gave a paper entitled "Fog and Smoke," in which, in the words of the *Daily Graphic* of July 26, "he said it required no science to see that there was something produced in great cities which was not found in the country, and that was smoky fog, or what was known as 'smog.'" The next day the *Globe* remarked that "Dr. des Vœux did a public service in coining a new word for the London fog."

soccer

Soccer, the most popular team sport everywhere except in the United States, was invented in England. The word *soccer* is a shortening and alteration of the official name of the game, *Association Football,* that is, football as played under the rules of the Football Association of England, founded in 1863. The abbreviation *Assoc.* for *Association* was shortened and the suffix -er added. This suffix is found elsewhere in British public school and university slang, as in *footer* for *football, rugger* for *rugby.*

soldier

Why do soldiers fight? One answer is hidden in the word *soldier* itself. Its first recorded occurrence is found in a work composed around 1300, the word having come into Middle English as *soudier* from Old French *soudoior* and Anglo-Norman *soudeour*. The Old French word, first recorded in the twelfth century, was derived from *sol* or *soud*, Old French forms of modern French *sou*, an old kind of coin. The name of this coin derives from

the obverse (left) and reverse sides of a c. 475 B.C. Roman gold solidus that was struck for the last Emperor of the Western Roman Empire, Romulus Augustulus

Latin *solidus*, a widely-used gold coin. Old French *sol* referred to a coin and also meant "pay," and a *soudoior* was a man who fought for pay. This was a concept worth expressing in an era when many men were not paid for fighting but did it in service to a feudal superior. Thus *soldier* is parallel to the word *mercenary,* which goes back to Latin *mercēnārius,* derived from *mercēs,* "pay," and meaning "working for pay." The word could also be used as a noun, one of whose senses was "a soldier of fortune."

soothsayer

The truth is not always soothing, but our verb *soothe* is related to *soothsayer,* the word for one who tells the truth, especially beforehand. The archaic adjective and noun *sooth,* "true, truth," comes from the Old English adjective and noun *sōth* with the same meanings. The Old English form derives from Germanic *ᴤanth-az, "true," which comes from Indo-European *ᴤont-, one of the participles from the Indo-European root -eᴤ-, "to be": the truth is that which is. Old English also formed a verb from ᴤōth, namely ᴤōthian, "to confirm to be true." This is the ancestor of soothe; its meaning changed from "to assent to be true, say 'yes' to" to "to humor by assenting, placate." Doing the latter on occasion requires something less than the truth.

south

Though a south-facing house on the north side of a street sometimes gets more sun, etymologically speaking, the sunny side of the street is the south side. "South" in Old English was ᴤūth. This came from an earlier *ᴤunth, from a still earlier *ᴤunthaz, "sunny," whose first element, *ᴤun-, meant "sun." As the first word in compounds, Old English ᴤūth was subject to shortening, showing up in Modern English with a short rather than long u. This is seen in place names like Suffolk, where the "south folk" were (compare Norfolk), Sutton, "south town," and Suᴤᴤex, the location of the "South Saxons" (whose eastern and western cousins were located in Eᴤᴤex and Weᴤᴤex, respectively).

See also **Sunday**.

speak

Because English is a Germanic language, first-year German produces many moments of recognition for English speakers and several puzzles. For example, when we learn the verb ᴤprechen, ᴤprach, geᴤprochen, "to speak," and the noun Sprache, "speech, language," we wonder whether we lost the *r* or the Germans put one in. Sounds are more often lost than added in language change, and this is the case here. In Old English the verb was *ſprecan,* the noun *ſprǣc,* both with an *r* as in German (and in the other Germanic languages). The *r*-less forms began to appear in the south of England and became common in the eleventh century; the forms with *r* disappeared completely by the middle of the twelfth. A similar loss of *r* after a consonant and before a vowel occurred in the Middle English noun *prang* and its variant *pronge,* "severe pain, sharp pain." *Pronge* survives today as *prong* (of a pitchfork, for example). The plural of *prang* appears in a poem composed about 1400 as *panguſ,* "sharp stabs of pain," and survives today as *pang,* "sharp, stabbing pain."

spell

Two of the words spelled *ſpell*—the noun *ſpell,* "an incantation," and the verb *ſpell,* "to give the letters of a word in proper order"—are etymologically related. Both words derive from the Indo-European root **ſpel-,* which means "to say aloud, recite, pronounce." The noun *ſpell* comes from Old English *ſpell,* which had a much wider meaning than its modern descendant; it was used with the senses "discourse," "narration," "sermon," and "story." In fact Old English *ſpell* appears as the second element of *goſpel,* meaning literally "good tidings." The meaning "incantation" did not appear until late medieval or early modern times, and the word *ſpellbound* is a compound that developed from this sense of *ſpell.* The verb *ſpell,* "to write the letters forming a word," is borrowed from Old French *eſpeller,* "to interpret, explain, spell." The

French word came from a Germanic derivative, *ʂpel-
lōn, of the same Indo-European root as the English
noun ʂpell. See also **glamour.**

spoof

We are indebted to a British comedian for the word
ʂpoof. Sometime in the nineteenth century
Arthur Roberts (1852-1933) invented a game called
Spoof, which involved trickery and nonsense. The first
recorded reference to the game in 1884 refers to its
revival. It was not long before the word ʂpoof took on
the general sense "nonsense, trickery," first recorded
in 1889. The verb ʂpoof is first recorded in 1889 as
well, in the sense "to deceive." These senses are now
less widely used than the noun sense "a light parody
or satirical imitation," first recorded in 1958, and the
verb sense "to satirize gently," first recorded in 1927.

spree

A spending spree seems a far cry from a cattle raid,
yet etymologists have suggested that the word
ʂpree comes from the Scots word ʂpreath, "cattle
raid." The word ʂpree is first recorded in a poem in
Scots dialect in 1804 in the sense of "a lively outing."
This sense is closely connected with a sense recorded
soon afterward (in 1811), "a drinking bout," while the
familiar sense "an overindulgence in an activity," as
in a ʂpending ʂpree, is recorded in 1849. Scots and
Irish dialects also have a sense "a fight," which may
help connect the word and the sense "lively outing"
with the Scots word ʂpreath, meaning variously,
"booty," "cattle taken as spoils," "a herd of cattle tak-
en in a raid," and "cattle raid." The Scots word comes

from Irish and Scottish Gaelic *spréidh,* "cattle," which in turn ultimately comes from Latin *praeda,* "booty." This last link reveals both the importance of the Latin language to Gaelic and a connection between cattle and plunder in earlier Irish and Scottish societies.

starve

And loveth hym [Christ], the which that right for love
Upon a crois [cross], oure soules for to beye [save],
First starf [died], and roos, and sit in hevene above.
—Chaucer, *Troilus and Criseyde,* circa 1380

The verb *starve* is descended from the Old English word *steorfan,* which simply meant "to die," the sense illustrated in the quotation given from Chaucer (containing a past tense, *starf,* of *sterven,* the Middle English descendant of Old English *steorfan*). Only in modern times did the verb develop more specific meanings. In Standard English, *starve* became restricted to the meaning "to die from lack of food." In northern English dialects *starve* also acquired the sense "to die of cold," but this usage no longer occurs in Standard English. Similarly, in many northern English dialects, a verb *clem* or *clam,* instead of the verb *starve,* is used in the meaning "to die of hunger."

story

The history of *story* and the story of *history* are related. Both words go back to the Latin word *historia,* in turn borrowed from Greek *historia,* which meant primarily "the recording of past events," but which could also designate any narrative, factual or fictional. *History* was borrowed into English directly from the Latin word, as well as from an Old French intermediary, *estoire* or *estorie,* also descended from Latin *historia.* But *story* came into English from the Old French intermediary alone, during the thirteenth century. At first English *story* referred, as did its Old French predecessor, principally to narrations of actual past events, or to what were then perceived as factual accounts (although, of course, the medieval sense of "fact" does not always conform to modern standards of verification). Already during the Middle English period *story,* like the Latin word *historia,* had a secondary application to any relation of events, real or imagined, intended for entertainment, which emerged in the fourteenth century. Gradually *story* shifted toward the sense of "fiction" generally associated with it today, leaving to *history* the sense "a remembered or researched account of observable phenomena." The two can still be used interchangeably in some contexts, but usually they are differentiated into virtually opposite senses.

The origin of the word *story,* "level of a building," is obscure, but it is perhaps the same word as *story,* "tale." Medieval churches and other large buildings were often adorned with series of stained-glass windows or tiers of sculpture that illustrated stories, as from the Bible or the lives of saints. The word *story* was perhaps transferred from the tale being told to the level of the building telling it.

suede

The word *suede* originates in the phrase *Suède gloves,* from the French phrase *gants de Suède,* literally "gloves from Sweden." In French *gants de Suède* denoted gloves made of undressed kidskin. English *suede* was extracted from the phrase *Suède gloves* and developed the meaning "undressed kidskin," then "leather with a napped surface."

sunbeam

Though the period of European history from the fifth to the eleventh century is often called the Dark Ages, writers and scholars of the time in fact did much to preserve and extend the light of civilization. A minor but felicitous contribution to the English language from this period is the word *sunbeam,* which is believed to have entered English in the ninth century through the work of Alfred the Great. A scholar as well as a king, Alfred undertook and oversaw the translation of a number of Latin works into the English of his time, now known as Old English. Among these was *The Ecclesiastical History of the English People,* a work composed by the Venerable Bede. The Latin phrase *columna lūcis,* which we would today translate as "a column of light," occurs several times in this work. Since the Old English translator did not have the word *column* in his vocabulary, he used *bēam,* which meant "a tree" or "a building post made from a tree" (our modern word *beam*). *Columna lūcis* thus became *sunnebēam,* or "sun post," which survives as our *sunbeam.* Though perhaps less stately than "column of light," *sunbeam* has brightened our language. From it the word *beam* alone came to mean "a ray or rays of light"; it subsequently became a verb meaning "to radiate." It now allows us not only to beam with pride or happiness but also to beam our broadcasts around the earth and even to the stars.

Sunday

Sunday comes from Old English *Sunnandæg*, an ancient translation of Latin *Diēs Sōlis*, "Sun's Day." The form *Sōlis* in this phrase is the possessive case of the Latin word for "sun," *sōl*. In fact, both English *sun* and Latin *sol* descend from the same Proto-Indo-European word, **sāwel-*, "sun." The element **-el-* was originally a suffix and alternated with **-en-*, yielding the variant forms **s(u)wen-* and an even more reduced **sun-* in the Germanic languages. Latin, however, shows another variant form, **səwōl-*, which develops into *sōl*. We can see this in English *solar*, from Latin *sōlāris*, "of the sun." The English word *solstice* contains Latin *sōl* and the element *-stitium*, "a stoppage," also seen, for example, in English *armistice.* The solstices are the two times in the year when northward or southward drift of the path of the sun through the sky stops and begins to return in the opposite direction.

In Greek, a Proto-Indo-European *s* became *h* at the beginning of a word before a vowel, and the derived form **sāwel-yo-* shows up as *hēlios*, "sun." The Greek word may be familiar to you as the name of the sun god, but it has also served as the source of the word *helium.* Researchers analyzing light from the outer layers of the sun during a solar eclipse in 1868 found evidence for a new element, unknown on our planet up until that time. The new element was named after the Greek god Helios, and it was not until 1895 that it was finally isolated on Earth.

For another appearance of the Proto-Indo-European word for "sun," *saəwel-,* in English see the word **south**.

supercilious

The English word *supercilious* ultimately derives from the Latin word *supercilium,* "eyebrow." *Supercilium* came to mean "the eyebrow as used in frowning and expressing sternness, gravity, or haughtiness." From there it developed the senses "stern looks, severity, haughty demeanor, pride." The derived Latin adjective *superciliōsus* meant "full of stern or disapproving looks, censorious, haughty, disdainful," as it has since it entered English as *supercilious* in the sixteenth century. The *super-* in the Latin word *supercilium* means "above," and *cilium* was the Latin word for "eyelid." In the Romance languages this word developed into the word for "eyelash." This development is probably reflected in the scientific use in English of the word *cilium,* whose plural is *cilia. Cilia* are minute hairlike appendages of cells or unicellular organisms that move in unison in order to bring about the movement of the cell or of the surrounding medium.

surly

That the word *surly* means "churlish" nicely indicates its fall in status. *Churlish* derives from the word *churl,* which in its Old English form *ceorl* meant "a man without rank, a member of the lowest rank of freemen," as well as "peasant." In Old English *ceorl* may have been a term of contempt; it certainly became one in Middle English, where *cherl* meant "base fellow, boor," with *churlish* descending in meaning accordingly. *Surly,* on the other hand, started life at the top of the scale. In Middle English and early Modern English, *surly* was only one spelling for this word; another, *sirly,* reflects its origin in *sir,* the term of

honor for a knight or for a person of rank or importance. *Sirly,* the form under which the early spellings
of the word are entered in the *Oxford English Dictionary,* first meant "lordly." *Surly,* entered as a separate
word in the *OED* and first recorded in 1566, meant perhaps "lordly, majestic" in its earliest use and was subsequently used in the sense "masterful, imperious,
arrogant." As the gloss "arrogant" makes clear, the
word *surly* could have a negative sense, and it is this
area of meaning that is responsible for the current
"churlish" sense of the word.

syphilis

In 1530 Girolamo Fracastoro, a physician, astronomer, and poet of Verona, published a poem entitled
"Syphilis, sive Morbus Gallicus," translated as
"Syphilis, or the French Disease." In Fracastoro's
poem the name of this dreaded venereal disease is an
altered form of the name of the hero Syphilus, a shep-
herd who is supposed to have been the first victim of
the disease. Where the name *Syphilus* itself came
from is not known for certain, but it has been suggested that Fracastoro borrowed it from a work of the
Roman poet Ovid, *Metamorphoses.* In Ovid's work
Sipylus (spelled *Siphylus* in some manuscripts) is the
oldest son of Niobe, who lived not far from Mount
Sipylon in Asia Minor. Fracastoro's poem about
Syphilus was modeled on the story of Niobe, a woman
who boasted that she more children than Leto, the
mother of Apollo and Artemis, and was punished. Fracastoro went on to use the term *syphilis* again in his
medical treatise *De Contagione,* published in 1546.
The word that Fracastoro used in Latin was eventually
borrowed into English, being first recorded in 1718.

The Greek word *surinx,* to which our word *syringe* goes back, meant "panpipe," a wind instrument consisting of a series of pipes or reeds played by blowing across the open ends, and "anything like a pipe," including things such as pores or even the passage through an elephant's trunk. *Syringe* was first applied to "a cylindrical tube for extracting or ejecting liquid" in the fifteenth century.

A *panpipe* gets its name from the Greek god Pan, patron of shepherds, who was depicted as half-man, half-goat. He was often shown holding a rustic panpipe, and the Roman poet Ovid tells a pretty fable of its origin in the same work mentioned in the previous note, *Metamorphoses.* Pan desired a beautiful nymph, Syrinx, who nevertheless sought to avoid his embrace. She fled and he pursued her.

a South American-style panpipe

Just as he was about to catch her, she was transformed into reeds, which sighed mournfully. Pan took the reeds and made the panpipe from them, that his lips might at last touch the nymph who had escaped him.

taboo

Among the many discoveries of Captain James Cook was a linguistic one, the term *taboo.* In a journal entry from 1777, Cook says this word "has a very comprehensive meaning; but, in general, signifies that a thing is forbidden . . . When any thing is forbidden to be eat, or made use of, they say, that it is *taboo.*" Cook was in the Friendly Islands (now Tonga) at the time, so even though similar words occur in other Polynesian languages, the form *taboo* from Tongan *tabu* is the one we have borrowed. The Tongans used *tabu* as an adjective. Cook, besides borrowing the word into English, also made it into a noun referring to the prohibition itself and a verb meaning "to make someone or something taboo." From its origins in Polynesia the word *taboo* has traveled as widely as Cook himself and is now used throughout the English-speaking world.

tadpole

The word *tadpole* is an old compound word whose meaning is no longer transparent. *Tad* is an alternative form of the word *toad*. *Pole,* recorded from the sixteenth to the nineteenth century, is a form of our word *poll,* meaning "head." *Tadpole* thus refers to "a toad that is all head," and the compound first appeared in English in the fifteenth century. *Poll* still means "head" (as in *poll tax*, sometimes also called a *head tax*) and also "a survey of public opinion" or "the place where votes are cast," among other senses more familiar to us than "head." *Poll* probably developed these senses at least partly through the notion of the head as the prominent part of a person in a crowd, a part that could be counted. A similar notion is found in the phrase "a head of cattle."

talent

The word *talent* entered English with several meanings, from several directions. It ultimately derives from the Greek word *talanton,* "balance, weight, talent (an ancient unit of weight), a sum of money," borrowed with that meaning into Latin as *talentum.* The Latin word entered Old English as *talente,* denoting the unit of measure and currency. Later it also entered Middle English with the sense "tendency, disposition, natural ability" from the Old French development, *talent,* of the Latin word. The meaning "ability, aptitude" comes from the metaphorical use of *talanton* in the parable recorded in Matthew 25:14-30. This parable tells how a master entrusted money to each of his three servants in his absence. The servant with five talents and the one with two talents both doubled their money and were rewarded on their master's return. The servant who had been given one talent buried the money and returned only the original amount, and for this he was reproached. The parable was interpreted as an exhortation to improve the natural gifts and abilities that God has given.

tantalize

The gods and heroes of ancient Greece and Rome still play a lively role in our language and culture, despite the dominant role of Christianity in western civilization over the past fifteen hundred years. *Tantalize,* for example, comes from *Tantalus,* the name of a legendary king of Lydia. He enjoyed the privilege of dining with gods, and various stories are told about how he offended the gods or abused this privilege. According to one tale, he stole the food of the gods, the divine nectar and ambrosia, and gave it to mortals. In another story, he kills his son Pelops and serves him to the gods in order to test them and see whether they can detect the offense. The gods therefore condemned him to suffer eternal hunger and thirst in the presence of food and drink that remained just out of his reach. The verb *tantalize* means basically "to cause to suffer the torments of Tantalus," although in a much milder form. *Tantalize* is first recorded in the

sixteenth century, during a resurgence of interest in classical texts and translation of those texts into English for the first time.

tattoo

Although the practice of tattooing the body is very old, the English word *tattoo* is relatively new. The explorer Captain James Cook (who also gave us the word *taboo*) introduced the word to English speakers in his account of a voyage around the world from 1768 to 1771. Like *taboo, tattoo* comes from Polynesian languages such as Tahitian and Samoan. The earliest use of the verb *tattoo* in English is found in an entry for 1769 in Cook's diary. Sailors introduced the custom into Europe from the Pacific societies in which it was practiced, and it has remained associated with sailors, although many landlubbers now get tattoos as well.

tavern

Investigating the etymology of words will sometimes reveal strange bedfellows, such as *tavern* and *tabernacle.* Both of these English words are ultimately derived from the Latin word *taberna,* "a hut or booth," a term that probably evolved in Latin from the word *trabs,* "a building post or timber." *Tavern* entered English during the thirteenth century by way of Old French, where the Latin word *taberna* had developed into *taverne.* In Middle English the word meant primarily, as it does today, "an establishment dispensing alcoholic beverages." *Tabernacle,* similarly, was borrowed into Middle English either from Old French *tabernacle,* an adaptation of the Latin word *tabernāculum,* or directly from this Latin source. *Tabernāculum,* a diminutive form of *taberna,* that is, "a small hut or booth, tent," had been used in Late Latin to name the tentlike moveable sanctuary which contained the Ark of the Covenant in the Old Testament. English borrowed the term in this context and has continued to use it nearly exclusively in religious senses. The connection between *tavern* and *tabernacle* is no longer evident, but they are etymological kin nonetheless.

tawdry

The word *tawdry* is an alteration of the name of Saint Audry, also known as Saint Etheldreda. Saint Audrey was queen of the Anglo-Saxon kingdom of Northumbria and founder of an important monastery in Ely, England. She died in 679 of a throat tumor, supposedly because she delighted in fancy necklaces as a young woman. There was an annual fair at Ely in her honor, at which cloth neckbands or neckties, called *tawdry laces,* were sold. The word *tawdry,* meaning "gaudy and cheap," became an adjective in its own right by the sixteenth century.

tea

"Here thou, great Anna! whom three realms obey, / Dost sometimes counsel take–and sometimes tea." When Alexander Pope wrote these lines from *The Rape of the Lock* in 1714, *tea* still rhymed with *obey.* This was true of many words spelled with *ea,* and it was just about in Pope's time that nearly all these words started changing their pronunciation from (ā) to (ē), as in our modern pronunciation of *tea,* (tē). Most Modern English words whose main vowel sound is spelled *ea* were pronounced with long vowels in Middle and Old English. Many of these vowels were shortened in the sixteenth and seventeenth centuries to their modern pronunciations, as in our words *dead* and *sweat.* But those words that were pronounced with an (ā) sound in Middle English did not undergo this sound change and kept their long vowels, undergoing the further change in Pope's time to the modern "long e" sound. There were several exceptions to this last sound change, most notably the words *break, great,* and *steak.* Interestingly, the old pronunciation is also retained in Irish family names, such as *Reagan, Shea, Beatty,* and *Yeats* (in contrast to British family names such as *Keats*).

telephone

The everyday word *telephone* illustrates some important linguistic and etymological processes. First, the noun *telephone* is one of a class of technological and scientific words made up of combining forms derived from classical languages, in this case *tele-* and *-phone. Tele-* is from the Greek combining form *tēle-* or *tēl-,* a form of *tēle,* meaning "afar, far off," while *-phone* is from Greek *phōnē,* "sound, voice." Such words derived from classical languages can be put together in French or German, for example, as well as in English. Which language actually gave birth to them cannot always be determined. In this case French *téléphone* (about 1830) seems to have priority. The word was used for an acoustic apparatus, as it originally was in English (1844). Alexander Graham Bell appropriated the word for his invention in 1876, and in 1877 we have the first instance of the verb *telephone,* meaning "to speak to by telephone." The verb is an example of a linguistic process called *functional* *shift.* This occurs when a word develops a new part of speech: a noun is used as a verb (*to date*), a verb as a noun (*a break*), an adjective as a noun (*the rich*), a noun as an adjective (*a stone wall*), or even an adjective as a verb (*to round*). When we *telephone* a friend, we are changing the syntactic function of *telephone*, making it a verb rather than a noun.

temple

Words that are identical in form do not always derive from the same source, and when they have different sources they are usually considered different words. The *temple* that refers to a place of worship, for example, does not have the same origin as the *temple* that refers to a side of the forehead. The *temple* where one worships comes from Latin *templum,* itself derived from the Indo-European root **tem-,* "to cut, divide." Latin *templum* probably referred originally to the fact that temples were on sacred ground that was "divided" (or separated) from ordinary ground. The *temple* of the head comes from the Latin word *tempus,* "temple of the head." Its origin is not certain; some have thought it to be a special use of the homonymous word *tempus,* "time," as a translation of Greek *kairios,* "(proper) time, opportunity, vital spot," but there is no hard evidence for this. What is known, and not uninteresting in itself, is how *tempus* eventually became *temple* in English. In Latin, the plural, *tempora,* was more frequently used than the singular *tempus* (it being more common to talk about paired body parts together rather than singly). There was a large class of Latin nouns ending in *-a* in the singular, and this led to a reinterpretation of *tempora* as a singular in later Latin, where it was also altered to **tempula.* This became *temple* in Old French, whence English *temple* (of the head) was borrowed, first appearing in 1310.

The classical Latin form survives in the English adjective *temporal* (as in *temporal bone* or *temporal muscle*).

testis

The resemblance between *testimony*, *testify*, *testis*, and *testicle* shows an etymological relationship, but linguists are not agreed on precisely how English *testis* came to have its current meaning. The Latin *testis* originally meant "witness," and etymologically means "third (person) standing by": the *te-* part comes from an older *tri-*, a combining form of the word for "three," and *-stis* is a noun derived from the Indo-European root *stā-* meaning "stand." How this also came to refer to the body part(s) is disputed. An old theory has it that the Romans placed their right hands on their testicles and swore by them before giving testimony in court. Another theory says that the sense "testicle" in Latin *testis* is due to a calque, or loan translation, from Greek. The Greek noun *parastatēs* means "defender (in law), supporter" (from *para-*, "by, alongside," as in *paramilitary*, and *-statēs*, from *histanai*, "to stand"). In the dual number, used in many languages for naturally occurring, contrasting, or complementary pairs such as hands, eyes, and ears, *parastatēs* had the technical medical sense "testicles," that is "two glands side by side." The Romans simply took this sense of *parastatēs* and added it to *testis*, the Latin word for "legal supporter, witness."

To the casual eye *testy* and *heady* seem to have no connection; a more thoughtful examination reveals that both words refer to the head. The *head* in *heady* is easy to see in both the form and meanings of the word. The earliest sense, first recorded in a work composed before 1382, is "headlong, headstrong," which is clearly a "head" sense; but so is the better-known current sense "apt to go to the head, intoxicating." To see the *head* in *testy*, we must look back to the Old French word *testu*, "headstrong," the source of our word. *Testu* is derived from the Old French word *teste*, "head" (modern French *tête*). In English, *testy* developed another sense, "aggressive, contentious," which passed into the sense we are familiar with today, "irritable."

they

Incredible as it may seem, the English pronoun *they* is not really an English pronoun. *They* comes from Old Norse and is a classic example of the profound impact of that language on English: because pronouns are among the most basic elements of a language, it is rare for them to be replaced by borrowings from foreign sources. The Old Norse pronouns *their, theira, theim* worked their way south from the Danelaw, the region governed by the Old Norse-speaking invaders of England, and first appeared in English about 1200, gradually replacing the Old English words *hīe, hīora, him*. The nominative or subject case (modern English *they*) seems to have spread first. William Caxton, who brought the printing press to England, used *they, hir, hem* in his earlier printed works (after 1475) and *thei, their, theim* in his later ones. This is clear evidence of the spread of these Norse forms southward, since Caxton did not speak northern English natively (he was born in Westminster). The native English objective case of the third person plural, *him* or *hem*, may well survive, at least colloquially, in Modern English *'em*, as in "Give 'em back!"

thimble

A thimble belongs on the thumb; the history of the word leaves no doubt about that. The Old English word *þȳmel*, the ancestor of *thimble*, is derived from Old English *þūma*, the ancestor of our word *thumb*. (The letter *þ* is called *thorn* and was used in Old and Middle English for the sounds now usually represented by *th* in modern spelling. The suffix *-el*, used for appliances or instruments, survives as *-le* in *thimble* and in similar words such as *ladle* and *bridle*. (The *b* after the *m* in *thimble* apparently developed sometime during the fifteenth century.) The earliest sense of *thimble* was "a covering for the thumb or finger." In Middle English *thymel* came to mean "a sheath of leather that protects the finger pushing the needle in sewing." Leather has since been replaced by metal, ceramic, and plastic.

third

Every native speaker knows that the cardinal *three* and the ordinal *third* are closely related, but many may wonder why the *r* comes before the vowel in the former and after in the latter. What we have here is metathesis, the switching of the order of two sounds. This is a common occurrence in languages, and especially so in English with the consonant *r*. In Old English, *three* was *thrīe,* and *third* was *thridda. Thridda* would have given us *thrid* in Modern English except for the metathesis of *r* and *i.* This metathesis began in Old English times in Northumbria: *thridda* appears as *thirdda* in Northumbrian manuscripts. The metathesis spread south during Middle English times and also affected many other words, including *bird* (originally *bridd* in Old English and in Chaucer's Middle English) and *nostril,* literally "nose hole" (from Old English *thyrl*). Metathesis even produced the curious form *throp* from *thorp,* "village," which survives in the proper name *Winthrop.*

Thursday

Thursday is Thor's day. This Germanic god was known as *Thunor,* literally "thunder," and *Thūrr* in Old English, and as *Thōrr* in Old Norse, and it is the Old Norse form that is generally most familiar today. Thor wielded the thunderbolt to destroy the monsters menacing the gods and men. In this he most closely resembled the Roman god Jove or Jupiter (whose etymological cousin is actually the god Tyr, see **Tuesday**). When the Germanic peoples adopted the Roman week, *Diēs Jovis,* "Jove's (or Jupiter's) day," was given to Thor and became *Thunresdæg,* literally "Thunder's Day." *Thōrr* and *thunder* both ultimately go back to Germanic **thunaraz.* The Germanic form

*thunaraz also hides in the English word *blunder-buss,* indicating an old-fashioned type of gun with a wide muzzle, and now often used metaphorically in the sense "a clumsy person." This word is an alteration of Dutch *donderbuss,* literally "thunder-gun." The *d* has been changed to *bl* in English, probably under the influence of *blunder,* since a *donderbuss* would spray shot pell-mell over a wide range.

The Indo-European root of the words *Thōrr* and *thunder* is *ʌtenə-,* "to thunder." We can be sure the Indo-Europeans knew thunderstorms in their homeland, wherever it was. This root appeared in Latin and the Germanic languages as *ten-,* without its initial *ʌ* (as occasionally happens with other roots beginning with *ʌ*). In Latin, the root took the form *ton-.* English *ʌtun* and *aʌtoniʌh* are both from Old French *eʌtoner,* formed from Latin *tonāre,* "to thunder." The metaphor is familiar from the English expression *thunder-ʌtruck.* The verb *detonate* ultimately derives from the Latin verb *dētonāre,* "to thunder forth, express in thunderous tones."

We also hear the root *ʌtenə-* reverberate in the word *tornado.* This word is an alteration of Spanish *tronada,* "thunderstorm," derived from *tronar,* "to thunder." *Tornado* was originally used by British voyagers to describe the violent storms of the tropical Atlantic, and it only later came to mean the whirlwinds occurring in the American Midwest. The voyagers heard the Spanish word and altered its form by folk etymology with the Spanish verb *tornar,* "to turn." *Tronada* and *tronar* are also from Latin *tonāre,* "to thunder." The intrusive *r* in the first syllable of Spanish words comes from the noun *tronido,* "thunder," the result of a metathesis of Latin *tonitruʌ.* After the *r* was moved around by English speakers, the word *tornado* later turned around and was reborrowed into Spanish. *Tornado,* a word for the most powerful winds on earth, is a worthy addition to the Indo-European family of Thor.

ticket

The resemblance in form between the words *ticket* and *etiquette* is not accidental; both have the same ultimate source, Old French *estiquet*. But because these words were borrowed into English at different times, they came into our language with different meanings. Old French *estiquet* meant "a note, label." Having been changed in form to *etiquet* in French, the word was adopted into English in the sixteenth century in a form without the initial *e*, *tiket* (first recorded in 1528). The earliest uses of the word in English were in the senses "a short written notice," "a notice posted in a public place," and "a written certification." The word is first recorded with reference to something like a ticket of admission in 1673. In French, meanwhile, the word (in the form *étiquette*) came in the eighteenth century to mean "a ceremonial, a book in which court ceremonies were noted down or labeled." The French word was borrowed again into English, this time in the form *etiquette*, which is first recorded in 1750.

tide

Tyde nor tyme tairieth no man.

—Robert Greene, *A Disputation Betweene a Hee Conny-catcher and a Shee Conny-catcher*, 1592

The words *tide* and *time* are related, both going back to the Indo-European root *dā-*, "to divide" (in the form *dai-* extended with an *i*.) Both words occur in Old English, as *tīd* and *tīma*, respectively. They were very close in meaning, both having senses such as "time, hour, period, season." Modern English *tide* is no longer much used alone in the sense "interval of time," though it still appears in archaic compounds such as *Christmastide* and *Yuletide.* The usual sense of *tide* nowadays, "the periodic variation in the surface level of the earth's waters," is a development of the original meaning of the word, since the tides rise and fall at predictable times of the day.

The Indo-European root *dā-, "to divide," can be seen elsewhere in English, as in the word *democracy,* built from Greek *dēmos,* "people, land," perhaps originally "a division of society."

tithe

A tithe is a tenth, etymologically speaking; in fact, *tithe* is the old ordinal numeral in English. Sound changes in the prehistory of English are responsible for its looking so different from the word *ten. Tithe* goes back to a prehistoric West Germanic form *tehuntha-, formed from the cardinal numeral *tehun, "ten," and the same ordinal suffix that survives in Modern English as -*th.* The *n* disappeared before the *th* in the West Germanic dialect area that gave rise to English and eventually yielded the Old English form *tēothe,* "tenth," still not too different from the cardinal numeral *tīen.* But over time, as the former became *tithe* and the latter *ten,* and as *tithe* developed the specialized meaning "a tenth part paid as a tax," it grew harder to perceive a relationship between the two. The result was that speakers of English created a new word for the ordinal, *tenth,* built with *ten* on the pattern of the other regularly formed ordinal numerals like *sixth* or *seventh.*

toady

The earliest recorded sense (around 1690) of *toady* is "a little or young toad," but this has nothing to do with the modern usage of the word. The modern sense has rather to do with the practice of certain quacks or charlatans who claimed that they could draw out poisons. Toads were thought to be poisonous, so these charlatans would have an attendant eat or pretend to eat a toad and then claim to extract the poison from the attendant. Since eating a toad is an unpleasant job, these attendants came to epitomize the type of person who would do anything for a superior, and *toadeater* (first recorded 1629) became the name for a flattering, fawning parasite. *Toadeater* and the verb derived from it, *toadeat,* influenced the sense of the noun and verb *toad* and the noun *toady,* so that both nouns could mean "sycophant" and the verb *toady* could mean "to act like a toady to someone."

Tokyo

The names of Japan's early and current capitals, *Kyoto* and *Tokyo,* appear to us to be made up of the same two elements reversed, but in fact they have only one element in common. The elements of *Tō-kyō* are old borrowings from Middle Chinese, the Chinese language as it was spoken in the middle of the first millennium A.D. In Japanese, the word-building element *tō* means "east" and *kyō* means "capital," so together they mean "east(ern) capital." Chinese has another word for "capital," pronounced *dū,* whose Middle Chinese ancestor was borrowed into Japanese as *to,* "capital, large city." This is found in the name *Kyoto,* which was Japan's capital from 794 to 1192. The first part of

Kyōto, kyō, is in fact the same word for "capital" found in *Tokyo. Kyōto* thus means "capital city."

The Japanese word-building element meaning "capital," now pronounced *kyō,* is a borrowing of a Middle Chinese word pronounced *kiajng.* Middle Chinese continued to develop into the modern dialects of Chinese, such as Mandarin, and *kiajng* can be seen as the *-king* in the city name *Peking,* which means "northern capital." The name of this city is nowadays usually written *Beijing,* using a system of transcription that better represents the sounds of Chinese as it is spoken today. Similarly, the name of the city of Nanking (nowadays Nanjing) means "southern capital." Although the *-kyō* in *Tōkyō* and *-jing* in *Beijing* do not sound much alike anymore, historically they are the same word.

tomato

Among the greatest contributions to world civilization made by the early inhabitants of the Americas are plant foods such as the potato and squash. The tomato, whose name comes ultimately from the Nahuatl language spoken by the Aztecs and other groups in Mexico and Central America, was another important contribution. When the Spanish conquered this area, they brought the tomato back to Spain and, borrowing the Nahuatl word *tomatl* for it, named it *tomate,* a form shared in French, Portuguese, and early Modern English. *Tomate,* first recorded in 1604, gave way to *tomato,* a form created in English either because it was assumed to be Spanish or because it came under the influence of the word *potato.* As is well known, people at first resisted eating this New World food because its membership in the nightshade family made it seem potentially poisonous, but it is now an important element of many world cuisines.

tooth

Eating, biting, teeth, and dentists are related not only logically but etymologically; that is, the roots of the words *eat, tooth,* and *dentist* have a common origin. The Proto-Indo-European root **ed-,* meaning "to eat" and the source of our word *eat,* originally meant "to bite." A participial form of **ed-* in this sense was **dent-,* "biting," which came to mean "tooth." Our word *tooth* comes from **dont-,* a form of **dent-,* with sound changes that resulted in the Germanic word **tanthuz.* This word became Old English *tōth* and Modern English *tooth.* Meanwhile the Proto-Indo-European form **dent-* itself became in Latin *dēns* (stem *dent-*), "tooth," from which is derived our word *dentist.* We find a descendant of another Proto-Indo-European form, **(o)dont-,* in the word *orthodontist.*

torpedo

The original meaning of *torpedo* in English was "electric ray," a fish that can produce an electric discharge to stun its prey or defend itself against predators. The term was borrowed with this meaning in the sixteenth century from the Latin word *torpēdō,* which denoted the same fish but which basically meant "numbness." *Torpedo* in English came to be used figuratively for someone or something with a numbing effect, as in Oliver Goldsmith's remark in *The Life of Richard Nash,* published in 1762: "He used to call a pen his torpedo whenever he grasped it, it numbed all his faculties." The torpedo we are most familiar with is a self-propelled missile, though the original form of the weapon was a drifting underwater mine. *Torpedo* was first applied to such instruments of war in the nineteenth century. The English word *torpor*, meaning "lethargy, apathy," is also a borrowing from Latin and belongs to the same family of words, exemplified by the Latin verb *torpēre*, meaning "to be stiff, numb."

torte

Torte, *tortellini*, and *tortilla* share a common ingredient, that is, derivation from the Late Latin word *torta*, denoting a kind of bread. Late Latin *torta* is the ancestor of *torta*, "cake," in Italian. German *Torte*, "a rich cake," which is the source of our word *torte*, may have come from Italian *torta*. Italian *torta* also served as the base for another Italian word, *tortelli*, indicating a certain kind of pasta. The diminutive of this word, *tortellini*, denotes small, stuffed pasta dumplings. The Late Latin word *torta* also became the Spanish word *torta*, "round cake," and its diminutive in American Spanish, *tortilla*, means "a thin, round unleavened bread, usually made from cornmeal." All of these words ultimately derive from the same Late Latin source, as one culture and its cuisine influenced another, but those that entered English did so at widely different times, *torte* in the sixteenth century, *tortilla* in the seventeenth century, and *tortellini* in the twentieth century.

travel

Travel and *travail* are variants of the same word, each maintaining one aspect of the original meaning of their source in Old French. Both are derived from the Old French verb *travailler*, which in turn comes from the Vulgar Latin verb *tripāliāre, "to torture on the rack," from a noun *tripālium, "rack" (the instrument of torture). This noun was probably derived from the word *tripālis, "having three stakes." Old French travailler originally meant "to torture, torment, trouble" and thus "to suffer, be troubled, become tired or worn out." Travailler hence came to mean "to tire out by a journey" and "to journey." Travail still refers to pain and suffering. Travel, originally only a variant form of travail, now exclusively describes "a journey, journeying," whether painful or pleasant. Interestingly, the words descended from Vulgar Latin tripālis, "torture rack," and *tripāliāre, "to torture," don't mean "travel" in the modern Romance languages, they mean "work," such as modern French travail and Spanish trabajo.

treason

Our word tradition refers to things that are handed on from generation to generation. It is a borrowing of Old French tradicion, itself a learned borrowing of the original Latin trāditiō, which described the same sorts of things. But Latin trāditiō could also denote "a handing over, a surrender, or a betrayal of persons or territory." It is this sense that was continued as Latin developed into the Romance languages: trāditiō became Old French traïson, whose Anglo-Norman equivalent treisoun was borrowed into English and became our word treason. At first, treason simply meant betrayal, but in the fourteenth century, the term's meaning shifted slightly to a new legal sense, "a subject's violation of allegiance to his lord."

trivial

The word *trivial* entered Middle English with senses quite different from its most common contemporary ones. We find in a work from 1432-50 the phrase *arte trivialle,* an allusion to the three liberal arts that made up the trivium, the lower division of the seven liberal arts taught in medieval universities–grammar, rhetoric, and logic. The history of *trivial* goes back to the Latin word *trivium,* formed from the prefix *tri-,* "three," and *via,* "road." *Trivium* thus meant "the meeting place of three roads, especially as a place of public resort." The publicness of such a place also gave the word a pejorative sense that we express in the phrase *the gutter,* as in "His manners were formed in the gutter." The Latin adjective *triviālis,* derived from *trivium,* thus meant "appropriate to the street corner, commonplace, vulgar." *Trivial* is first recorded in English with a sense identical to that of *triviālis* in 1589. Shortly after that *trivial* is recorded in the sense most familiar to us, "of little importance or significance," making it a word now used of things less weighty than grammar, rhetoric, and logic. The plural noun *trivia* "insignificant matters, trifles" is just the plural of the Latin noun *trivium,* "crossroads," used in the sense "commonplace things."

Tuesday

Tuesday is Tiw's day. But who is Tiw? Tiw, as he was known in Old English, or Tyr, as he was known in Old Norse, was the god of war among the early Germanic peoples. Etymologically at least, Tiw, Zeus, and Jupiter are related. The name of both the Germanic god and the Roman god is derived from the Indo-

illumination from a 13th-century Icelandic manuscript depicting Tyr and the Fenris wolf

European root **dyeu-,* meaning "to shine," with many derivatives referring to the heavens. See **Zeus.**

The word for "god" in Indo-European, **deiwos,* was derived from this root **dyeu-* and is attested all across the Indo-European world, from Sanskrit *deva,* "god," in India to Irish *Día,* "God," in the very west of Europe. In Latin, **deiwos* developed into two words, *dīvus,* "pertaining to the gods," source of English *divine* and the Italian operatic *diva,* and *deus,* "god," source of English *deity.* In the Germanic languages, however, **deiwos* developed into the name of the god Tiw or Tyr.

Although their names are derived from the same root, Tyr and Jupiter do not immediately resemble each other much at all. Tyr, whom the Old Norse texts call the bravest of the gods, lost his right hand in the maw of the monstrous Fenris wolf. The wolf was destined to kill the god Odin, and to forestall the end of the world, the gods attempted to trick him into being bound by playing a game: they would put fetters on him and he would break them to show off his tremendous strength. The gods promised to loose the wolf if he could not break them. Fenris did not wholly trust the gods, so they agreed that Tyr would put his right hand into the wolf's mouth as security. The gods then put an unbreakable bond, fashioned by the magic of dwarfs, on the wolf. The wolf struggled and discovered he could not get free. The world was saved for the moment, but Tyr lost his hand.

The Old Norse texts say of Tyr, "he is one-handed, and he is not called a reconciler of men." On account of his bravery and patronage of warriors, Tyr was identified with the Roman god of war, Mars, when the names of the days of the week were borrowed by the early Germanic peoples. Jupiter and his thunderbolt were instead associated with Thor (see **Thursday**), and Latin *Diēs Martis,* "Mars's Day," became Tiw's Day. (See more at **Saturday**).

tulip

Although we associate tulips with Holland, both the flower and its name originated in the Middle East, where both are associated with turbans. Tulips were brought to Europe in the sixteenth century; the word *tulip,* which earlier in English appeared in such forms as *tulipa* or *tulipant,* came to us by way of French *tulipe* and its obsolete form *tulipan* or by way of New Latin *tulīpa,* from Ottoman Turkish *tülbend,* "muslin, gauze." (Our word *turban,* first recorded in English in the sixteenth century, can also be traced to Ottoman Turkish *tülbend.*) The Turkish word for "gauze," with which turbans can be wrapped, seems to have been used for the flower because a fully opened tulip was thought to resemble a turban.

turkey

The bird *Meleagris gallopavo,* commonly known as the *turkey* and familiar as the centerpiece of the Thanksgiving feast, is a native of the New World. It acquired the name of an Old World country as a result of two different mistakes. The name *turkey,* or *turkey cock,* was originally applied to an African bird now known as the *guinea fowl* (*Numida meleagris*), which at one time was believed to have originated in Turkey. When European settlers first saw the American turkey, they identified it with the guinea fowl and gave it the name *turkey.* There are many other examples of this sort of transference of old names to newly encountered species by speakers moving into a new area. The large thrush called a *robin* in the New World (*Turdus migratorius*) is an entirely different bird from the robin of the Old World (*Erithacus rubecula*), but they both have a breast of a reddish-orange color.

tweed

Changes in word forms are not always the result of patterned changes in consonants and vowels over time. In the case of the word *tweed,* as in many others, human error may have played a part. *Tweed* may be the result of a misreading of *tweel,* an originally Scots form of *twill. Tweed* might also be a misreading of an abbreviated form of *tweeled,* a form of *twilled.* Association with *Tweed,* the name of the river that is part of the border between England and Scotland, probably helped support the misreading, which was originally a trade name. Harris Tweed, a particular type of tweed, is still trademarked and must be woven from yarn dyed and spun in the Outer Hebrides of Scotland. *Tweed* is said to have first been used around 1831, but it is not recorded until 1847.

tycoon

It has been claimed that in today's global economy some business leaders have more power than heads of states. It is etymologically fitting that such leaders are sometimes called *tycoons. Tycoon* came into English from Japanese, which had borrowed the title, meaning "great prince," from Chinese. Use of the word was intended to make the shogun, the commander in chief of the Japanese army, more impressive to foreigners (his official title *shōgun* merely meant "general"). It worked with Matthew C. Perry, who opened Japan to the West in 1854; Perry carried out his negotiations with the shogun, thinking him to be the emperor. In fact, the shogun did rule Japan, although he was supposedly acting for the emperor. The shogun's title, *taikun,* was brought back to the United States after Perry's visit. Abraham Lincoln's cabinet members used *tycoon* as an affectionate nickname for the president. The word soon came to be used for business and industry leaders—at times being applied to figures like J. P. Morgan, who may indeed have wielded more power than many princes and presidents.

typhoon

The history of *typhoon* presents an extraordinary example of how many words are blown from shore to shore on their long journey in coming into English, sometimes even colliding with other words. *Typhoon* traveled from Greece to Arabia to India, and also arose independently in China, before assuming its current form in our language. According to early Greek sources, *Tuphoeus* had a hundred heads and was the father of the winds. He was subdued by Zeus after a tremendous battle. *Tuphōn*, a terrible whirlwind, was the son of Tuphoeus and in turn became the father of many other monsters of Greek myth, such as Cerberus, the Hydra, and the Sphinx. Later the two figures, father and son, were conflated, and the word *tuphōn* was used as a common noun meaning "whirlwind, typhoon." It was borrowed into Arabic during the Middle Ages, when Arabic learning both preserved and expanded the classical heritage and passed it on to Europe and other parts of the world. *Ṭūfān,* the Arabic version of the Greek word, passed into languages spoken in India, where Arabic-speaking Muslim invaders had settled in the eleventh century. Thus the descendant of the Arabic word, passing through an Indian language into English (first recorded in 1588) in forms such as *touffon* and *tufan*, originally referred specifically to a

drawing of a detail from a Greek vase painting showing Zeus (left) attacking Typhon with a lightning bolt

severe storm in India. The modern form of *typhoon* was influenced by a borrowing from the Cantonese variety of Chinese, namely the word *taaîfung*, and was respelled to look more like Greek. *Taaîfung,* meaning literally "great wind," was coincidentally similar to the Arabic borrowing and is first recorded in its English guise as *tuffoon* in 1699. The various forms coalesced and finally became *typhoon,* a spelling that first appeared in 1819 in Shelley's *Prometheus Unbound.*

ukulele

The ukulele, which we usually associate with Hawaii, is actually a modification of the braguinha, a small Portuguese instrument of the guitar family. This instrument was probably brought to Hawaii in 1879 by Portuguese settlers from Madeira. Some of the Portuguese families began manufacturing the instrument and modified it in various ways so that it ultimately became the ukulele we know today.

The word *ukulele,* however, is of native Hawai'ian origin. In Hawaiian, *'ukulele* means "jumping flea," from *'uku,* "flea," and *lele,* "jump." (The symbol ' represents a glottal stop, the sound you make in the middle of the word *uh-oh.*) How did the instrument come to have this name? One story has it that Edward Purvis, vice-chamberlain to King Kalakaua of Hawaii in the late nineteenth century, was quite fond of this new adaptation of the braguinha and helped spread its popularity at the king's court, which was devoted to music. Purvis was nicknamed *'ukulele* because he was small and nimble and a lively musician, and the nickname was then transferred to his favored instrument. This explanation, based on oral tradition reported by Samuel H. Elbert and Edgar C. Knowlton Jr. in *American Speech* 32 (1957), may well be correct.

Hawaiian belongs to the Malayo-Polynesian branch of the Austronesian language family, whose name means "of the southern islands." The Malayo-Polynesian languages are spoken over a vast area—from Madagascar in the west, through the Indonesian archipelago, Malaysia, and the Philippines, all the way to Hawaii and Easter Island—a testimony to the seafaring accomplishments of the Malayo-Polynesian peoples. During the course of the development of Hawaiian, many consonant sounds found in the Malayo-Polynesian protolanguage underwent radical changes. Proto-Malayo-Polynesian *k became a glottal stop (written '), and similarly Proto-Malayo-Polynesian *t became Hawaiian k. For example, the English word *taboo* comes from Tongan *tabu,* "forbidden," and the word is similarly *tabu* in other Polynesian languages. In Hawaiian, however, the word appears as *kapu,* with the change of t to k. If we take the word *'uku,* "flea," and roll back time by undoing these changes, then we get a protoword *$kutu$. In fact, *kutu* is still the word for "flea" or "louse" in many of the relatives of Hawaiian to the west, such as Maori and Malay. Does this word *kutu* sound familiar? It has been suggested that Malay *kutu* is the source of English *cootie.* The two descendants of the Proto-Malayo-Polynesian *kútuh,* "flea, louse," may have thus diverged and been carried far across the seas, only to meet up again in the same language, English. Malayo-Polynesian words have voyaged even more widely than their speakers.

See also **taboo, wiki.**

The history of the word *uncouth* reveals the propensity of human beings to react with hostility and aversion to something unknown or strange. *Uncouth* is the descendant of the Old English word *uncuth*, which meant simply "unknown, unfamiliar." It was descended from a Germanic combination of the negative prefix *un-* and **kunthaz,* the past participle of **kunnan,* "to know." The rather neutral meaning "unfamiliar, strange" for *uncouth* eventually developed into the meaning "odd, awkward," which further developed into "crude, unrefined," probably the most familiar modern sense of the word. *Couth,* meaning "known, familiar"–the descendant of Old English *cuth* from Germanic **kunthaz* by itself–did exist at one time but is now obsolete. The Germanic verb **kunnan* also meant "to know how to, to be able to." It developed into Old English *cunnan* and survives in Modern English as *can,* "be able to."

A new adjective *couth* has very recently been formed as an antonym of *uncouth* in the sense "crude, unrefined." We find both words in this sentence taken from the March 28, 1963, edition of the Manchester *Guardian:* "Modern idiom and slang is used with reckless abandon and the couth and uncouth punch each other about the ears with unrelenting monotony."

unkempt

Unkempt is a variant form of *unkembed,* derived from the past participle of a verb *kemb,* "to comb." *Kemb* has mostly disappeared from dialects of Standard English, although its past participle is still used occasionally, as in "a nicely kempt beard." The verbs *kemb* and *comb* (the latter derived from the noun *comb*) are closely related. *Comb* and *kemb* go back to the Germanic word **kambaz*, "comb." *Kambaz* became *camb* in Old English, which in turn became our Modern English word *comb*. The Germanic verb **kambjan*, meaning "to comb," was derived from **kambaz*. The *j*, pronounced *y*, in **kambjan* caused the preceding *a* to become *e*, yielding the Old English *cemban*, "to comb," that survives in Modern English *unkempt*.

upholster

The word *upholster* has a tortuous history, but its story begins with the simple English verb *uphold*, meaning "to support" and apparently also "to keep in repair." The noun suffixes *-ster* and *-er* were added to this verb, producing *upholdster* (or *upholdester*) and *upholder*, which originally meant "a dealer in or repairer of furniture." A new noun, *upholdsterer* or *upholstere*, with much the same meaning, was formed by adding the suffix *-er* to the noun *upholdster*. The verb *upholster* was formed from *upholsterer* by deleting the suffix *-er*. Although the noun *upholsterer* is recorded from the seventeenth century, the verb *upholster* is not recorded until the nineteenth century.

uranium

Some chemical elements, such as ytterbium and berkelium, derive their names from the places they were discovered, but the element uranium owes its name to an earlier scientific discovery, that of the planet Uranus. Sir William Herschel, who discovered Uranus in 1781, wanted to name the planet *Georgium sidus*, "the Georgian planet," in honor of George III;

others called it *Herschel.* Eventually convention prevailed and the planet came to be called *Uranus,* like *Mercury* and *Pluto* the name of a heavenly deity in classical mythology. This god, called *Ouranos* in Greek (Latinized as *Uranus*), was chosen because he was the father of Saturn (Greek Kronos), the deity of the planet next in line, who himself was the father of Jupiter (Greek Zeus), the deity of the next planet. The name of this new planet, *Uranus,* was then used in the name of a new chemical element discovered eight years later by M.H. Klaproth. Klaproth, a German scientist, gave it the Latin name *uranium* in honor of the discovery of Uranus. *Uranium* passed into English shortly thereafter, being first recorded in the third edition of the *Encyclopedia Britannica,* published in 1797.

victual

Victual was borrowed from Old French *vitaille*, the normal development of which is represented by the present pronunciation (rhyming with *little*) of the English word. As early as circa 1300 the Old French word was spelled with a *c* in the form *victaille*, reflecting the fact that the word goes back to Late Latin *vīctuālia*, "provisions." Forms of the English word, including *victual*, are also spelled with this *c*. They also contain the *u* in Latin *vīctuālia*, which is first reflected in French and English forms in the fifteenth century. However, the original pronunciation of *victual* remained unchanged by these respellings. The written form *vittle*, which adheres more closely to the actual sound of the word, is still sometimes used.

villain

The word *villain* exhibits in its history the low opinion in which peasants were held by their social superiors. It is ultimately derived from Latin *vīlla,* "the headquarters of a farm or country estate." From *vīlla* came the Vulgar Latin word **vīllānus,* denoting one who worked on a farm or estate. This Vulgar Latin word was the ancestor of Old French *vilain,* "feudal peasant, low rustic or common person." The Old French word has given us *villein,* "feudal peasant," and *villain,* "feudal peasant, wicked person," both originally the same word in English. *Villain* at first meant "low rustic or common person," but in early Modern English, this sense developed even more pejoratively into "a wicked person."

vixen

Why does the word *fox* begin with *f* but its female counterpart, *vixen,* begin with *v*? The answer lies in English dialects. In the speech of Devon, Somerset, and Cornwall, counties of southern England, words that begin with the voiceless fricative sounds (f) and (s) are pronounced instead with voicing, as (v) and (z). (The local rendering of the county name *Somerset,* in fact, is "Zomerzet.") The voicing is due to a Middle English sound change and may have roots even earlier. At least three examples of this dialectal pronunciation have entered Standard English: *vat, vane,* and *vixen.* The first of these is a variant of an earlier word *fat;* the pronunciation with (f) was still used in the nineteenth century before being displaced by the southern pronunciation (văt). *Vane,* which used to mean "flag," has a cognate in the German word for "flag," *Fahne,* showing the original *f. Vixen,* finally, represents the southern pronunciation of a word that goes back to Old English *fyxe,* the feminine of *fox.* It was formed by a change in the root vowel of *fox* and the addition of a suffix *-e* or *-en.* Besides being one of the rare southern English dialect forms to have come into Standard English, *vixen* is also the only survival of this type of feminine noun in the modern language.

vogue

The history of *vogue* demonstrates how the sense of a word can change dramatically over time even while flowing, as it were, in the same channel. The Indo-European root of *vogue* is **wegh-,* meaning "to go, transport in a vehicle." Among many other forms derived from this root was the Germanic stem **wēga-,* "water in motion." From this stem came the Old Low German verb *wogōn,* meaning "to sway, rock." This verb passed into Old French as *voguer,* which meant "to sail, row." The Old French word yielded the noun *vogue,* which probably literally meant "a rowing," and so by extension "a course," and figuratively "reputation" and later "reputation of fashionable things" or "prevailing fashion." The French, who have given us many fashionable things, passed this noun on as well, it being first recorded in English in 1571.

vulgar

The word *vulgar* now brings to mind off-color jokes and offensive epithets, but it once had more neutral meanings. *Vulgar* is an example of pejoration, the process by which a word develops negative meanings over time. The ancestor of *vulgar,* the Latin word *vulgāris* (from *vulgus,* "the common people"), meant "of or belonging to the common people, everyday," as well as "belonging to or associated with the lower orders." *Vulgāris* also meant "ordinary," "common" (of vocabulary, for example), and "shared by all." An extension of this meaning was "sexually promiscuous," a sense that could have led to the English sense of "indecent." Our word, first recorded in a work composed in 1391, entered English during the Middle English period, and in Middle English and later English we find not only the senses of the Latin word mentioned above but also related senses. What is common may be seen as debased, and in the seventeenth century we begin to find instances of *vulgar* that make explicit what had been implicit. *Vulgar* then came to mean "deficient in taste, delicacy, or refinement." From such uses *vulgar* has continued to go downhill, and at present "crudely indecent" is among the commonest senses of the word.

walrus

Etymologically, the walrus seems to be a "whale-horse." The word *walrus* entered English in the eighteenth century, borrowed directly from Dutch. The word came into Dutch from a Scandinavian source. A look at the word for "walrus" in several modern Scandinavian languages reveals that it is a compound of the words for "whale" and "horse." Thus in Swedish, for example, the word *valross,* "walrus," combines *val,* "whale," and *ross,* a word meaning "horse" that still survives in dialect and descends from the Old Norse word *hross,* "horse, mare."

Some have suggested that the Scandinavian words originated in a word for "walrus" in a non-Indo-European language of northern Europe such as Saami. This hypothetical word may have sounded to Scandinavians very much like their words for "whale" and "horse" put together. Because of this resemblance in sound, Scandinavians began to use this combination as a name for the animal. In the Old Norse word *hrosmhvalr,* "walrus," we find two elements: *hvalr,* "whale," and *roѕm-*. But this is *roѕm-* is mysterious in sense and derivation. It may have come from a source such as Saami *morѕ*, "walrus," probably the source of *morѕe,* an uncommon English word for the walrus. *Morѕe* is also the usual word for "walrus" in French, as is *morž* in Russian. Other etymologists believe that the animal was, in fact, originally called a "whale-horse," or perhaps "horse-whale," by the Scandinavians from the very beginning. They cite the Old Norse word for "walrus," *hroѕѕhvalr,* and the Old English word *horѕchwæl,* both of which are compounds of words for "horse" and "whale." According to this theory, forms such as Swedish *valroѕѕ* may have arisen by simple inversion of Old Norse *hroѕѕhvalr.*

war

The chaos of war is reflected in the semantic history of the word *war.* War can be traced back to the Indo-European root **werѕ-,* "to confuse, mix up." In the Germanic family of the Indo-European languages, this root gave rise to several words having to do with confusion or mixture of various kinds. One was the noun **werza-,* "confusion," which in a later form, **werra-* was borrowed into Old French, probably from Frankish, a largely unrecorded Germanic language that contributed about two hundred words to the vocabulary of Old French. From the Germanic stem came both the form *werre* in Old North French, the form borrowed into English in the twelfth century, and *guerre* (the source of *guerrilla*) in the rest of the Old French–speaking area. Both forms meant "war." Meanwhile another form derived from the same Indo-European root had developed into a word denoting a more benign kind of mixture, Old High German *wurѕt,* meaning "sausage." Modern German *Wurѕt* was borrowed into English in the nineteenth century, first by itself (recorded in 1855) and then as part of the word *liverwurst* (1869), the *liver* being a translation of German *Leber* in *Leberwurst.*

warlock

The history of *warlock* can be traced to Old English, and the word may be even older. There is, however, a discontinuity between the Old English and Modern English words in both form and meaning. The Old English ancestor of *warlock* was *wǣrloga,* probably derived from *wǣr,* "covenant, pledge," and *lēogan,* "to lie, speak falsely," and perhaps already compounded from the Germanic ancestors of these words before the Old English period. *Wǣrloga* meant "oath-breaker," "wicked person," "damned soul," and "devil." These meanings persisted until the end of the medieval period. The regularly derived modern form of Old English *wǣrloga* would be *warlow,* which actually does occur in Middle English. During the fourteenth century, *warlow* developed the meaning "sorcerer, wizard." It had its greatest currency in northern England and Scotland, where it survived well into the modern period. *Warlock* in its current sense, "wizard," acquired new life throughout the English-speaking world through its appearance in the works of Sir Walter Scott and Robert Burns. The precise reason for the alteration of the second syllable is unknown.

water

Water is wet, even etymologically. The Indo-European root of *water* is **wed-,* "wet." This root could appear in several guises—with the vowel *e,* as here, or as **wod-,* or with no vowel between the *w* and *d*, yielding **ud-*. All three forms of the root appear in English either in native or in borrowed words. From a form with a long *e*, **wēd-*, which by GRIMM'S LAW (see glossary) became **wēt-* in Germanic, we have Old English *wǣt*, "wet," which became Modern English *wet*. The form **wod-*, in a suffixed form **wod-ōr*, became **watar* in Germanic and eventually *water* in Modern English. From the form **ud-* the Greeks got their word for water, *hudōr*, the source of our prefix *hydro-* and related words like *hydrant*. The suffixes **-rā* and **-roʌ* added to the form **ud-* yielded the Greek word *hudrā*, "water snake" (borrowed into English as *hydra*), and the Germanic word **otraz*, the source of our word *otter*, the water animal.

wedlock

Wedlock, however indissoluble its bonds are considered to be, has no etymological connection with locks of any kind. The element *-lock* is a respelling, perhaps influenced by the word *lock*, of the Old English suffix *-lāc*, which forms nouns of action expressing the practice or performance of something. The suffix occurs in only a handful of Old English compounds and has not survived except in the word *wedlock*. The Old English term *wedd* denoted a pledge or a security of any kind, but the compound *wedlāc* seems even in Old English times to have been restricted to marriage vows.

Wednesday

Wednesday is Woden's day. You may be more familiar with the Germanic god Woden by the Old Norse form of his name, *Odin* (or *Óðinn*), from Norse mythology. Odin helped create the human race by giving breath to an ash and an elm tree, which became the first man and woman. Odin is lord of the heavenly hall where he gathers together those who die gloriously on the battlefield to carouse in the afterlife. He roams the world in disguise as a traveler. He is also said to have discovered the runes after a mystical experience while hanging from the tree, Yggdrasil, that formed the axis of the ancient Norse cosmos. He is depicted

illumination from a 13th-century Icelandic manuscript depicting Odin astride his eight-legged horse Sleipnir

as one-eyed, since he gave one of his all-seeing eyes to the giant Mimir in exchange for being able to drink from Mimir's well of wisdom. He is also said to arouse warriors and instill animalistic fury in them (see **berserk**). Odin also retrieved the magic mead of inspiration, which gives eloquence to the poets of the world, after the mead had been taken by a giant. Sailors called upon Odin for protection as the god of cargoes. When the Romans encountered the Germanic tribes, they thought this Germanic god resembled their god Mercury. Mercury (who absorbed various characteristics of the Greek god Hermes) led the souls of the dead from this world to the afterlife. He protected travelers. He was the god of writing and commerce, and he was known for his cleverness and eloquence. Therefore, when the ancient Germanic peoples adopted the Roman week (see **Saturday**), the fourth day of the week, *Diēs Mercuriī,* "Mercury's Day," was given to Woden/Odin and became Old English *Wōdnesdæg.*

Old English *Woden* and Old Norse *Óðinn* came from Germanic **wōd-eno-* from the Indo-European root *wet-,* meaning "to blow, inspire, arouse." (The **t* in this root changed to a **d* by the working of GRIMM'S LAW and VERNER'S LAW, which are explained in the glossary.) Odin's connection with inspiration is illustrated by the myth of the mead told above.

In Greek, the same Indo-European root, **wet-,* was continued in the word *atmos,* "breath, vapor," a contraction of an earlier **awetmos.* The English word *atmosphere* is derived from this word and Greek *sphaira,* "ball, sphere."

weird

> M acbeth: Saw you the weird sisters?
>
> Lennox: No, my lord.
>
> . . . .
>
> Macbeth: Infected be the air whereon they ride?:
> And damn'd all those that trust them!
>
> —Shakespeare, *Macbeth,* Act IV, Scene 1

When Macbeth refers to the witches on the heath as the "weird sisters," he does not mean that they are merely odd. The word *weird,* which can feel a bit like slang nowadays, is in fact quite ancient, and its history includes more than one strange twist of fate. The phrase *weird sisters* originally referred to the Fates, the three goddesses who decree the destiny of each person. The Greeks called them the *Moirai,* the Romans called them the *Parcae,* and they were known as the *Norns* to the speakers of Old Norse. The Anglo-Saxons used their word *wyrd,* ancestor of our word *weird,* to translate the Latin name for these goddesses. *Wyrd* by itself was a noun originally meaning "fate," and it was derived from the Indo-European root **wert-*, "to turn." The Anglo-Saxons also shared in the ancient European mythological conception of a person's fate as a thread being spun out by the goddesses and finally cut at the moment of death. The original sense of the noun *weird* was extended to include women who prophesied or possessed other attributes of the Fates, namely witches.

We owe our use of *weird* to Shakespeare's use of the noun in the phrase *weird sisters,* where it was interpreted as an adjective. The great prestige of Shakespeare preserved this use of *weird,* which was picked up and extended to its probably most current meaning, "strange," by nineteenth-century poets and writers.

went

Why do we say *went* and not *goed*? *Go* has always had an unusual past tense, formed from a completely different root from its present tense. The replacement within a series of inflected forms of one form by a completely unrelated form is called *suppletion.* (Another, even more extreme example of suppletion in English is found in the paradigm *be, am, are, was,* whose forms are originally from four different verbal roots.) The past tense of *go* in Old English was *ēode,* formed from an unrelated root that has no other verb forms in English. Its modern replacement, *went,* derives from old forms of the modern verb *wend.* In Middle English the original past tense and past participle of *wenden,* "to go, turn," were *wended* and *wend,* respectively. The forms *wente* and *went* appeared around 1200 and gradually displaced the older *wended* and *wend.* The new past tense *wente* also took on a new use as the past tense of *go*, replacing *ēode.* By the beginning of the Modern English period, around 1500, *went* was no longer used in any other way and was therefore felt to be the normal past tense of *go;* at the same time, *wend* acquired the new form *wended* for its past tense and past participle, meaning "turned."

werewolf

The *wolf* in *werewolf* is current English; the *were* is not. *Werewulf,* "werewolf," occurs only once in Old English, about the year 1000, in the laws of King Canute: "lest the madly ravenous werewolf too savagely tear or devour too much from a godly flock." The *wer-* or *were-* in *wer(e)wulf* means "man"; it is related to Latin *vir,* which has the same meaning and is the source of *virile* and *virility.* Both the Germanic and the Latin words derive from Indo-European **wīro-,* "man." *Wer-* also appears, though much disguised, in the word *world. World* is first recorded (written *wiaralde*) in Old English in a charter dated 832; the form *worold* occurs in *Beowulf.* The Old English forms come from Germanic **wer-ald-,* "were-eld" or "age of man." The transfer of meaning from the age of humans to the place where they live has a parallel in the Latin word *saeculum,* "age, generation, lifetime," later "world."

whiskey

Many connoisseurs of fine whiskey wouldn't dream of contaminating their libations with water, but they really can't avoid it. Not only is water used in distilling whiskey, but the words *whiskey* and *water* share a common Indo-European root, **wed-,* "water, wet." This root could appear in several guises, as *wed-, *wod-, or *ud-. *Water* is a native English word that goes back by way of prehistoric Common Germanic *watar to the Indo-European suffixed form *wod-ōr, with an *o*. *Whiskey* is a shortened form of *usquebaugh*, which English borrowed from Irish Gaelic *uisce beatha* and Scottish Gaelic *uisge beatha*. This compound descends from Old Irish *uisce*, "water," and *bethad*, "of life," and means literally "water of life." (It thus means the same thing as the name of another drink, *aquavit*, which comes from Latin *aqua vītae*, "water of life.") *Uisce* came from the Indo-European suffixed form *ud-skio-*. Finally, the name of another alcoholic drink, *vodka*, came into English from Russian, where it means literally "little water," as it is a diminutive of *voda*, "water"—a euphemism if ever there was one. *Voda* came from the same Indo-European form as English *water*, but is differently suffixed: *wod-ā*. Whiskey, water, and vodka—etymology can mix a potent cocktail.

whore

Derivatives of Indo-European roots have often acquired starkly contrasting meanings. A prime example is the case of the root *kā-, "to like, desire." From it was derived a stem *kāro-, from which came the prehistoric Common Germanic word *hōraz, with the underlying meaning "one who desires" and the effective meaning "adulterer." The feminine of this, *hōrōn-, became *hōre* in Old English, the ancestor of Modern English *whore*. In another branch of the Indo-European family, the same stem *kāro- produced the Latin word *cārus*, "dear." This word has several derivatives borrowed into English, including *caress*, *cherish*, and *charity*, in Christian doctrine the highest form of love and the greatest of the theological virtues. Another derivative of the root *kā- in Indo-European was *kāmo-, a descendant of which is the Sanskrit word for "love," kāmaḥ, appearing in the name of the most famous treatise on love and love-making, the Kāmasūtra.

wiki

Anyone who has not yet encountered a *wiki* while web surfing will sometime soon, for *wikis* are proliferating quickly. In fact, the word *wiki* comes from a word for "quick." A *wiki* is a collaborative website whose content can be edited by anyone with access to it, and the word *wiki* is a good example of how the invention of new technologies requires the invention of new words. *Wiki* is an abbreviation of *WikiWikiWeb,* the name that American computer programmer Ward Cunningham chose in 1995 for his new code permitting the easy development of collaborative websites. Mr. Cunningham explains that a name such as *quick web* or the like would have been appropriate for a system that makes webpages quickly. He coined the word *WikiWikiWeb* from Hawaiian *wikiwiki,* "fast, speedy" (a reduplication of *wiki,* "fast"), with the thought that *WikiWikiWeb* was more fun to say than *quick web.* *Wikiwiki* was the first native Hawaiian word that Mr. Cunningham learned on his first visit to the islands, when he was instructed by the airport counter agent to take the *wikiwiki bus* between terminals. Since this word was new to Mr. Cunningham, the agent explained that *wikiwiki* meant "quick." Mr. Cunningham himself advocates the pronunciation *wee-kee* for the new word, since it is closer to the original Hawai'ian, rather than a pronunciation *wick-ee.* The word *wikiwiki* in Hawaiian is akin to Tahitian *viti* and *vitiviti,* "deft, alert, well done." The Hawaiian word has a *k* where the Tahitian has a *t,* a regular correspondence between Hawaiian and the other Austronesian languages. To learn more about this correspondence and other Austronesian loanwords in English, see **ukulele.**

window

The source of our word *window* is a vivid metaphor. *Window* comes to us from the Scandinavian invaders and settlers of England in the early Middle Ages. Although we have no record of the exact word they gave us, it was related to Old Norse *vindauga,* "window," a compound made up of *vindr,* "wind," and *auga,* "eye," reflecting the fact that at one time windows contained no glass. The metaphor "wind eye" is of a type beloved by Norse and Old English poets and is called a *kenning;* other examples include "oar-steed" for *ship* and "whale-road" for *sea.* Recently we have restored to the 800-year-old word *window* a touch of its poetic heritage, using it figuratively in such phrases as *launch window, weather window,* and *window of opportunity* or *vulnerability.*

winsome

Winsome people easily win friends, so it is not surprising that *winsome* and *win* have a common root. Their shared element *win-* comes from the Indo-European root **wen-,* meaning "to desire, strive for," which has a number of descendants in the Germanic languages. One was the prehistoric Germanic noun **wini-,* meaning "friend" (literally, "one who desires or loves" someone else), which became *wine* in Old English and is preserved in such names as *Winfred,* "friend of peace," and *Edwin,* "friend of (family) possessions." A different form of the root with a different

suffix became Old English *wynn*, "pleasure, joy," preserved in *winsome*. Finally, the verb *win* itself is from
this root; its meaning is an extension of the sense "to
strive for," namely, "to strive for with success, be victo-
rious." Outside of the Germanic branch of Indo-
European, we also see the root, for example, in Latin
venus or *Venus*, "love, the goddess of love," and the verb
venerāre, "to worship," the source of English *venerate*.

wizard

The word *wizard* is a compound formed from the
adjective *wise*, "learned, sensible," and the suffix
-*ard*. The word, first recorded in the fifteenth century,
originally meant "a wise man." The suffix -*ard*, however, almost always has a pejorative or disparaging
sense, as in the words *coward, drunkard, laggard,* and
sluggard. Wizard was thus often used to mean "a wise
man" in a bad sense: "a man who uses his knowledge
to evil ends." From this use it came to mean "sorcerer."
However, the positive sense, "someone who is uncan-
nily adept at something," is quite old as well, being
attested from the seventeenth century.

write

Every western Indo-European language except English derives its verb for "to write" from Latin
scrībere: *écrire* in French, *escribir* in Spanish, *scrivere*
in Italian, *scríbaim* in Old Irish, *ysgrifennu* in Welsh,
skriva in Breton, *skrifa* in Old Norse, *skrive* in Danish
and Norwegian, *skriva* in Swedish, *schreiben* in German, *schrijven* in Dutch. The Old English verb "to
write" was *wrītan*, from a Germanic root, **writ-*, that
derived from an Indo-European root, **wreid-*, mean-

ing "to cut, scratch, tear, sketch an outline." German still retains this meaning in its cognate verb *reissen,* "to tear." Only Old English employed *wrītan* to refer to writing, that is, scratching on parchment with a pen. English shows a similar contrariness in its verb *read,* being almost the only western European language not to derive its verb for that concept from Latin *legere.*

xenophobia

We don't greet *guests* with *hostility* and *xenophobia*, but instead with *hospitality*. Amazingly, however, these four words actually contain the same Proto-Indo-European root, **ghos-*. The English word *guest* descends from Proto-Indo-European **ghostis*, "guest-friend, a person with whom one has reciprocal duties of hospitality," an actual full word we can confidently reconstruct for the protolanguage. The word **ghostis* was the central expression of the guest-host relationship that was highly important to ancient Indo-European societies. The guest-friendship was a bond of trust accompanied by ritualized gift-giving, and it created an obligation of mutual hospitality and friendship that, once established, could continue in perpetuity and be renewed years later by the same parties or their descendants. The bond created by guest-friendship resembled kinship. A famous example is the story of the Trojan warrior Glaukos and the Greek warrior Diomedes in the *Iliad,* who agree not to fight each other when they realize that Glaukos's grandfather Bellerophon (of Chimera-killing fame) and Diomedes's grandfather Oineus had know each other many years before. The two warriors instead embrace and exchange armor as a testimony to the guest-friendship still binding their families two generations later.

In the Germanic branch of Indo-European, this friendly meaning of *ghoₛtiₛ has been preserved all the way down to English, where it appears as *guest,* a borrowing of Old Norse *geₛtr.* The same meaning was also preserved in Latin *hoₛpeₛ,* "host." This word, however, is the continuation of an Indo-European compound *ghoₛti-potiₛ "lord of guests." You can find the second element *poti-,* meaning "powerful," in many other words we have borrowed from Latin, such as

potent. Hoₛpeₛ developed into Old French *hoₛte,* from which we get our word *hoₛt,* "someone who receives guests."

In many ancient societies, a householder had a sacred duty to offer hospitality to strangers. Strangers are potential friends, but they are also potential enemies, and

detail from a c. 540 B.C. amphora attributed to the Inₛcription Painter

this explains the development of Proto-Indo-European *ghoₛtiₛ, "guest-friend" into Latin *hoₛtiₛ, "enemy." *Hoₛtiₛ* is the source of our word *hoₛtile,* as well as *hoₛt* in the sense of "army." The Greek word for "stranger, guest-friend" was *xenoₛ* (the *x* is pronounced as *kₛ*). This comes from Proto-Indo-European *ghₛenwoₛ, whose the strange-looking cluster of consonants at the beginning, *ghₛ-,* is another form of the root *ghoₛ-.* The very foreign-looking English word *xenophobia,* "fear or hatred of foreigners," is derived from Greek *xenoₛ.*

Xmas

X*mas* has been used for hundreds of years in religious writing, where the *X* represents a Greek chi. The Greek form of chi is χ (minuscule) or X (majuscule). Chi is the first letter of Greek Χριστος (transliterated as *Khrīstos* or *Chrīstos*), which is the source of English *Christ*. The symbol *x* or *X* has long been used as an abbreviation for *Christ*. However, people unaware of the Greek origin of this *X* often mistakenly interpret *Xmas* as an informal shortening pronounced something like *eks-mass*. Many therefore frown upon the term *Xmas* because it seems to them a commercial convenience that omits *Christ* from *Christmas*.

The Greek word *chrīstos* means "anointed" and is a translation of Aramaic *məšiḥā* or Hebrew *māšiaḥ,* which also mean "the anointed one." These Aramaic and Hebrew words are the ultimate source of the English word *messiah.*

x-ray

Wilhelm Röntgen (1845-1923), the German scientist who discovered x-rays, gave them the name *X-Strahlen,* which was translated into English as *x-rays.* He used *x*, the symbol for an unknown quantity, because the nature of x-rays was not known at the time. In 1901, Röntgen received the very first Nobel Prize in physics for his discovery.

The use of the letter *x* as a symbol for an unknown quantity originates with the French philosopher and mathematician René Descartes (1596-1650).

yacht

When we talk about the sea in English, we may find ourselves using at one least one of the many words that English borrowed from Dutch: *brackish, corvette, deck, dock, freebooter, harpoon, hoist, maelstrom, mesh* (of a net), *reef, school* (of fish), *skipper, sloop, tackle, trawl,* and *walrus.* The word *yacht* probably also comes—at least partially—from Dutch *jaght,* now spelled *jacht.* Norwegian too has a word *jakt* of similar meaning, and it is possible that both languages contributed to the formation of English *yacht.* Both the Dutch and the Norwegian word ultimately derive from Middle Low German *jachtschip,* or "hunting ship." (If you know standard German, you may recognize the cognate of *Jagd,* "hunt," in this word, or even the root found in the surname *Yeager,* originally *Jäger,* the German equivalent of the English surname *Hunter.*) The original Dutch *jacht* was a fast, light boat, which fulfilled the practical purpose of hunting down smugglers. In English, the Dutch form of the word received a big boost in 1660 when the Dutch East

India Company gave Charles II of England a *jacht* of this type. However, he used it for pleasure *cruises*—another word from Dutch!

Yacht is the only common English word in which *ch* is silent. In Dutch, however, the written *ch* is actually pronounced as a separate sound, like the one you make when you clear your throat—it is the sound *ch* at the end of the German pronunciation of the composer *Bach.* English is closely related to Dutch and German, and it used to have the same sound, too, in such words as *bought, cough,* and *taught* that are now spelled with a silent *gh.* Then over the course of the fifteenth century, the pronunciation of this sound in English began to change. In some words it simply disappeared. Sometimes, however, the original throat-clearing sound became *f,* as in *draught* (also spelled *draft*) and *laugh.* (The German and the Dutch word for "to laugh" is still *lachen,* with a throaty *ch.*) By the time the English borrowed the Dutch word *jacht,* they could no longer say the original *ch* very well, so it was left out of the pronunciation. But the spelling of the word stayed the same.

Yankee

The origin of *Yankee* has been the subject of much debate, but the most likely source is the Dutch name *Janke,* meaning "little Jan" or "little John," a nickname that dates back to the 1680s. Perhaps because it was used as the name of pirates, the name *Yankee* came to be used as a term of contempt. It was used this way in the 1750s by General James Wolfe, the British general who secured British domination of North America by defeating the French at Quebec. The name may have been applied to New Englanders as an extension of an original use referring to Dutch settlers living along the Hudson River. Whatever the reason, *Yankee* is first recorded in 1765 as a name for an inhabitant of New England. The first recorded use of the term by the British to refer to Americans in general appears in the 1780s, in a letter by Lord Horatio Nelson, no less. Around the same time it began to be abbreviated to *Yank.* During the American Revolution, American soldiers adopted this term of derision as a term of national pride. The derisive use nonetheless remained alive and even intensified in the South during the Civil War, when it referred not to all Americans but to those loyal to the Union. Now the term carries less emotion—except of course for baseball fans.

yoga

The word *yoga* comes from Sanskrit *yogaḥ,* "joining together, connection, harnessing of one's mental faculties." The word literally meant "a yoking together" and is descended from the Indo-European root **yeug-,* "to join, yoke." **Yeug-* descended into Germanic as *yuk-,* represented in Old English by *geoc,* the ancestor of Modern English *yoke.* The root **yeug-* is continued by words in most of the branches of the Indo-European language family, which indicates that the speakers of Proto-Indo-European pulled their plows and drew their wagons with draft animals.

yolk

This word, meaning "the yellow part of an egg," is descended from Old English *geolca. Geolca* is a noun derived from the adjective *geolu,* the ancestor of *yellow. Yolk* and *yellow* go back to the Indo-European root **ghel-,* meaning "to shine." From this root are derived various words denoting colors, such as

English *yellow* and Greek *khlōros,* "pale green, green-ish-yellow," the source of *chloro-* in *chlorophyll.* From **ghel-* also comes the English word *gold,* as well as the word denoting "bile" (a greenish secretion), *gall.*The element *-choly* in the word *melancholy* is also from the root **ghel-. Cholē* was the Greek word for "bile." In the ancient Greek and Roman theories of medicine, the relative quantities of four substances, called *humors,* within a person were thought to determine the person's character. The four humors were called in English *blood, phlegm, yellow bile,* and *black bile.* Too much black bile, or in Greek, *melankholiā,* was thought to result in a gloomy and pensive character.

Yule

The word *Yule* continues Old English *geōl,* "Christmas Day, Christmastide." It is related to Scandinavian words such as Old Norse *jōl,* which denoted a pagan midwinter festival that lasted thirteen days. After the Anglo-Saxons were converted to Christianity, the name *Yule* was used for the feast of Christmas. The use of native words for Christian traditions was encouraged in the Anglo-Saxon church; another example is the use of the term *Easter* for the feast of Christ's resurrection. See **Easter.**

Z

za

When young people today speak casually of ordering a *za,* "pizza," they are unwittingly producing an expression that is quite interesting to language historians. *Za* derives from the full form *pizza* by a process known as *clipping.* Two types of clipping are common in English: dropping the syllable or syllables not receiving the primary word stress, as in *fridge* from *refrigerator;* and dropping all syllables after the first syllable, as in *ab, dis,* and *vibe,* whether or not the first syllable was originally stressed. In the case of *za,* the syllable that was dropped was originally stressed and was the first syllable, which is unusual. *Rents* for "parents," is another recent example of the same kind of clipping. Interestingly, we don't need to stay in the realm of contemporary youth slang to see the results of this unusual process. The words *phone, bus,* and *wig* (from *telephone, omnibus,* and *periwig*) belong to Standard English but had their start as slangy or catchy neologisms formed by clipping stressed syllables, just like *za.* Who knows whether in fifty years *za* and *rents* will be as widely accepted as *phone* and *wig* are now?

Zen

Although the practice of Zen is an approach to life that seems characteristically East Asian, the word *Zen* itself is ultimately Indo-European, reflecting the origins of Buddhism in India. *Zen,* which has been in English since 1727, is the Japanese pronunciation of a Chinese word, now pronounced *chán* in Mandarin Chinese, meaning "meditation." *Chán* comes from Pali *jhānaṃ,* from Sanskrit *dhyānam,* "meditation," from the Sanskrit root *dhyā-,* or *dhī-,* "to see, observe." The Indo-European root behind the Sanskrit is *dheiə-, or *dhyā-, "to see, look at." This root also shows up in Greek, where *dhyā- developed into *sā-,* as in the Common Greek noun *sāma, "sign, distinguishing mark." This became *sēma* in Attic Greek, the source of English *semantic.*

zero

The word *zero* is not only synonymous with the word *cipher* but goes back to the same source, the Arabic word *sifr,* which meant "empty." The Arabic word is in turn a translation of the Sanskrit term for "zero," *śūnya-,* literally "empty." *Zero* came into English in the seventeenth century from Italian *zero,* a contracted form of earlier *zefiro,* while *cipher* came into English via Old French from Medieval Latin *cifra.* Although *zero* was borrowed as a synonym of *cipher,* the two words have diverged in meaning. *Cipher* has developed the sense "a code," whereas *zero* is used primarily as the name of the numeral, or of quantities represented by it, especially in scientific use.

Zeus

Homer's *Iliad* calls him "Zeus who thunders on high" and Milton's *Paradise Lost*, "the Thunderer," so it is surprising to learn that the Indo-European ancestor of Zeus was a god of the bright daytime sky. *Zeus* is a somewhat unusual noun in Greek, having both a stem *Zēn-* (as in the philosopher *Zeno*'s name) and a stem *Di-* (earlier *Diw-*). In the *Iliad* prayers to Zeus begin with the vocative form *Zeu pater,* "O father Zeus." Father Zeus was the head of the Greek pantheon; another ancient Indo-European society, the Romans, called the head of their pantheon *Iūpiter* or *Iuppiter* (Jupiter). The *-piter* part of his name is just a reduced form of Latin *pater,* "father," and *Iū-* corresponds to the *Zeu* in Greek: *Iūpiter* is therefore precisely equivalent to *Zeu pater* and could be translated "father Jove." *Jove* itself is from Latin *Iov-,* the stem form of *Iūpiter,* an older version of which in Latin was *Diov-,* showing that the word once had a *d* as in Greek *Diw-.* An exact parallel to Zeus and Jupiter is found in the Sanskrit god addressed as *Dyaus pitar: pitar* is "father," and *dyaus* means "sky." We can equate Greek *Zeu pater,* Latin *Iū-piter,* and Sanskrit *Dyaus pitar* and reconstruct an Indo-European deity, **Dyēus pəter,* who was associated with the sky and addressed as "father." Comparative philology has revealed that the "sky" word refers specifically to the bright daytime sky, as it is derived from the root meaning "to shine." This root also shows up in Latin *diēs,* "day," borrowed into English in words like *diurnal.* Closely related to these words is Indo-European **deiwos,* "god," which shows up, among other places, in the name of the Old

English god *Tīw* in Modern English *Tuesday,* "Tiw's day." (See more at **Tuesday**.) *Deiwos* is also the source of Latin *dīvus,* "pertaining to the gods"–whence English *divine* and the Italian operatic *diva*–and *deus,* "god"–whence *deity.*

zither

a zither

What do the zither and the guitar have in common, etymologically speaking? A zither is a stringed musical instrument from Austria. The German word *Zither* comes from Latin *cithara,* borrowed from Greek *kithara,* which also denoted a kind of stringed instrument. Greek *kithara* has other descendants in Modern English, such as *cittern,* which entered English in the sixteenth century, and *guitar,* which entered English in the seventeenth century through Spanish *guitarra.* Both are musical instruments in the same family as the zither, but the word *zither* enters English much later, in the nineteenth century.

Glossary

ablative A grammatical case (see below) indicating separation, direction away from, sometimes manner or agency, and the object of certain verbs. It is found in Latin and other Indo-European languages. See **limbo**.

accent The relative prominence of a particular syllable of a word. Different languages have different types of accent. English, for example, has a stress accent, in which prominence is given to the syllable by greater intensity and duration. Other languages, such as Japanese, have a pitch accent, realized by varying the pitch or tone of the syllable. The prehistoric ancestor of English, Proto-Indo-European had a pitch accent, which shows its effects in Verner's Law (see below).

acronym A word formed from the initial letters of a name, such as WAC for Women's Army Corps, or by combining initial letters or parts of a series of words, such as *radar* for *radio* detecting and ranging. See **scuba**.

Anglo-Norman The dialect of Old French, derived chiefly from Norman French, that was used by the Normans who lived in England after the Norman conquest of England in 1066 and by the descendants of these settlers.

Algonquian A family of languages spoken or formerly spoken in an area from Labrador to the Carolinas between the Atlantic coast and the Rocky Mountains. The Algonquian languages include Arapaho, Cheyenne, Cree, Menomini, Ojibwa, and Shawnee, among many others. For examples of words borrowed from Algonquian languages, see **opossum** and **quahog**.

article The part of speech used to indicate nouns and to specify their application. An indefinite article, such as English *a* or *an,* does not fix the identity of the noun that it modifies. In English, the indefinite articles are *a* and *an.* A definite article restricts or particularizes a noun. In English, *the* is the definite article. Articles are often tightly bound to the nouns they accompany in languages, so much so that the noun and its article are borrowed as one word. See **an** and **alcohol.**

alteration A catch-all term for an irregular, unexpected change in the pronounced form of a word. Such changes often result from the influence of another word that is similar in sound or meaning to the word that is altered. For examples, See **female, goatee, gringo, tomato.**

attestation An occurrence of a word or phrase, usually in a written text, but also in more recent times in sound recordings. An attestation of a word proves the existence of the word when the text was written or the recording was made. Many dates of first attestation are given in this book, but it often happens that scholars find yet earlier dates through further research. If a word has several possible etymologies, knowing the date of first attestation of a word can often help us eliminate the false ones. See an example at **hooker.**

Australian Aboriginal language Any of the many indigenous languages of Australia. Over 250 distinct Aboriginal languages are recognized, belonging to several unrelated families. Many of Australian languages are extinct or near extinction, but they have given a wealth of words to the English language. See **boomerang, kangaroo.**

Austronesian A large, widespread family of languages, including Malagasy (the language of Madagascar), the indigenous languages of Taiwan, and many of the languages of Indonesia and the islands of the Pacific. See **taboo, ukulele, wiki.**

back-formation A new word created by removing an affix from an already existing word, as *vacuum clean* from *vacuum cleaner,* or by removing what is mistakenly thought to be an affix. For examples, see **eavesdrop, pea, kidnapper.**

Bambara A language belonging to the Niger-Congo language family of Africa. Bambara is spoken in Mali and several other West African countries.

blend A word produced by combining parts of other words. See **chortle, smog.**

borrowing The adoption of a word from one language for use in another. Often the introduction of unfamiliar concepts, creatures, or objects leads to borrowing, as when English borrowed such words as *opossum, pow-wow,* and *wigwam* from the indigenous languages of North America. In other cases, the borrowed word may compete with the native or be used to express just one of the original senses of the native word. For an interesting example of such borrowing, see beef.

case A distinct form of a noun, pronoun, or adjective that is used to express one or more particular grammatical relationships to other words in a sentence. In the English sentence *I love him, I* is in what is called the nominative case, which specifies that *I* is the subject of the verb. *Him* is in the accusative case, which specifies that *him* is the direct object of the verb. The older Indo-European languages such as Latin, Greek, and Sanskrit often had many cases. See **limbo.** Old English nouns had four cases, and their differing forms expressed such concepts as subject, direct object, indirect object, and possessor of a noun. The Old English case system has mostly disappeared except for the pronouns and the possessive forms like *his, her,* and *Alice's,* but it has left other interesting traces in such words as **shadow.**

causative A form of a verb indicating that the subject of the verb causes the object to perform the action of the verb. In Proto-Indo-European, many verb roots made causative forms, especially by using a form of the root with the vowel *o* in it. The root *men-* "to think" (source of our word *mind*), made a causative form *mon-eye-ti,* "he makes (someone) think," which became Latin *monēre,* "to remind, warn, advise," source of our words *admonish, monitor,* and *demonstrate.* English has several traces of this ancient system. See **drench.**

clipping (or *clipped form*) A word formed by dropping one or more syllables from a polysyllabic word, such as *gas* from *gasoline* or *phone* from *telephone.* Clipping is often used to create new slang, but some older words that are originally clippings include **canter, fan, mob,** and **mutt.** For examples of clipped forms in which the beginning of a word is removed, see **bus, cute, za.**

cluster Two or more successive consonants in a word, as *cl* and *st* in the word *cluster.* Many of the less common clusters in English words are found in borrowings from foreign languages.

cognate Related in origin, as certain words in closely related languages descended from the same ancestral root; for example, English *name* and Latin *nōmen* are cognate words, from Indo-European **nōmen-.* For a few surprising sets of cognates, see **chai, ukulele,** and **Zeus.**

coinage An invented word (rather than one that has developed naturally from earlier words). Coinages may be wholly new or be fashioned out of elements from other preexisting words. For examples, see **nerd, quark, robot, smog, spoof, wiki.**

compound A word that consists either of two or more elements that are independent words, such as *loudspeaker, baby-sit,* or *high school,* or of specially modified combining forms of words, such as Greek *philosophia,* from *philo-,* "loving," and *sophia,* "wisdom." The variety of compounds included in this book shows how productive this process is in the creation of new words. Some words are old compounds, even though the individual elements may not be immediately recognizable any longer: **crisscross, garlic, gossip, pedigree, tadpole, walrus, warlock.** In other words, one of the elements may be instantly recognizable, but the other may be obscure to someone who does not know the etymology. See **bridal, gangplank, landscape, midwife, ombudsman, quicksilver, werewolf.**

contamination A word whose form has been influenced by other words of similar sound or meaning. For examples of the various changes that can take place through contamination, see **female, lobster.**

creole A language derived from a pidgin that has become the native tongue of a community. A pidgin is a simplified system of communication that is usually a mixture of two or more languages, has a rudimentary grammar and vocabulary, and is used for communication between groups speaking different languages, often for trade purposes. A pidgin is not spoken as a first or native language. When a pidgin becomes the native tongue of a community, it develops into a creole, also called a *creolized language.* Creoles are just as grammatically complex as human languages that do not derive from an earlier pidgin, such as English. Most creole languages contain elements from the languages of the colonial powers of Europe, such as Dutch, English, Portuguese, and French. The word **jukebox** is from Gullah, a creole based on English.

derive To form (a word), or (of words) to be formed from, and in particular by use of a method of word formation that is common or productive in a language, such as adding suffixes. English has borrowed so many Latin and Greek words that the common derivational processes in these languages, such as making verbs with the suffix *-ate* or *-ize* or nouns with *-ation* can be considered part of English grammar now. Some English words with surprising derivations include **fornication, naughty,** and **oscillate.**

dialect A regional or social variety of a language distinguished by pronunciation, grammar, or vocabulary, especially a variety of speech spoken in a particular region and differing from the standard literary language or speech pattern of the culture in which it exists. Standard American English is just one dialect among many other English dialects. Some English borrowings from other languages have not been taken from standard dialects of these languages but from other dialects. In particular, English has many loans from Anglo-Norman, a variety of French different from Parisian French. For an example, see **catch.**

dialect borrowing (or **mixture**) Borrowing of a word or phrase from one dialect of a language into another dialect. For examples, see **bury, raid.**

diminutive A word formed with a suffix that indicates smallness or, by semantic extension, qualities such as youth, familiarity, affection, or contempt, as *-let* in *booklet, -kin* in *lambkin,* or *-et* in *nymphet.* The formation of words with diminutive suffixes is often a very productive source of new words in many languages. See **banquet, bumpkin, caterpillar, gauntlet, leprechaun, Yankee.**

diphthong A complex speech sound that begins with one vowel and gradually changes to another vowel within the same syllable, as *oi* in *boil* or *i* in *fine.* English dialects often differ in the ways certain diphthongs are pronounced. For an example, see **heist.**

dissimilation The process by which one of two similar or identical sounds in a word becomes less like the other, such as the *l* in English *marble* (from French *marbre*). For examples, see **charming, colonel, filibuster, glamour, tavern.**

doublet One of two words derived from the same historical source by different routes of transmission, such as *skirt* from Scandinavian and *shirt,* the native English development of the same Germanic word. Because English has borrowed words from a great variety of languages, it has many interesting pairs of doublets, such as those discussed at the words **catch, cattle, croissant, jaunty, lawn, poison,** and **sherbet.**

etymology The origin and historical development of a word, a part of a word, or even a phrase, as shown by determining its basic elements, earliest known use, and changes in form and meaning; tracing its transmission from one language to another; identifying its cognates in other languages; and reconstructing its ancestral form where possible.

false splitting (or **recutting**) A change in the number of sounds in a word that happens when speakers reinterpret the boundary between two closely connected words, such as an article and a following noun. Even though this change is sporadic, it is surprisingly common in the languages of the world. For examples, see **apron.**

family A group of languages descended from the same parent language, such as the Indo-European language family or the Austronesian family.

feminine A grammatical gender relating to or belonging to words or forms that refer chiefly to females or to things grammatically classified as female.

folk etymology Change in the form of a word or phrase resulting from a mistaken assumption about its composition or meaning, as in *ʃhamefaced* for earlier *ʃhamfaʃt,* "bound by shame," or *cutlet* from French *côtelette,* "little rib." Folk etymology is a powerful and common process that we can see operating in the history of many words, such as **artichoke, caprice, cockroach, crayfish, hangnail, humble pie,** and **penthouse.**

gender A grammatical category used in the classification of nouns, pronouns, adjectives, and, in some languages, verbs. It may be arbitrary or based on characteristics such as the sex of the being described or whether it is alive or inanimate. The gender of a word may determine the form taken by other words in a sentence, such as adjectives describing a noun. In English, the pronoun *he* has masculine gender, *ʃhe* feminine gender, and *it* neuter gender. In other languages, such as French, all nouns are classified as being either masculine or feminine gender, even those referring to inanimate objects or other things without obvious male or female characteristics. In French *la main,* "the hand," is feminine, while *le braʃ,* "the arm," is masculine. *Le pied,* "the foot," is masculine, while *la jambe,* "the leg," is feminine.

Germanic The branch of the Indo-European language family that includes English and its closest relatives. The word is also used as a name for the proto-language ancestral to all the Germanic languages. The Germanic languages are divided into three subgroups. The West Germanic languages include English, High German, Low German, Yiddish, Dutch, Afrikaans, Flemish, and Frisian (the closest relative of English, spoken in the Netherlands and Germany.) The modern North Germanic languages include Norwegian, Icelandic, Swedish, Danish, and Faroese, all descended from various dialects of Old Norse. During the medieval period English borrowed a large number of words from Old Norse. The East Germanic group is now extinct but included the language of the Goths. See **Gothic.**

Grimm's Law A formula describing the regular changes undergone by Indo-European stop consonants during the history of the Germanic languages. By the workings of Grimm's law, Indo-European *p, t,* and *k* became Germanic *f, th,* and *h.* Indo-European *b, d,* and *g* became Germanic *p, t,* and *k.* Indo-European *bh, dh,* and *gh* (see *voiced aʃpirate* in this glossary*)* became sounds that eventually appear in English as *b, d,* and *g.* Grimm's Law often provides the key to understanding how English words are related to those in other languages such as Latin and Greek. For examples of the workings of Grimm's Law, see **fee, fire, island, queen, water, whore.**

High German German as indigenously spoken and written in Austria, Switzerland, and central and southern Germany, especially the standard variety of German used as the official language in Germany and Austria and as one of the official languages in Switzerland. The term is a translation of German *Hochdeutsch,* from *hoch,* "high," and *Deutsch,* "German," and refers to the mountainous terrain of the area in which it originated, not to its social status or a supposed superiority to other dialects.

Indo-European A family of languages consisting of most of the languages of Europe as well as those of Iran, the Indian subcontinent, and other parts of Asia. English and the other Germanic languages are Indo-European languages. The parent language of the Indo-European languages, Proto-Indo-European, is sometimes also called simply Indo-European. See the chart on pages 346–347.

Irish Also called Irish Gaelic. The indigenous language of Ireland, belonging to the Celtic branch of the Indo-European language family. The literary tradition in the Irish language has continued unbroken from the late sixth century. Today most Irish speakers can speak English as well, which has resulted in the borrowing of several terms from Irish into English. The dialect of English used in Ireland is often called Hiberno-English.

Latin The Indo-European language of the ancient Romans and the most important cultural language of western Europe until the end of the seventeenth century. The spoken Latin of the later Roman Empire is called Vulgar Latin (see below). A very large percentage of English words is from Latin, borrowed either directly or from the Romance languages.

loan translation A form of borrowing from one language to another whereby the individual parts of a given word are literally translated into their equivalents in the borrowing language. Also called a *calque.* See **sunbeam.**

Low German The German dialects of northern Germany. The term is a translation of German *Niederdeutsch,* from *nieder,* "low," and *Deutsch,* "German," and refers to the lowland terrain of northern Germany, not to any supposed inferior status or value of the dialects. It is sometimes difficult to tell whether an English word is ultimately from Dutch or Low German. See **vogue** for a word from Low German.

masculine A grammatical gender relating to or belonging to words or forms that refer chiefly to males or to things grammatically classified as male.

melioration The linguistic process by which a word over a period of time grows more elevated in meaning or more positive in connotation. For examples, see **fond** and **nice**.

metathesis Transposition within a word of letters, sounds, or syllables, as in the change from Old English *brid* to modern English *bird* or in the confusion of *modren* for *modern*. See **third**.

Middle Chinese The Chinese language during the Sui and Tang dynasties (581–907). See **chai, Japan,** and **Tokyo**.

neuter Relating or belonging to the gender of words or forms that refer chiefly to inanimate objects or to things that are grammatically classified as neither male nor female. The pronoun *it* in English is a neuter pronoun.

New Latin Latin as used since about 1500, especially as a language of science.

Old French The French language from the ninth to around the end of the fourteenth century. There was extensive borrowing from Old French into Middle English, especially during the fourteenth century.

Old Norse A language or group of dialects that is the ancestor of the modern languages of Scandinavia. After the middle of the fourteenth century the dialects are different enough that we refer to them as individual languages, such as Icelandic, Norwegian, and Danish. Speakers of Old Norse made substantial colonies in the north of the British Isles and gave English many new words, such as **bylaw** and **their**.

palatalization One of the most common changes that happens to the sounds of a language, in which an original *k* or *d* sound becomes a *ch* or *j* sound, produced with the blade of the tongue near the hard palate. In the history of English, an Indo-European **k* became an Old English *ch* if it occurred before the vowels *e, i,* and *y*. In the history of French, a Latin *c* (which had a *k* sound) became a *ch* before the vowel *a* in some dialects of Old French. For some examples of this common process in various languages, see **chase, churl, ciao, drench, maharajah**.

parent language A language from which a later language is derived. Sometimes the parent language of a language family is not attested, and linguists learn about its characteristics through reconstruction. Latin is the parent language of Italian, French, and the other Romance languages. Proto-Indo-European is the parent language of English, Latin, Greek, and all the other Indo-European languages.

participle A form of a verb that in some languages, such as English, can function independently as an adjective, as the past participle *baked* in "We had some baked beans" or the present participle *drooping* in "He watered the drooping flowers." English has in fact accepted a great number of words that were participles in other languages, such as *adolescent.* For an interesting survival of an old Indo-European participle in English, see **tooth**.

pejoration The process by which the meaning of a word becomes negative or less elevated over a period of time, as seen in *silly,* which formerly meant "deserving sympathy, helpless or simple" and has come to mean "showing a lack of good sense, frivolous." See **lewd** for another example.

pejorative Imparting a negative, disparaging, or belittling meaning to a word. For examples of pejorative prefixes and suffixes, see **coward** and **disaster**.

prefix A word element that can only occur attached to the front of a word and is used to form a new word or indicate the grammatical role of the word in the sentence, such as *dis-* in *disbelieve.* See **nest** for an interesting example of the use of prefixes in the history of an English word.

reconstruction A hypothetical word, ending, sound, or system of grammar that is proposed by linguists in order to account for the history of a language. Based on the evidence of words meaning "god" in many Indo-European languages, such as Sanskrit *devaḥ* and Latin *deus,* as well as the name of the Germanic god known as Tiw in English, linguists can reconstruct a word for "god," **deiwos*, in Proto-Indo-European. Since this form is not attested, it is marked with an asterisk. Linguists also believe that regular rules govern the evolution of a reconstructed form, such as **deiwos*, into attested forms, such as Latin *deus.* For more on this reconstruction, see **Zeus**.

reduplication A word formed by doubling the initial syllable or all of a root or another word. For an example, see **namby-pamby**.

respelling A change in the spelling of word, especially in order to make the supposed historical origin of the word clearer. In the past, spelling was generally not as fixed as it is today. Especially during and after the Renaissance, many writers sought to make words from Latin look as much like the original Latin word as possible, and they inserted "silent letters" and otherwise modified words in order to accomplish this. See **posthumous**. Other respellings result from simple mistaken etymologies. See **delight**.

Romance language One of the languages descended from Vulgar Latin, the Latin language as it was spoken in the later Roman Empire. Words have made their way to English from many Romance languages, including Portuguese, Spanish, Catalan, French, Italian, and Romanian. For an interesting example of how a word borrowed from a Romance language may differ from cognates borrowed directly from Latin, see **cattle**.

root The element that carries the main component of meaning in a word and provides the basis from which a word is derived by the addition of other elements such as suffixes or by the changing of the sounds in the word. Most of the words in Proto-Indo-European were derived from a simple root that often has the shape *consonant-vowel-consonant*. For some examples of how the words in English and the other Indo-European languages were made from roots, see **empty, orgy, paradise,** and **whore**.

Saami Any of the languages of the Saami, a people of nomadic herding tradition inhabiting Lapland. Saami is related to Finnish and Estonian and belongs to the larger Uralic language family, which also includes Hungarian and many other languages of Eurasia. Another name for Saami, less preferred nowadays, is *Lapp.*

schwa A vowel having the sound of the final vowel of English *sofa.* In English, the vowel *schwa* is very common and typically occurs in syllables with no accent. It is written with the symbol ə.

Scots The dialect of English used in the Lowlands of Scotland.

Scottish Gaelic The Celtic language of Scotland, closely related to Irish.

semantic change Change in the meaning of a word over time. There are many different kinds of semantic change, such as specialization and reinterpretation, or the meaning can be extended to become more general, as in **revamp**. For a few interesting examples of semantic change, see **bless, harlot, hearse, pay, scan, scold,** and **war**.

Semitic language family A family of languages including Akkadian, Arabic, Hebrew, many of the major languages of Ethiopia and Eritrea, and Aramaic (the language of daily life among the Jews in Roman times). It is a subgroup of the larger Afro-Asiatic language family, which includes Ancient Egyptian and many other languages of Africa. English has large number of words that are ultimately of Semitic origin or related to Semitic words. See **alcohol, Betelgeuse,** and **lion**.

specialization A kind of semantic change in which the meaning of the word becomes narrower or more specific, as in the history of **deer**.

sound change Over the history of a language, generally all instances of a single sound will develop in the same way if the surrounding sounds in the words do not interfere and cause yet another kind of change. For example, as sound changes build up over the centuries, languages that come from the same parent language can begin to look quite different. But the fact that sound change is mostly regular allows us to establish correspondences, such as Grimm's Law, which demonstrate that quite dissimilar words in different languages are ultimately from the same root. However, some sound changes appear to be sporadic and defy linguists' attempts to find any regularity in them. For some interesting examples of how sound change can transform a word, see **beef, queue, speak, tea.**

stem The main part of a word, to which suffixes changing the meaning of the word, or endings indicating grammatical information, may be added. In the English word *dictionaries,* we can see four different separable elements: a root, two suffixes, and an ending: *dic-tion-arie-s.* The Latin root *dic-,* meaning "to say" (from Proto-Indo-European **deik-,* "point"), is also seen in the English words *dictate* and *edict.* In Latin a noun was made from this root with the suffix *-tiōn-* meaning "the act of saying," which English has borrowed as *diction.* In medieval times, an additional suffix, *-ārium,* was added to this stem to make a new word *dictiōnārium,* "book of words," which English borrowed as *dictionary.* When we want to make a plural of this noun in English, we add an additional ending, *-s.* In Proto-Indo-European, most stems were formed in the same way as in the Latin word, by adding suffixes to a root, and then grammatical endings were added. Linguists usually write stems with *n*-dashes or hyphens after them. This means that the stem is not a word in itself, but requires the addition of an ending if it is to be used in a sentence.

suffix A word element that can only occur attached to the end of a word or stem, forming a new word or indicating the grammatical role of the word in the sentence, such as *-ness* in *gentleness, -ing* in *walking,* or *-s* in *sits.* For examples of the variety of suffixes found in English, see **coward, cuckold, cushy, cynic, water.**

suppletion The use of another unrelated word to express certain grammatical forms, such as the past tense or a degree of comparison, of a word. For example, the comparative of *good* is not *gooder,* but *better.* Another example of suppletion in English is provided by the verb *go.* See **went.**

syllable A unit of spoken language consisting of a single uninterrupted sound formed by a vowel or diphthong (or occasionally a consonant functioning as a vowel, as the *n*-sound in the usual pronunciation of *button,* where there is no *o*-vowel or schwa pronounced) alone, or by any of these sounds preceded, followed, or surrounded by one or more consonants.

taboo avoidance The avoidance of a word by speakers because of social custom or emotional aversion. Taboo avoidance often affects words that are similar in sound. See **donkey**.

tone The pitch of a word used in some languages to determine its meaning or to distinguish differences in meaning. For example, in Mandarin Chinese, the syllable *ma* with a high level tone means "mother," but when pronounced with a rising tone, it means "hemp." When pronounced with a tone that falls and then rises again, it means "horse," and when pronounce with a sharply falling tone, it means "scold." Chinese and other languages of East Asia are famous for having tones, but the use of tone is found in languages all over the world, such as Punjabi in India, Swedish, and many of the indigenous languages of Mexico and South America.

Verner's Law A law stating that the Proto-Germanic noninitial voiceless sounds *f, th, x* (a sound like *ch* in German), and *s* became voiced in voiced environments when the previous syllable was unstressed in Proto-Indo-European. For example, both the *th* and the *d* of English **third** are descended from Proto-Germanic voiceless *th, but the second was voiced by Verner's Law and eventually became *d*. See also **freeze**.

vocative A grammatical case used in certain languages to indicate the person or thing being addressed. See **Zeus** for an example of the use of the vocative case.

voiced Uttered with vibration of the vocal cords, as the sounds (b) and (d). Changes affecting the voicing of consonants are frequent in the history of languages. Grimm's Law drastically altered the voiced and voiceless consonants of Proto-Indo-European on the way to Germanic. For another example of a change in the voicing of consonants, see **vixen**.

voiced aspirate Uttered with a breathy or murmured vibration of the vocal cords, as the sounds transliterated *bh* and *dh* in Hindi and many other languages of northern India. The voiced aspirate *dh* sounds somewhat similar to the *dh* in the English word *adhere*–a *d* followed by a puff of air. Proto-Indo-European also had voiced aspirated consonants, and Grimm's Law altered these consonants on the way to Germanic and eventually English.

voiceless Uttered without vibration of the vocal cords, as the sounds (p) and (t). Compare **voiced**.

Vulgar Latin The common speech of the ancient Romans, which differs somewhat from the written standard dialect of Latin used in Roman literature. Although the ancient graffiti surviving from Roman times in places like Pompeii is frequently obscene, the word *vulgar* in the term *Vulgar Latin* refers to its use by the *vulgus*, Latin for "the common people," not to any intrinsic obscenity of the language. Vulgar Latin, rather than literary Latin, is the ancestor of the Romance languages. It is also sometimes called *Proto-Romance*. In the Romance languages, many words look as if they are the modern continuations of everyday Latin words, but the original Latin words happen not to be attested in Roman literature. Because they are unattested, such words are classified as Vulgar Latin rather than simply as Latin. For a sampling of such words, see **caterpillar, desert, dinner, dress, ennui, fey, mosquito, scarce,** and **temple**.

Wolof A language of belonging to the Niger-Congo language, a very large language family of Africa. Wolof is spoken in Senegal and several other West African countries.

Yiddish The language traditionally spoken by Ashkenazic Jews of Central and Eastern Europe, resulting from a fusion of elements derived principally from medieval German dialects and secondarily from Hebrew and Aramaic, various Slavic languages, and Old French and Old Italian. Yiddish has made substantial contributions to the popular vocabulary of English. See **glitch** for an example.

The Indo-European Family of Languages

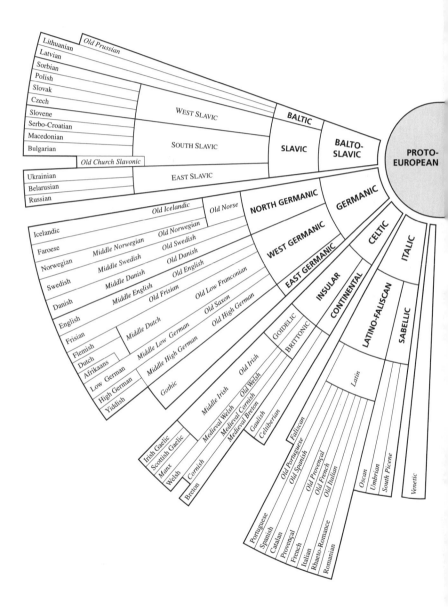

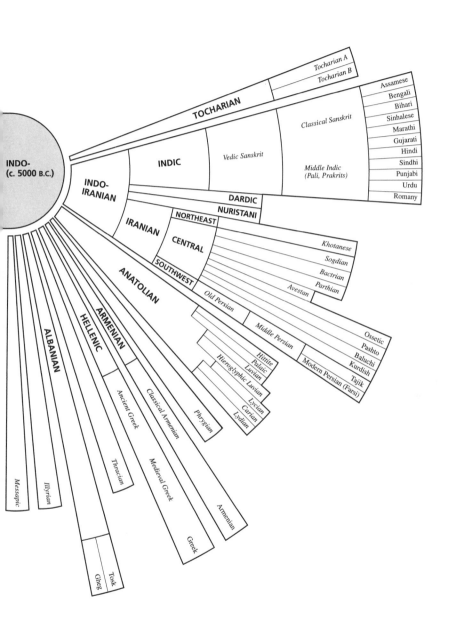

INDO-
(c. 5000 B.C.)

TOCHARIAN
- Tocharian A
- Tocharian B

INDIC
- Vedic Sanskrit
- Classical Sanskrit
- Middle Indic (Pali, Prakrits)
  - Assamese
  - Bengali
  - Bihari
  - Sinhalese
  - Marathi
  - Gujarati
  - Hindi
  - Sindhi
  - Punjabi
  - Urdu
  - Romany

INDO-IRANIAN

DARDIC

NURISTANI

IRANIAN
- NORTHEAST
- CENTRAL
- SOUTHWEST
  - Old Persian
  - Avestan
  - Khotanese
  - Sogdian
  - Bactrian
  - Parthian
  - Middle Persian
    - Ossetic
    - Pashto
    - Baluchi
    - Kurdish
    - Tajik
  - Modern Persian (Farsi)

ANATOLIAN
- Hittite
- Palaic
- Luvian
- Hieroglyphic Luvian
- Lycian
- Carian
- Lydian
- Phrygian

ARMENIAN
- Ancient Greek
- Classical Armenian
- Medieval Greek
- Armenian

HELLENIC
- Thracian
- Greek

ALBANIAN
- Illyrian
- Tosk
- Gheg

Messapic

Picture Credits

abracadabra Tech-Graphics **Amazon** The Granger Collection, New York
artichoke Laurel Cook Lhowe **atlas** The Granger Collection, New York
avocado © 2004 PhotoDisc, Inc./Getty Images **barnacle** Laurel Cook
Lhowe **caprice** © 2004 PhotoDisc, Inc./Getty Images **chai** Patrick Taylor
dandelion Elizabeth Morales **digitalis** © 2004 PhotoDisc, Inc./Getty
Images **fascism** Gail E. Piazza **gauntlet** Chris Costello **gun** The Granger
Collection, New York **iconoclast** Art Resource, New York/Réunion des
Musées Nationaux **kangaroo** © 2004 PhotoDisc, Inc./Getty Images
lemur Laurel Cook Lhowe **mail** Courtesy, American Antiquarian Society
maudlin Corbis/Elio Ciol **opossum** © 2004 PhotoDisc, Inc./Getty Images
pan out Corbis/Bettmann **pompadour** Corbis/Bettmann **pretzel** Laurel
Cook Lhowe **reindeer** Corbis/Joe McDonald **rune** The Granger Collection,
New York **sequoia** Library of Congress (LCUSZ62-1292) **soldier** The
Granger Collection, New York **syringe** © 2004 PhotoDisc, Inc./Getty
Images **tadpole** Cecile Duray-Bito **tantalize** Corbis/Bettmann **Thursday**
Corbis/Bettmann **Tuesday** The Granger Collection, New York **typhoon**
Art Resource, New York/Foto Marburg **Wednesday** The Granger
Collection, New York **xenophobia** Courtesy of the J. Paul Getty Museum
zither © 2004 PhotoDisc, Inc./Getty Images